340

12-6-78

Being and the Messiah

Being
and the Messiah

The Message of St. John

José Porfirio Miranda

Translated by John Eagleson

Note to the English Translation

The basis for this translation was the author's original Spanish manuscript, which varies slightly from the published Spanish edition. Subheadings have been added by the translator. The author has graciously reviewed and revised the translation.

Special thanks are gratefully extended to Naomi Noble Richard, who assisted in preparing the final English version with her remarkable skill.

Library of Congress Cataloging in Publication Data

Miranda, José Porfirio
  Being and the Messiah.

    Translation of El ser y el Mesías.
    Bibliography: p.
    Includes indexes.
    1. Bible. N.T. Johannine literature—Criticism,
interpretation, etc. 2. Existentialism. 3. Communism.
I. Title.
BS2601.M5413   230   77-5388
ISBN 0-88344-027-X
ISBN 0-88344-028-8 pbk.

Originally published in 1973 as *El ser y el mesías*

Copyright © 1973 by Ediciones Sígueme, Salamanca, Spain

English translation copyright © 1977 by Orbis Books

Orbis Books, Maryknoll, NY 10545

Printed in the United States of America

Contents

2030544

Preface

Each of us must decide on which side of the scale we will place the sum total of our actions. We cannot escape responsibility for our personal role in history if it contributes to the oppression of the poor and the helpless.

The time has come when all those who write or speak about Christ must also state whether they are struggling for the church or for Christianity.

The worst possible response would be to object that these two realities are identical. This would be like maintaining that what is good for our political party is good in itself and that what is bad for our political party is bad in itself, or that the end justifies the means. No authority can decree that everything is permitted; for justice and exploitation are not so indistinguishable. And Christ died so that we might know that not everything is permitted.

But not any Christ. The Christ who cannot be co-opted by accommodationists and opportunists as the historical Jesus. This book is dedicated to him.

Chapter 1

Revolution and Existentialism

In his *Critique de la raison dialectique*, Jean-Paul Sartre makes this remarkable comment: "To fire workers because a factory is closing is a sovereign act that tacitly assumes the fundamental right to kill."[1]

Dialectical reason, in its contemporary form, occurs in Marxism, and in this Marxist form it deserves to be criticized—for its superficiality. For we cannot bring about true revolution if we have not determined the root causes of oppression and exploitation. Firing workers for capitalistic reasons such as lowering costs is only a visible manifestation, a demonstrable, tangible effect of exploitation; it is not the cause, it is not the root of oppression. On the other hand, the feeling that we have the fundamental right to kill lies at a deeper level of human existence. Its manifestations change over time, but the feeling that produces these manifestations does not change.

In the same place Sartre has this to say about the bourgeois of the capitalist period: "There is, then, a meaning which redounds upon him from the future and henceforth will constitute the sense of all that he does, namely, no matter what he does he *must* suppress." There is an attitude that can overpower us and establish itself at our center; it makes us suppress, degrade, mistrust, and trample upon others. The historical contribu-

1

tion of existentialism is that it forces us to consider such a basic attitude very seriously—to discover it, to analyze it, to see how it affects all we do, to determine either its meaning or its absurdity.

The most interesting and threatening aspect of such an attitude is that the bourgeois themselves are not always aware of their deepest motivation. We can deduce it, however, from observing all that they do as members of their class. Moreover, this belief that we have the fundamental right to kill can exist on an unconscious level in all of us—even noncapitalists; and thus any consideration of such an attitude poses a threat to us.

THE ROOTS OF OPPRESSION

It would be so simple to divide the world into good people and bad, like the characters in cowboy movies. We must recognize that Marxism continuously verges on this kind of oversimplification. Compare Vittorio de Sica's *Miracle in Milan* with Luis Buñuel's *The Young and the Damned*. Buñuel avoids the temptation of romanticizing the proletariat, as if this class, immune to the contagions and commercialism of consumer society, were the depository of all sweetness and light. With de Sica, on the other hand, the rich are bad, the poor are good—a romanticism characteristic of the Marxism of his day.

Let me repeat: It would be much simpler to describe the world in this way. Indeed, it would even appear to be more revolutionary, because with this descriptive instrument it would be easier to revolutionize the people. And some will say that this alone is enough to justify such a Manichean approach, that the only important thing is to bring about the revolution, and if a Manichean schema hastens the revolution, this proves that such a schema is true.

But it would not bring about true revolution. This is the crucial point. We can rightly object to this Manichean approach because it is ineffective. Moreover, the only efficacy that matters is made impossible by such an approach.

One more coup d'état is of no interest to us, one more addition to the long list of political revolts, even if the majority of the population supports it. We are not concerned with some superficial mini-revolution whose inevitable outcome is to reproduce in grander proportions the very capitalistic world that it intended to eliminate.

Existentialist honesty would put an end to all romanticism and dogmatism: It would force us to acknowledge, for example, that if we took an objective poll of the Mexican people today, we would find that their desires, aspirations, and values were precisely those engraved on their soul by capitalism.

Let there be no confusion between the existentialist thesis that we sustain here and the perennial conservative argument that holds that before true revolution can occur people must "first" change, that people must "first" be converted. That is simply an argument for the indefinite postponement of revolution. No, here we want to take revolution seriously. The assault on power and the expropriation of the means of production must occur as soon as possible, that is to say, as soon as the organization of the exploited is strong enough. But the problem of revolution is not solved by the assault on power, and this problem is our concern here.

Three years after his successful assault on power, Lenin wrote the following:

The old society was based on the principle: rob or be robbed; work for others or make others work for you; be a slave-owner or a slave. Naturally people brought up in such a society assimilate with their mother's milk, one might say, the psychology, the habit, the concept which says: you are either a slave-owner or a slave, or else, a small owner, a petty employee, a petty official or an intellectual—*in short, a man who is concerned only with himself and does not care a rap for anybody else.*[2]

Lenin was no revolutionary romantic. His was no black-and-white diagnosis of society. It was very clear to him that the proletariat itself had been profoundly contaminated by capitalism. Revolution cannot be reduced to taking power and expropriating the goods of production:

It is a victory over our own conservatism, indiscipline, petty-bourgeois egoism, a victory over the habits left as a heritage to the worker and peasant by accursed capitalism. Only when *this* victory is consolidated ... will a reversion to capitalism become impossible, will communism become really invincible.[3]

Lenin, the theoretician of revolution par excellence, avoided the Manichean temptation of commonplace Marxism. It was quite clear to Lenin that the proletariat itself, the exploited themselves, both workers and peasants, had been imbued with the spirit of the bourgeoisie, with the desire for personal gain characteristic of private producers:

The small commodity producers ... surround the proletariat on every side with a petty-bourgeois atmosphere, which permeates and corrupts the proletariat, and constantly causes among the proletariat relapses into petty-bourgeois spinelessness, disunity, individualism.[4]

The concrete-and-steel jungle, the war of all against all, has been imposed by the capitalists, and they have made all of us participants. This they have accomplished through the mass communications media and the contagion of commonplace attitudes (in any rural hamlet, for example, the rich person is admired, imitated, and envied). But their principal instrument has been the capitalist economic machinery itself, which makes certain attitudes and behavior essential to survival.

The Manichean approach of the Marxist parties, which ingenuously divides the world into good people and bad, is an apparently handy expedient that up to a point seems to facilitate the revolution, for it saves the toil of honest thinking. But this approach is not compatible with the authentic revolutionary thought of Marx and Lenin. Nor does it really carry us toward true revolution, for it prevents us from understanding the actual situation. The apparent revolutionary efficacy of this approach and its apparent capacity for inciting the masses against "the bad people," are indeed just that—apparent. For it permits those of us who are not rich to disregard how deeply each of us is an accomplice to the capitalism that has brainwashed us all.

Once we surmount our cherished oversimplifications, it becomes clear, although painful to admit, that capitalism, which benefits only a privileged minority, could not have endured if it had not convinced even the exploited majority of its goodness. To accomplish this, capitalism has had to poison the majority from within; by its very criteria of good and bad the majority has become an accomplice.

True revolution is impossible if we do not understand that the capitalism that we must defeat has already captured the vital core within each of us. To deny this is to prevent true revolution and to assure—as in Di Lampedusa's *The Leopard*—that everything changes in such a way that everything remains the same.

The invaluable merit of existentialism—as developed by Kierkegaard, Heidegger, and Sartre—is to have focused philosophically on this terrible but inescapable fact: In one way or another, we are all guilty. (We must not confuse this human responsibility with Catholic and Protestant teaching on original sin, which is very different from biblical teaching on the subject.) Concern, not mathematical intellect, is truly the instrument for knowing reality. The revolution must oppose an entire tranquillizing, alienating tradition, which used philosophy to put us to sleep. The problem is more difficult than Marx's eleventh thesis on Feuerbach indicates, for

Marx himself philosophized; *he had to do so* to change the world. If a revolution breaks only with the history of the last century, it is of but little value. We must destroy an oppression that has lasted thousands of years.

Hoederer's words to Jessica in Sartre's *Dirty Hands* might at first seem disheartening: "I suppose that you're half victim and half accomplice, like everybody else." Such a notion may not help to arouse the multitudes. But disheartening or not, inflammatory or not, existentialism rightly acknowledges this overwhelming truth. Unless we realize the pervasiveness of the evil we want to combat, there is no hope that the coming revolution, which indeed has already begun, will be a true revolution. If we imagine ourselves to be immune to this evil, the one thing we can be sure of is that when we accomplish the revolution we will be re-establishing stronger than ever the bourgeois oppression we carry inside ourselves. This thought may indeed be disheartening at first. But a clear consciousness of the fact that we too have been implicated in inhumanity is indispensable if we really want the world to change. If we do not risk this consciousness, then deep down we have no hope. And so we struggle for the sake of struggling, to stick with our group, so that no one will say we gave up.

The idea of guilt in general and of one's own guilt in particular is missing from the accepted ideologies of contemporary Marxist parties. It is likewise absent from the thought of other, quite commendable, organizations that claim to have adopted Marx's thought as an instrument of revolutionary analysis. Let us briefly consider this point.

Marx's criticism of Feuerbach's materialism should cause all sincere followers of Marx to re-examine their entire ideology: premises, first principles, deductive process, conclusions. For many Marxists quite evidently are professing the pre-Marxist materialism of Feuerbach, whose most important political and philosophical thesis was that material conditions determine human behavior and inescapably mold our attitudes. In his third thesis on Feuerbach, Marx takes a different direction, stating that the educator itself (namely, the material conditions) has to be educated and re-educated by the revolutionary. If this thesis (which is inseparable from the other ten) contradicts what present-day Marxists understand by materialism, then they should clearly acknowledge the contradiction and choose between Marx and materialism.

EXCHANGE-VALUE

But the normative and conclusive criterion of Marx's thought is found in his masterwork, *Capital*. Here he says that the basic determinant of all past and present economies is exchange-value. Anyone claiming to understand relationships of production without reference to the theory of value is not a good Marxist. Indeed, in the introduction to *Capital* Marx emphasizes that the purpose of the entire work is to discover in what value consists, for humankind has been fruitlessly trying to clarify this for two thousand years.

Refuting Adam Smith, Marx says that exchange-value is a "mode of existence" of a commodity "which has nothing to do with its corporeal reality."[5] It is "an imaginary ... mode of existence of the commodity."[6]

In sum, according to *Capital* the decisive factor in history is the economic factor, and the most decisive element within this economic factor is exchange-value. But exchange-value is not identical with the material reality of the commodities. Rather it is part of the community's way of thinking; it is a concept, produced by the human spirit in its social and collective dimensions.

We are not dealing with a marginal, subordinate point in Marx. It is the central theme of his work, and the depth and extent of its implications have escaped Marxists and anti-Marxists alike. Let us consider this point carefully.

The *use-value* of an article is indeed determined by its material properties, that is to say, its flavor, color, form, resistance, weight, consistency, etc. However its *exchange-value* is determined by people's willingness to exchange other articles for it. This is so much the case that exchange-value is expressed in terms of other articles, for example, a ton of wheat is worth as much as five pairs of shoes, or as much as a rug, or as much as a transistor radio. Exchange-value consists in these multiple equivalencies of objects to each other.

The expression of value in monetary terms is only an abbreviated way of showing these equivalencies. When we say that a hundred bushels of wheat are worth four hundred dollars, our statement has meaning only because we implicitly refer to a specific quantity of other goods that we could buy with that sum of money. Money is only an intermediate mechanism in the exchange of commodities. The exchange-value of any article is the amount of other things we can barter for it. Therefore its exchange-value is not inherent in the material properties of the article, but is extrinsic to them.

This point is further proved by the fact that an article's exchange-value can vary without any variation in its material properties. A ton of wheat may be worth five pairs of shoes at one time and eight pairs of shoes at another, though neither the quality of the wheat nor the quality of the shoes has changed in the slightest degree. Clearly, then, exchange-value is not inherent in the wheat or the shoes.

Exchange-value is a set of relationships, varying with time and place and according to subjective preferences, that people, by their imagination and conceptualization, establish among things that can be bartered. It is a table of multiple equivalencies that the human mind projects upon things as a means of ordering them. For this reason Marx holds that the exchange-value of a commodity is utterly unrelated to its corporeal reality: *Nur eine eingebildete, das heisst bloss soziale Existenzweise der Ware, die mit ihrer körperlichen Realität nichts zu schaffen hat.* In sum, exchange-value is a construct of the human spirit and this exchange-value is the dominant element in all economic systems, which in turn, Marx says, are the determining factor of history.

Why did humankind invent a table of equivalencies called exchange-value and project it upon reality? The answer seems quite simple: in order to exchange commodities. The scarcity of certain goods among a specific human group would be the reason why that group would want to enter into commercial dealings with other groups. And scarcity has characteristics of a purely material nature that would sufficiently explain the existence of exchange-value.

But the answer is not so simple, for people invented the table of equivalencies in order not only to exchange commodities, but also to exchange them to their own advantage. Marx says, "What, first of all, practically concerns producers when they make an exchange, is the question, how much of some other product they get for their own."[7] Therein lies the poison.

Let us enlarge the dimensions of the question. One of the commodities that people exchange is labor-power, and so we say, for example, that the day's wages of a farm worker are worth three pounds of wheat, or three yards of cloth, or fifty bricks. The value of labor-power is included with the other values in the table of equivalencies, and it too is variable.

Following Petty, Cantillon, Smith, and Ricardo, Marx holds that the basis for the equivalencies that we have established among diverse commodities is the amount of labor it normally requires in a given period of history for the production of each commodity. The price of an orange rises when—perhaps because of changing climate or methods of cultivation—it takes more hours of labor than formerly to produce a sack of oranges. The value of cloth goes down when—perhaps because of technological advances—it takes fewer hours of normal labor to produce a yard of cloth. Thus at the basis of all the equivalencies we always find labor. This means that when we trade *to our advantage* we are always valuing the labor of others as less than our own labor.

Marx and his four above-mentioned predecessors very correctly discerned that a relationship exists between exchange-value and labor. The other four, however, remained trapped in the fetishistic belief that exchange-value is a material reality, and so they were unable to ask the necessary question: What is the nature of this relationship? Only someone who, like Marx, realized that exchange-value is simply a product of the mind, a very functional entity of reason, a societal tenet, an invention of culture, could ask the decisive question: What was it invented for? What is the reason for this relationship between value and labor? To us it is clear that the difficult task was to formulate the question, for the answer is obvious: The reason for the relationship is to make others work, *because* it is impossible to extract surplus-value from someone who does not work.

Marx himself did not fully understand that he had found the key to history when he discovered that exchange-value is a mental construct and not an inherent property of commodities. But Sartre expresses it very well: "Alienation transfers, then, the principal characteristic of oppression—which *must* be merciless or it disappears—to the process itself, and thus alienation expresses its human origin. . . . This is what deceived Engels in his hurried responses to Dühring. . . ."[8] "But it is not things that are merciless, it is people. . . ."[9] "Neither the indelible marks of oppressive praxis nor the masters' premeditated consent to their own violence can ever be dissolved into the practico-inert necessity of alienation."[10]

THE NECESSARY MINIMUM

It is not scarcity and matter that are decisive in history, but rather greed and oppression. That Marx was aware of this when he wrote Book One of *Capital* is clear from his discussion of "necessary labor." Out of what they produce by their day's labor the workers receive in return what they need to reproduce their labor-power. The remainder of what they produce is surplus-value, and the entrepreneur keeps it. But how does one determine what amount of goods is "necessary" for the sustenance and reproduction of a worker? Here materialism would have to respond: This is a physical, biological datum. Marx, on the contrary, answers:

> The number and extent of his so-called necessary wants, as also the modes of satisfying them, are themselves the product of historical development, and depend therefore to a great extent on the degree of civilisation of a country, more particularly on the conditions under which, and consequently on the habits and degree of comfort in which, the class of free labourers has been formed. In contradistinction therefore to the case of other commodities, there enters into the determination of the value of labour-power a historical and moral element.[11]

The limit to exploitation is not the level of consumption below which the proletariat will die of hunger. The necessary minimum is not a physiological datum; rather it is derived from the prevailing culture, morality, civilization. History offers abundant examples of the fact that "necessary" does *not* mean physiologically necessary: The proletariat has frequently received either more or less than what is necessary to survive.

But then how is the necessary minimum determined? In effect, says Marx in the above citation, the necessary minimum is the point below which the proletarians rebel because less remuneration is absolutely intolerable to them. For each period of history and for each country the limit to exploitation is determined by convictions and customs derived from the cultural and religious tradition and by social, juridical, and political pressures. The upper limit of remuneration, of what is "necessary," must always be fixed below the total value of the worker's labor-power, or there will be no remainder, no "surplus-value," no margin of profit for the exploiting classes. The definition of "necessary," then, is a datum of merciless oppression on the one hand and of resignation and impotence on the other.

Scrutinizing the realities of history and society with a thoroughly materialistic mentality, Marx discovered two concepts that could not be reduced to matter: (1) Exchange-value, which is an invention of human intelligence and constitutes the determining factor in all economy; and (2) the fact that the "necessary necessities" are determined by morality, custom, and culture, and that without this determination there can be no extraction of surplus-value.

THE DESIRE FOR PERSONAL GAIN

There is a third immaterial force operating in history, whose discovery by Marx and Lenin is perhaps even more important: the desire for personal gain as an *eradicable* motivation for human behavior and particularly for work. It is well known that in general terms Marx wanted to bring about a society based on the policy "from each according to his ability, to each according to his needs." This means that the communist movement wants to break the link between the diversity of remunerations and the diversity of contributions through labor. If this connection can be broken, labor will become truly human, for it will be motivated by impulses other than the desire for income.

In his *Critique of the Gotha Program,*[12] Marx, as summarized by Lenin, refers to "the *course of development* of communist society, which is *compelled* to abolish at first *only* the 'injustice' of the means of production

seized by individuals, but which is *unable* at once to
eliminate the other injustice, which consists in the distribution of consumer goods 'according to the amount of
labour performed' (and not according to needs)."[13]

Indeed, in the first phase of communism, Marx says,

Equal right here is still in principle—*bourgeois right.* . . . In
spite of this advance this *equal right* is still constantly stigma-
tized by a bourgeois limitation. The right of the producers is
proportional to the labor they supply; the equality consists in
the fact that measurement is made with an *equal standard*,
labor.[14]

It is clear that for Marx and Lenin it is still an inju st-
ice, a mutilated right, when incomes vary according to
the diverse kinds and levels of labor. Only in the higher
phase of communism, when "the narrow horizon of
bourgeois right [is] crossed in its entirety," can true
justice be achieved: "From each according to his ability,
to each according to his needs!"[15]

In other words, Marx and Lenin found that capitalism, as well as previous economic arrangements, ap-
peals to people's desire for personal gain to make them
work more and better, or simply to make them work at
all. But Marx and Lenin are convinced that this motivation can be eliminated from history. They believe it a
wretched concept of human nature that holds that the
desire for personal gain is inherent to the human race,
that people cannot live together, collaborate, or work
without the selfish, utilitarian stimulus of self-interest,
and that because self-interest is necessary for human
society it is therefore ineradicable.

At this point it is clear that the materialists—their
palaver notwithstanding—must find recruits elsewhere, for Marx and Lenin are no longer members of the
group. As Sartre says, "We must make a de facto choice:
Either 'each looks out for his own interest,' which means
that division among people is *natural*, or it is the division
among people . . . which causes self-interest (particular
or general, of the individual or the class) to appear as a

real characteristic of relationship among people."[16] If we affirm that there is a "law of self-interest" that governs people as the law of gravity governs stones, then we are denying the possibility of revolution, for communist society cannot be achieved if the desire for personal gain is not eliminated.

Moreover, the thesis that self-interest is an essential part of human nature is contradicted by the existence of truly selfless people. A single exception is enough to invalidate a universal affirmative proposition. As Sartre says, "Self-interest as a fact of nature is a perfectly unintelligible datum. Moreover, any induction that posits it as an a priori reality of human nature is perfectly unjustifiable. Indeed, if conflicts of self-interest are the engine of history, then the overall pattern of history becomes completely absurd. In particular, Marxism becomes nothing more than an irrational hypothesis."[17] It is evident that this criticism applies to present-day Marxism, and not to Marx and Lenin, at least insofar as these thinkers remain true to their discoveries that we have described.

But we must add that Christian theologians partake of the same conservatism and fatalism as afflicts the materialists when they identify self-interest with an original sin that—notwithstanding all the official statements to the contrary—has come to be seen as an integral part of human nature. According to Genesis and to Paul's Epistle to the Romans, original sin is a contingent event and therefore eradicable from human society. But dogmatic theology—in order to justify a socioeconomic system that motivates people through a desire for personal gain—has gone so far as to hold that the peccatum originale originatum, manifesting itself as selfishness, is essentially inseparable from the human being. This thesis is especially inconsistent for Catholic theologians, for the Council of Trent affirmed that original sin can be abolished and therefore its effects can be abolished as well.

THE ROLE OF EXISTENTIALISM

If we insist that the tendency to oppress and injure others is natural—that is, that we are not free to do otherwise—then we cannot become aware of how thoroughly capitalism has infected us all, and it will be impossible for the coming revolution to uproot oppression from human society. If we do not confront reality, we cannot hope to change in any profound way. Existentialism's invaluable contribution is to show us reality and thereby to make possible a true revolution.

Mexico harbors fewer illusions than many other nations about the miraculous power frequently attributed to revolution. (I hope the non-Mexican reader will indulge my occasional allusions to Mexico; my country brought about the first social revolution of this century, and the results are there for all to see.) Even if all the means of production had been taken over by the state, we do not believe that we would thereby cease to be the bundle of complexes, involutions, and aggressions that we are. We hold the world record for violence and we wretchedly submit to "what people say," and these characteristics are the result of something more than private ownership of productive goods.

Capitalist oppression could not have endured if all of us, or nearly all of us, had not been its accomplices. Sartre puts it very well: "We must agree with the statement by J. Romains, 'In war there are no innocent victims.' "[18] Benítez, Garibay, and Fuentes are deceiving themselves when they deduce from the present situation that we are obliged to support Echeverría.[19] But the reluctance of certain intellectuals to join the new revolution is due, although they are perhaps unaware of it, to their need of assuring that this time human beings themselves are transformed, and this transformation depends on "ideas" to a degree much greater than leftist movements and guerrilla groups are willing to concede. By "ideas" I mean an awareness of reality, and reality is worldwide. The coming revolution will be worldwide or it will not be a true revolution.

The mission of existentialism at this moment, then, is to make the summons of conscience inescapable. Only in this way can the revolution be global in its scope and total in its effect.

Let us note very carefully that existentialism's role is not to inculcate that disease we call " a sense of guilt." But the voice of conscience does indeed exist, and any philosophy which tries to make us believe that it does not, reducing it to our subjectivities, betrays the revolution, for it prevents the revolution from getting at the heart of the matter. As Heidegger ironically says, "The 'common-sense' interpretation of conscience, which 'sticks rigorously to the facts,' uses the fact that conscience does not speak aloud as a pretext for dismissing it as undemonstrable or nonexistent."[20]

Very well, conscience is not demonstrable like the phenomena of light waves or sound waves or electricity. But neither science nor positivist philosophy has the right to impose rules of evidence derived from the physical sciences on the phenomenon of conscience, rules that a priori exclude the inescapable fact of conscience. The merit of existentialism is that it prevents capitalistic positivism from continuing to deceive us through the stratagem of establishing rules that (like all the game rules of the bourgeois system) predetermine the conclusions before the investigation has begun.

This positivist stratagem has very little use for seeing things as they really are. Existentialism has discovered a new field of being, a field in which being, in order to be able to be, demands of us a decision. This being, this new way of being, can absolutely not be observed by someone who maintains the neutral, "objective" attitude of an observer. This being depends on our resolution in order to exist.

It is, then, ironic that the sciences have overlooked this field of being, since it is the most characteristic and distinctive object of human knowledge, and since humans exist in the fullest sense only when they make a decision concerning this being. Human knowing and being differs from animals' knowing and being precisely in this: Humans exist in the fullest sense only when they are touched by the voice of conscience and make decisions according to it.

It is not only the positive sciences that have helped conceal the existence of conscience; so, paradoxically, has moral science. It has done this in two ways. First, it has confused the moral imperative with a judgment of advantageousness or long-range utility, which have nothing to do with morality. Second—and Heidegger and Sartre argue against this specifically—it has diverted our attention from the basic guilt to casuistic inventories of faults. We will briefly clarify each of these two points.

THE MORAL IMPERATIVE

Conscience is unmistakable. If I jump into the river to save a drowning child, truly risking my life, no one can convince me that I am doing it to win a heavenly reward, or to achieve inner tranquillity, or for fear of hell, or to avoid future remorse. I jump because the child is drowning and *must be saved*. If I refrain from robbing a defenseless widow of what little money she has, I have a concrete experience of obeying an imperative that prevents me from robbing. My own future happiness in no way is my motive. The only real motive is *this must not be done*. There is no question of reward or punishment, nor of some ultimate personal benefit.

Kant made clear the distinction between the imperative of conscience and the other imperatives. The imperative of conscience is unconditional. It does not say, "If you want to be happy, do this." It says simply, "Do this." Other imperatives are explicitly or implicitly conditional: "If you want to be esteemed an honorable person, don't do this"; "If you want to avoid the pains of hell, do that."

But western moralists have been the best propagandists for the long-range utilitarianism characteristic of Greek eudemonism. They believe that moral purity is maintained by postponing the reward and punishment till the next life. But they are wrong, for an imperative is moral because it is grounded in itself, not in advantages or disadvantages resulting from the conduct it prescribes. Do you ask why the existence of a reward troubles me? It does not at all. The fact is, however, that when we act morally, *it is not for that reason* that we do so. There may in fact be a reward, but it is not for the reward that I save the child. When I acted to save the child, the idea of reward did not even occur to me. In the West, preachers have distracted our attention from true conscience, whose only motivation is its own imperative. Otherwise, it is not specifically moral.

FUNDAMENTAL GUILT

Western moral teaching has presented perhaps an even greater impediment to conscience by its preoccupation with casuistry. We broach the subject directly with a point often made by Heidegger: "Only he who already understands can listen."[21] Only he who *is* already moral pays any attention to the minute, casuistic precepts of ethics. Expressed negatively, the point is even stronger: The authors of treatises and the confessors—through their cheapening of ethics with their handy lists and recipes—have contributed to the tranquillization of the human conscience by silencing our profound guilt. As Heidegger says, "The existing person, whose being is concern, accuses himself of individual, specific faults, but the truth is that he *is* guilty at the very root of his being; without this primordial culpability as an ontological condition, the person could not be guilty of individual, specific faults."[22] A human being could not commit concrete sins, which casuistry then compiles into lists, if in some way that person were not, at a deeper level, guilty. Any revolutionary philosophy that disregards this fundamental fact unwittingly collaborates with capitalism's mass communications media, whose purpose is to "distract" us. The first meaning of "to divert" is "to turn aside," "to deflect," "to deviate." This implies deceiving us, diminishing us, denying us the possibility of being fully human, to turn us aside from the real problem, from the true path of revolution.

The guilt on which existentialism has focused is not formless or ill-defined, nor does it consist, as de Waelhens says, in our coming from nothingness and returning to nothingness.[23] Heidegger defines this being-guilty as *Grundsein für einen Mangel im Dasein eines Andern,* "Being-the-basis for a lack of something in the being of another."[24] He goes on to say that guilt "does not happen merely through law-breaking as such, but rather through being responsible for another's being endangered, or led astray, or even ruined. In this way one can become culpable toward others without breaking the 'public law.' "[25]

In our relationships with other human beings, existentialism insists, we are fundamentally guilty, even before committing concrete abuses that the authors of the treaties on morality can register and catalog. The debasement of the existentialist concept of guilt resembles the debasement of the biblical concept of original sin: Saint Paul expressly calls original sin "injustice" (Rom. 5:19, 21; 1:18, 28–32) and describes it in detail solely by giving specific examples of its occurrence in human relationships (Rom. 1:28–32; 3:10–18). But later commentators falsify Paul's notion by misrepresenting "injustice" as vague irreligiosity or ill-defined and nonspecific immorality.

The important point is this: There is always among people an underlying deviation, a mistrust, a readiness to trample upon the other. This can be strengthened and increased till it becomes in Sartre's words, "the feeling that we have the fundamental right to kill." But whether it reaches this point or not, it is this basic deviation that causes the hell we call human civilization.

But, we repeat, this deviation can be eradicated. If it could not—if we were not free to be otherwise—we would not experience it as guilt. The new field of being, discovered by existentialist philosophy, demands our decision in order to be able to be. The moment that evil appears as a "natural," irremediable datum, we have fallen back into the old field of being, the field of "objective" philosophy, the field of neutral, "observable" objects, the field of the "in itself." "The coefficient of adversity in things cannot be an argument against our freedom, for it is *by us*—*i.e.*, by our preliminary positing of a goal—that this coefficient of adversity arises."[26] Let there be no objection based on immutable essences: "It is freedom which is the foundation of all essences since man reveals intra-mundane essences by surpassing the world toward his own possibilities."[27] "*Freedom* is an objective quality of the Other as the unconditioned power of modifying situations. . . . In this sense the Other appears as the one who must be understood from the standpoint of a situation perpetually modified."[28]

The voice of conscience precedes its exercise in particular circumstances. Critics of the Kantian formalism of moral science, such as Max Scheler, would have done well to consider whether Kant was not in fact trying to see beyond inventories of faults to the concept of fundamental guilt. If he was, then existentialism is the legitimate extension of the *Critique of Practical Reason*.

Hegel wrote after Kant. It has often been noted that Hegel's *Phenomenology* reveals that his entire philosophy is a theodicy inspired by apologetics. But exactly the same is true of Marxism if it cleverly conceals the fact of guilt in past and present history. If Marxism does not make us aware of the evil that has taken root in us, if Marxism cannot make us aware of sin, then Marxism does not go beyond Hegelian dialectics. According to Hegel, all that has happened in history has been good because it has been necessary; all that is real is rational; everything has its justifiable reason for being, and we are, as Leibniz says, in the best of all possible worlds. The justification for capitalism and the civilization we have inherited is inherent in the Hegelian dialectic, which is a divinization of past and present. There can be no break; there is no basis for revolution. If theological prejudices prevent Marxism from confronting the unsettling fact of guilt, then it is ingenuously repeating Hegelian theology, which is a transposition of the "defense of God by the world that he made" undertaken by Leibniz.

Of course we are dealing with the sin of humankind. But the Marxists who in this matter are unable to hear *tua res agitur* are not serious thinkers. It is superficial to imagine that the spirit of oppression and exploitation has left us unscathed and has infected only that small sector of the population known as entrepreneurs. Both the question of guilt and the problem of death make the existentialist standpoint unavoidable for Marxists who are conscious of realities beyond their own system. Capitalism would not triumph or even endure if selfishness, the desire for personal gain, and the petty bourgeois spirit were not effectively inculcated even in its victims. To conceal this from the proletariat is to hinder the abolition of capitalism.

TRUE REVOLUTION

The true revolutionary abjures reformist palliatives, because these divert the efforts of the people most capable of fomenting rebellion against the bourgeois system into rejuvenating and refurbishing it; such palliatives thus constitute the system's best defense. By the same token, the revolutionary must find any change in the socioeconomic system to be a priori inadequate, if that change does not involve a radical revolution in people's attitudes toward each other. If exchange-value (that "imaginary entity") and the desire for personal gain continue to exist, they will inevitably create other oppressive and exploitative economic systems. They have in fact already done so, for these two "mental" factors, which Marx discovered at the heart of capitalism, were responsible not only for capitalism but also for every other economic system that ever preceded it, as Marx himself demonstrates. The contemporary revolutionary must reject workers' housing developments as a mere social tranquillizer, because inadequate housing is merely an effect, and to correct effects while leaving intact the cause, namely, the capitalist system, is to perpetuate injustice. By the same token, the revolutionary henceforth must reject as superficial the abolition of capitalism, if the "mental" causes that engendered it remain operative.

To confront these causes is the mission of existentialism. But it is of utmost importance to note that by confronting guilt (*der Mut zum Schuldigsein*, as Heidegger says), existentialism *brings about* the revolution of philosophy, the revolution that Marx *postulated* in his eleventh thesis on Feuerbach: "The philosophers have only *interpreted* the world, in various ways; the point, however, is to *change* it." Contemporary Marxism has not perceived that existentialism is bringing about this revolution of philosophy, and that this revolution cannot occur without existentialism. For their part the existentialists have not perceived that they are implementing Marx's eleventh thesis on Feuerbach.

It was characteristic of all previous philosophy to deal with precisely that field of being which does not depend on our free will in order to be what it is. It is a being that does not disturb us, that does not upset us, precisely because it does not require us to make any decision. It is the "objective" part of reality. But the reason it does not require us to make a decision is that any change in the "objective" part of reality is contingent on change in the other parts or fields of being that do indeed require our decision. Since the objective part of reality does not summon us, it *therefore* constitutes a cosmos in which "all is well": What is real is rational and what is rational is real; *tout est pour le mieux dans le meilleur des mondes.*

This philosophic tradition still dominated Hegel, but Nietzsche, Marx, and Kierkegaard rebelled against and broke with it. Of the three, Kierkegaard was the most conscious of the novelty of this method, which was to detect which fields of being can exist only if I make a decision. For Kierkegaard all other "parts" of being are irrelevant.

The individualism of existentialist philosophy should not prevent us from recognizing that it contains the beginning of the new method by which philosophy can transform reality. So too Hegel's apologetic tendencies should not prevent us from seeing that he laid the foundation for this new method by taking human history as a proper subject of philosophy. Just as Kierkegaard corrected Hegel by denying that historical reality is necessary and deducible, in the same way we must free Kierkegaard's revolutionary philosophy from its individualistic limitations and rid Marxism of its residue of Hegelian necessitarianism, which justifies all crimes past and present as necessary.

I think that the moment has arrived for philosophy —without ceasing to be philosophy—to play a decisive role in changing the world. Heidegger says that "when the person is resolute, he can become the 'conscience' of others."[29] This is undoubtedly true, but there is more involved. "It is freedom which is the foundation of all essences."[30] It is a priori reasoning to postulate that the traditional field of being—which requires no decision of ours in order to be what it is—has no connection with the new field of being—which depends on our free choice in order to exist. Such a compartmentalization of reality would have to be demonstrated, not simply presupposed. Perhaps certain "parts" of reality do not summon us to make a decision because changes in them are contingent on the parts of reality that do require our decision in order to be what they are. We will take up this question in chapter 9.

Platonic philosophers have always tried to impose the necessity of essences on history. The Hegelian necessity of history is identical to Aristotelian deduction, and Aristotelian deduction is a disguised affirmation of Socratico-Platonic recollection: There is nothing new; what seems new was always known by us, even though we were not aware of it; everything is deducible from the self; neither time, history, nor any event is *able* to constitute a break within the continuity of my recollection. Thus existentialism is a true revolution in philosophy. But by denying that historical reality is necessary existentialism makes humankind confront guilt.

In his accurate commentary on Kierkegaard, Jean Wahl says:

It is the presupposition of the entire Christian concept of time that the existing person is a sinner. In contrast with the Socratic disciple, whose teacher has only to awaken the memory, the Christian disciple feels an absolute rupture between what he was before the word of the teacher and what he will be after it. Up to that point he was in sin, and not, like the Socratic disciple, in ignorance.[31]

As we shall see, this coincidence between Christianity and atheistic philosophies like those of Heidegger and Sartre is not fortuitous and anecdotal, as Heidegger and Sartre would have us believe.

There is no place here for disappearing tricks or subjective approaches. The being discovered by existentialism is unavoidable: If we abdicate our unconditional resolution to confront our guilt, we automatically abandon our investigation of this field of being. Unbounded decision is the key to our inquiry. The question Heidegger asks is valid: "Is there any other way at all by which an entity can put itself into words with regard to its being?"[32] From Kant we know that the basis for the moral imperative cannot be proven, nor is this imperative grounded in anything or supported by anything. It is grounded in itself. We heed it or we do not; that is all.

NOTES

1. Jean-Paul Sartre, *Critique de la raison dialectique* (Paris: Gallimard, 1960), 1:713.

2. V.I. Lenin, "The Tasks of the Youth Leagues," speech delivered October 2, 1920, in *Selected Works* (New York: International Publishers, 1967), 3:470; emphasis added.

3. Ibid., "A Great Beginning," published as a pamphlet in July 1919, in *Selected Works*, 3:205.

4. Ibid., " 'Left-Wing' Communism—An Infantile Disorder," in *Selected Works*, 3:357.

5. Karl Marx, "Theories of Productive and Unproductive Labour," in *Theories of Surplus-Value (Volume IV of Capital)*, trans. Emile Burns (Moscow: Progress Publishers, 1963), part 1, chapter 4, section 3, 1:171.

6. Ibid.

7. Karl Marx, "The Fetishism of Commodities and the Secret Thereof," in *Capital*, trans. Samuel Morre and Edward Aveling (New York: International Publishers, 1967), book 1, chapter 1, section 4, 1:74.

8. Sartre, *Critique*, 1:699.

9. Ibid.

10. Ibid., p. 700.

11. Marx, "The Buying and Selling of Labour-Power," in *Capital*, book 1, chapter 6, 1:171.

12. Published in 1875, after *Capital* and therefore representing more mature thinking in Marx.

13. Lenin, "The State and Revolution," chapter 5, section 3, in *Selected Works*, 2:338.

14. Marx, "Critique of the Gotha Program," section 1, in *On Revolution*, The Karl Marx Library, vol. 1, ed. Saul K. Padover (New York: McGraw-Hill, 1971), p. 495.

15. Ibid., p. 496.

16. Sartre, *Critique*, 1:277.

17. Ibid.

18. J.-P. Sartre, *L'être et le néant* (Paris: Gallimard, 1943), p. 640 [Eng. trans.: *Being and Nothingness*, trans. Hazel E. Barnes (New York: Citadel, 1968), p. 530].

19. Benítez, Garibay, and Fuentes are Mexican intellectuals who supported President Echeverría and convinced many other intellectuals to do the same.

20. Martin Heidegger, *Sein und Zeit* (Tübingen: Niemeyer, 1960), p. 296 [cf. Eng. trans.: *Being and Time*, trans. John Macquarrie and Edward Robinson (New York: Harper & Row, 1962), p. 343].

21. Ibid., p. 164 [Eng. trans.: p. 208].

22. Ibid., p. 286 [cf. Eng. trans.: p. 332].

23. Alphonse de Waelhens, *La philosophie de Martin Heidegger*, 7th ed. (Louvain: Nauwelaerts, 1971), p. 165.

24. Heidegger, *Sein und Zeit*, p. 82 [cf. Eng. trans.: *Being and Time*, p. 328.].

25. Ibid., p. 282 [cf. Eng. trans.: pp. 327–28].

26. Sartre, *L'être et le néant*, p. 562 [cf. Eng. trans.: *Being and Nothingness*, p. 458].

27. Ibid., p. 514 [Eng. trans.: p. 414].

28. Ibid., p. 417 [Eng. trans.: p. 326].

29. Heidegger, *Sein und Zeit*, p. 298 *(Das entschlossene Dasein kann zum "Gewissen" der Anderen werden)* [cf. Eng. trans.: *Being and Time*, p. 344].

30. Sartre, *L'être et le néant*, p. 514 [Eng. trans.: *Being and Nothingness*, p. 414].

31. Jean Wahl, *Études kierkegaardiennes* (Paris: Vrin, 1949), p. 357.

32. Heidegger, *Sein und Zeit*, p. 315 [cf. Eng. trans.: *Being and Time*, pp. 362–63].

Chapter 2

The Vindication of Atheism

In the first chapter we indicated the difference between concrete faults and a state of fundamental guilt (or original shame, as Sartre calls it). And we said that the latter is a condition of possibility for the former—that is, the underlying condition that makes the concrete fault possible. If we did not habitually have a basic attitude of distrust, remoteness, and enmity, we would not commit concrete acts of envy, contempt, exploitation, subjugation, murder.

The reader should be aware of the transcendental method employed in making this distinction. We understand perceptible realities more thoroughly to the degree that we discover the condition or conditions of possibility of these realities. In the transcendental method, we attempt to detect those underlying human realities without which there could not exist the acts and facts whose existence we can directly verify.

In this chapter we want to describe a condition of possibility of the fundamental consciousness of guilt, which we considered in the first chapter.

THE ETHICAL GOD

In any history of philosophy two of Kant's works are recognized as being of paramount importance in the development of human thought: *Critique of Pure Reason* and *Critique of Practical Reason.* Modern philosophy, initiated a century and a half earlier by Descartes, reaches an apex in these works; without their stimulus the philosophizing of the nineteenth and twentieth centuries would be unthinkably different.

The chief contribution to modern thought of these two books occurs in their combination to demonstrate a single thesis: namely, the true God has no connection with ontology (the true God is not *a* being nor *the* being nor the *supreme* being); *rather* God is identified with the ethical imperative. The crux of the Kantian message is contained in this adversative "rather," but historians of philosophy have not sufficiently emphasized this, nor have post-Kantian philosophers themselves sufficiently grasped the contrast between the ontic order and the moral order. The Greek and Scholastic mania for ascribing a state of being to everything real has infected even those western thinkers who claim that they are anti-Hellenic—not to mention the common *homo occidentalis*, who incurably philosophizes in indirect proportion to his recognizing himself as a philosopher.

Out of this prevailing confusion between the ontic and ethical orders, an extremely interesting contemporary phenomenon has emerged: The philosophers of atheism are rejecting an ontic god in the name of ethics, and the atheism of our day—although its proponents do not recognize the fact—has come paradoxically to consist in rejecting, in the name of the true God, a god who is not God. It is also apparent that as long as Christians and Jews do not understand the reason for atheism they cannot understand the God revealed in the Bible.

Heidegger asserts that we must avoid a "theological exegesis of conscience."[1] If he is here referring to God as understood in the classic theological treatises, he is absolutely right. But the God of the treatises in no way resembles the God of the Bible, whose being is ethical and without whom no conscience is possible. If the Absolute Imperative in the otherness of the neighbor did not go unheard, then the fundamental consciousness of guilt would not be possible. Unfortunately, Heidegger knows little of the history of philosophy and theology, as he demonstrates by asserting that the notions of eternal truths and an absolute subject are residues of theology in philosophy.[2] But precisely the contrary is true: Theology took the notion of eternal truths from Platonic philosophy, and in so doing ceased to be Christian; theology took the idea of the absolute subject from Descartes, Spinoza, and Hegel, not vice versa. Thus the judgment of Heidegger (and Sartre) on theology's role is of very little value.

The concept of an ethical God is in no way an attempt to "win back" the atheists to Christianity, for the ethical God cannot be reclaimed by and is not reconcilable with the history of Christianity. Moreover, an ethical God implies the destruction of all known historical churches, and it is these churches that are concerned about "winning back." The concept of an ethical God vindicates historical atheism.

Morality's keystone and inescapable conclusion is that no end, no matter how sublime or divine or eternal, justifies causing—or indifferently allowing—an innocent person to suffer. Infinite retribution in another life does not compensate for even a small injustice in this life. And if the god of theology proclaims that it does compensate, then he is an immoral god and in conscience we are obliged to rebel against him.

Here we are not dealing solely with the scandal of evil in the world, nor is the incisive verdict of conscience reducible to the classic problem of evil. We are dealing with injustice, and there is no compensation for injustice. Any god who has not come to undo the hell that we have made of this life is a cruel god, even if there is another life. Even if the god of the theologians is not responsible for the barbarous world in which we live, the mere fact that he intervenes in our history for ends other than the abolition of human injustice qualifies him as amoral and merciless. The anti-idolatrous confutations of Jeremiah, Deutero-Isaiah, and the Psalms all cry out against such divine indifference, basing their fiery protests entirely on the revelation of Exodus. The omnipotence of an amoral god could *compel me* to submission, but not *oblige* me to obedience. Not only should we refuse to worship and obey such a god, we should also be morally obliged to struggle against him, even if faced with certain defeat and condemnation to eternal torment. It is moral right, not physical power, that we are obliged to obey.

The truly moral person is one who believes that his moral obligation is the only God. This is what the Bible teaches.

THE GOD OF THE BIBLE

Gerhard von Rad's investigations of the earliest biblical writings clearly show that the primitive revelation of Yahweh had nothing to say about creation or the origin of the world.[3] The God who originally revealed himself to Israel was the God of the Exodus, and his self-revelation was simply an obligatory intervention on behalf of the oppressed against their oppressors. The legislation contained in the most ancient biblical tradition was conceived as a necessary part of this primordial revelatory intervention; the sole intention of these original laws was to prevent the re-establishment among the Israelites of the slavery and injustices that they had previously endured at the hands of the Egyptians.[4] Laws governing cultus, sexual behavior, food purification, and other purification rites were introduced at a later date.

The creation of the world was not mentioned in Yahweh's original self-description. Moreover, the authors of the Bible took for granted that the normal course of the world's history had no connection with

Yahweh and that he could not be held responsible for things that occurred before his intervention. This is clearly proven by the fact that Yahweh breaks into human history to correct it radically. And it is the "outcry" of the oppressed (cf. Exod. 3:7) that makes this God intervene to revolutionize history.

We do not mean to deny the *later* biblical teaching that Yahweh is the creator of humankind and the world. But scientific exegesis does not—as dogmatic theology does—indifferently juxtapose teachings in such a way that one cannot tell which of them is the central truth in function of which the other truths must be understood. For example, the "omnipotence" of the God of the Bible must be understood in a way completely different from the triumphalistic meaning it has in the West. A God whose sole definitional intervention consists in struggling against injustice and innocent suffering can only be the moral imperative in itself; and human free will is more powerful, so to speak, than the absolute moral imperative. Indeed the biblical description of the creation of man and woman (Gen. 1:26–4:16) is dedicated principally to emphasizing this autonomous human power.

For the authors of the Bible the createdness of the world and history are of secondary or tertiary importance, and we must reassert this very clearly today. The creation story is told first, not because of its importance, but because creation came first chronologically. Our understanding of Yahweh as Creator must not be allowed to blur or weaken our understanding of the essential nature of the protest and imperative of Yahweh (the God of the Exodus). Involved here, I believe, is an elementary principle of hermeneutics, a principle in force since the science of documentation first dealt with the biblical authors as real authors who compose a work, and not as mere compilers or archivists. It can help us grasp the relative importance of Yahweh as Creator if we keep in mind that the teaching that the world originated in the divinity was conceived outside of Israel and the Bible (cf. the Epic of Enuma Elish). There was a time when every reasonable thinker in Asia Minor professed this teaching (just as any reasonable contemporary of ours believes that Hitler was a monster—pardon this comparison *a viliori*), and the biblical accounts that have come down to us were redacted during that time.

How the truth of creation can be harmonized with the revealed fact that Yahweh is essentially the realization of justice clearly constitutes a problem for the authors of the first three chapters of Gensis. But it constitutes a problem precisely because they neither abandon nor minimize the sole revelatory definition of Yahweh as the God of the Exodus.

It is worth noting that in the fourth and eighteenth chapters of Genesis itself the one who manifests himself is simply the God of the Exodus, nothing more.

HUMAN CAUSALITY

When the Yahwist and the Priestly document say that Yahweh created man free, they wish more to emphasize that man is free than that God created him. Note how the Yahwist, after man's disobedience, has Yahweh say: "The man has become like one of us, knowing good and evil" (Gen. 3:22). These words enable us to understand what the Priestly writer meant when he has God say, at the moment of creating man: "Let us make man in our image and likeness to rule the fish in the sea, the birds of heaven, the cattle, all wild animals on earth, and all reptiles that crawl upon the earth" (Gen. 1:26). Because man is made in the likeness of God he has complete freedom of action.

Because of their unsound tendency toward abstraction, theologians have found in the first chapters of Genesis only this: God created everything that is. The authors' idea was very different. In the Yahwistic narration (Gen. 2:4–4:26) the emphasis is on man's causality, not God's; it was already known that the world originated in the divinity. I do not deny that Yahweh is the one who cursed the ground (Gen. 3:17), but the author of the account, addressing himself to man, insists: "Accursed shall be the ground *on your account*" (Gen. 3:17; see also Gen. 8:21: "Never again will I curse the ground because of man").

The theme is human causality. And the implications of the theme are so far-reaching that not only is our Greek, western mentality disconcerted by them, but also the materialists themselves are today still unable to accept them: Human work, human action, causes the pains of pregnancy and childbirth; barren unproductive lands are explained by human causality; death is due to human action. The first two affirmations occur in Gen. 3:16–19. The third is implicit in the placing of the account of Cain and Abel (Gen. 4:1–11) after the account of "the man," for the punishment threatened in Gen. 2:17 ("on the day that you eat from it [the tree], you will certainly die") was still pending, and Gen. 3:3 and 3:4 indicate that the author had not forgotten it. The connection is deliberate, as indicated by Gen. 4:11, which is the first curse in history directed against man: "Now you are accursed, *more than* the ground." (The Hebrew expression should be translated either in this way or: "Now you are accursed, *rather than* the ground.") In few translations, ancient or modern, does this phrase make any sense, for the translators have overlooked its connection with Gen. 3:17. The idea the Yahwist wants to express is this: Death entered history in the form of fratricide; it was not connatural to man as God made him.

In general terms Paul understood very well the emphasis of the Yahwistic narrative: "It was *through one man* that sin entered the world, and through sin death" (Rom. 5:12); "since it was man who brought death into the world, a man also brought resurrection of the dead" (1 Cor. 15:21); "as the issue of one misdeed was condemnation for all men, so the issue of one just act is justice and life for all men" (Rom. 5:18).

The point we must truly understand in the Yahwistic and Pauline concept of origins is human causality. This is the powerful message that the biblical authors were trying to convey, and if we let ourselves be distracted from it by the truth that God created all that is, then we prevent the Bible's message from reaching us. If an author asserts that injustice is the cause of death in the world, readers who disregard this unprecedented message to concentrate on human createdness and finitude are being ridiculous. Even today, in the last third of the twentieth century, the world lacks ears to hear that if injustice can be abolished from human history, then death too can be abolished. We cannot contend against death if we do not even see that death can be contended against.

But let us return to the biblical concept that responsibility for the world and history is not Yahweh's; if it is not, then the etymological sense of "omnipotence" cannot be applied to the God of the Bible. Of course the theological treatises, when asserting God's "omnipotence," usually include escape clauses noting that omnipotence means that God can do "whatever is possible" (God is not able, for example, to do something self-contradictory). But then, lest there be a merely verbal question, the biblical narrative requires us to amplify tremendously what is included under the theologians' definition of "impossible."

When God intervenes his principal activity is directed to the conscience. And through people's consciences he achieves his true intervention: "Cain, Cain, where is your brother Abel?" (Gen. 4:9); "Your brother's blood that has been shed is crying out to me from the ground" (Gen. 4:10).

The God of the Exodus is the God of conscience. The liberation of the slaves from Egypt was principally a work of the imperative of liberty and justice implacably inculcated into the Israelites: "I have indeed turned my eyes towards you; I have marked all that has been done to you in Egypt, and I am resolved to bring you up out of your misery in Egypt, into the country of the Canaanites, . . . a land flowing with milk and honey" (Exod. 3:16–17). This is practically the only message Yahweh sent to the Israelites through Moses. The instrument of liberation was the word of Moses; therefore Yahweh said to him: "I will help your speech and tell you what to say" (Exod. 4:12). But what God tells him is over and again the same: "Say therefore to the Israelites, 'I am Yahweh, and therefore I will release you from your labors in Egypt. I will rescue you from slavery there'" (Exod. 6:6). Moses protests to Yahweh that the Israelites do not want to listen to him (Exod. 6:12; 4:10), and from Yahweh's answers we perceive the basic intention of God's intervention: the inexorable inculcation of the imperative of liberty and justice (see Exod. 3:7–10; 3:16; 4:10–17; 5:21–23; 6:5–9; 6:12; 14:11–12; 15:25–26).

The pharaoh too was enjoined over and again of his obligation to free the slaves (Exod. 5:1; 6:11, 13, 29; 7:1–2; 7:16; 7:26; 8:16; 9:1, 13; 10:3). The hammering insistence of the narrative of the plagues itself is a pedagogical device to show how obstinate the hardening of the heart against the moral imperative can be; its intent is made clear (Exod. 7–13) by the recurrent theme of the "hardening of pharaoh's heart."

But the supreme injunction regarding the imperative of justice consists in the very literary composition of Exodus, in which the whole process of the liberation of the slaves issues into legislation that assures that the oppression once suffered at the hand of foreigners would not be repeated by compatriots. This idea, generative of the whole Exodus account, provides the literary unity for Exodus 18, in which Moses is for the first time described as a legislator. This idea is most explicit in the following very ancient legal texts: Exod. 22:20–26; 23:9; Lev. 19:33–34; 25:35–38; 19:35–36; 25:39–42; 25:47–55; Deut. 15:12–15; 16:9–12; 24:17–18; 24:19–22.

The only truly revelatory intervention of the God of the Bible in human history is the moral imperative of justice, and this imperative remains the sole manifestation of Yahweh's definitive presence in history.

Thus, Deuteronomy 4 explains the reason for the legislation prohibiting images of Yahweh: God is present only in his words (Deut. 4:12), referring to the ten "words" that we call the ten commandments (Deut. 4:13). In Rom. 1:18–32 Paul considers this explanation, given originally to the Israelites, valid for the whole human race. He asserts that all people know the same God and that they hinder this knowledge by their injustice. People have no need for civil or religious legislation to teach them the moral imperative; this is proved by the fact that the pagans, "who do not possess the law... are their own law, displaying the effect of the law inscribed on their hearts. Their conscience is called as witness, and their own thoughts argue the case on either side, against them or even for them" (Rom. 2:14–15).

In order that the moral imperative of justice, in which God consists, might arise in history, only one thing is needed: the otherness of the neighbor who seeks justice.

THE OTHER AS ABSOLUTE

Sartre is quite justifiably indignant at the slogan of the Polish government: "Tuberculosis slows down production."[5] As Sartre says, people matter, not production. A Marxism that overlooks the absolute in the outcry of the neighbor in misery must "ground" the imperative in its effect on productivity, just as the developmentalist Mexican government, or any bourgeois government, must legitimate expenditures on behalf of the poor before the supreme tribunal of capitalist productivity.

In reality, all that is needed for the imperative to arise is a person who needs our solidarity and our help, the "other" who is not I and cannot—either in a Socratic or a Hegelian way—have been implicit in what I already was nor, therefore, in what I already knew. This otherness is irreconcilable with monism of any form, whether spiritualistic monism or materialistic monism, whether atheistic monism or "theistic" monism—whose objective god does not summon us from the "other" but rather hermetically seals the solipsism of the self. Insofar as monism remains as a Hegelian residue in Marxism, to that degree Marxism is unable to rebel against the human misery of both the past and present. Moreover it must justify this misery, because in monism there is no break either with the past or with the present.

It is most important to emphasize at this juncture that the dualism of a spiritualistic worldview has no connection with the otherness that concerns us here. The former does not break through the immanence of the self, nor does it recognize realities other than those already conceived by its apparatus of spiritual categories and deductions. The same can be said for the pseudodualism of worldviews that affirm the existence of a world other than our own.

Only the summons of the poor person, the widow, the orphan, the alien, the crippled constitutes true otherness. Only this summons, accepted and heeded, makes us transcend the sameness and original solitude of the self; only in this summons do we find the transcendence in which God consists. Only this summons provides a reason for rebellion against the masters and the gods in charge of this world, those committed to what has been and what is. The irreducible moral imperative is the only convincing reason for atheism, and this imperative is the God of the Bible.

It is on this point that present-day Marxism is not radical enough. In Marxist communism, there can be no justification for care of the old, the mentally retarded, the born cripples. The god known as productivity has no place for them in the world. How sad that precisely when the human being is really at stake the Marxist foundations are inadequate. Marx's effort to provide "to each according to his needs" and not according to his productivity is to be applauded, but the limitations of present-day Marxism offer no philosophical basis for such provision. Breaking the link between income and output—a link systematized but not invented by capitalism—is indispensable to a true revolution against the past and the present and all their gods and masters. This Marx perceived clearly. What he failed to see is that providing for each according to his needs presupposes caring for people simply because they exist, which in turn presupposes an absolute imperative unknown in his system of thought. This is not some insignificant marginal issue from which Marx can prescind.

It has become a commonplace thesis that revolution will be radical to the degree that it is based on man himself, that is, to the degree that man himself is its root. We do not question this thesis; rather we wish to take it absolutely seriously. In an individualistic sense, "man himself" is a criterion based on the Socratic theory of recollection and positing a person sufficient unto himself with his concepts, memories, and Aristotelian or Hegelian deductions. "Other" people are of no concern to him. Nor is he concerned with contingent facts (of which the whole of history consists), except to deny them as such, as Hegel did. No revolution can be based upon this "man himself," for such a basis would allow for no change in the individualism and utilitarianism that have prevailed to date.

The man in whom radical revolution has its roots is the "other." The basis for this revolution cannot even be the collectivity of which I am a part and which I call "humanity," as belonging to me. For such a view really involves nothing more than an expanded egoism, a utilitarianism recast with worldwide dimensions. And this is not revolution, but rather the complete triumph of the capitalist criterion—"rightly understood" and organized.

The "man himself" on whom the radicalness of the revolution depends is the other person, his otherness itself taken with unconditional seriousness insofar as it cannot be resorbed by the self, insofar as it cannot be made into a part of myself, precisely insofar as it transcends me. In this irreducible otherness, and only in it, is Yahweh. Any other objectivity which we might wish to ascribe to God converts God into an idol, into a non-God. Furthermore, this otherness of the neighbor in need, in order that it be nonresorbable, must be God for me.

Exhortations to love of neighbor and arguments for humanism have followed one another in endless succession throughout our history; Marxism and existentialism are the latest in a long series. But as long as the outcry of the neighbor in need is not God for us we are condemning humankind to an eternal return of revolution alternating with oppression.

Sartre and Heidegger should consider it very significant—since philosophy is one expression of real history—that at the end of their lives Engels and Neitzsche professed the eternal return of all things as a concept of history. Marx himself flirted with this notion in another form when he spoke of an imaginary primitive communism; in this sense the communism he hoped to achieve would have been a return to origins. I do not see how Sartre and Heidegger can avoid a similar conception if the conscience that they posit is not the definitive intervention of the Absolute. Without such intervention, there is nothing to stop the cycles and circumvolutions.

RELIGION AND THE ETERNAL RETURN

Marx held that it was useless to oppose religion as long as the social alienations that produce it perdure. But I believe it is indeed necessary to combat it, and in fact the anticultus of Jesus Christ and the prophets was a struggle against religion. As long as people project the Absolute into some "objective," escapist dimension like cultus, god is an extension of the self and does not transcend the self; such a god does not break through the sameness of the self with real otherness. Only if God locates himself in the very appeal of the "other" can the world be changed.

Perhaps the greatest disaster of history was the resorption of Christianity by the framework of religion. It is difficult to imagine a greater falsification of Christianity; and the masters of this world could not have invented a more effective stratagem for preventing the revolution of oppressed humanity. Religion does not alter the prevailing order; it has always had an accepted place in society; the successive gods, no matter what their names, are of absolutely no importance. Christianity fell into this pattern because of the understandable weakness of the persecuted as well as the subtle, invincible strength of the oppressors.

The anthropological, apologetic thesis that all people are innately religious is in a certain sense true, but it has no relation to Christianity. Or rather, it is related insofar as religiosity can resorb and annihilate Christianity. It is as if we were told that all people are innately alienated. So what?

Far from challenging consumeristic society, religion constitutes an integral part of it. We need only glance at the work of the urban planners: parks, schools, bus stations, theatres, churches, stores, parking lots, packing houses, sports arenas. A society that wants to preserve itself has to attend to the various needs of the people—religious needs, recreational needs, nutritional needs, etc. For many centuries religious authorities have taken advantage of this fact. But the message of the Bible has no place in such a program, it does not fit; it does not satisfy these needs nor was it meant to. Yahweh does not come to occupy a place reserved for him in the cosmos by the social structure. He comes to revolutionize this cosmos and this entire social structure from their very foundations.

Therefore Yahweh rejects cultus, because it would be a way of domesticating him, of reducing him to religion. See Matt. 5:23; 1 Cor. 11:20–22; Matt. 7:21–23; Amos 5:21–25; Isa. 1:10–20; Hos. 5:1, 2, 6; 6:6; 8:13; Mic. 6:6–8; Jer. 6:18–21; 7:4–7, 11–15, 21–22; Isa. 43:23–24; 58:2, 6–10; etc. In these passages, Yahweh does not demand interpersonal justice "in addition to" cultus, nor does he ask that cultus be reformed, nor does he require—as the theology of the status quo has unrepentantly interpreted the above passages—that cultus be continued but with better internal dispositions on the part of the worshippers. The message of these passages can be summarized in this way: *I do not want cultus but rather interpersonal justice.* Anything we do to find some other meaning in this message is pure tergiversation. We quote Amos 5:21–25 as representative:

I hate, I spurn your pilgrim-feasts;
I will not delight in your sacred ceremonies.
If you present sacrifices and offerings
I will not accept them,
nor look on the buffaloes of your shared-offerings.
Spare me the sound of your songs;
I cannot endure the music of your lutes.
Let right roll on like a river
and justice like an ever-flowing stream.
Did you bring me sacrifices and gifts,
you people of Israel, those forty years in the wilderness?

Religion lubricates the cycles of the eternal return in history. Rebellion against religion is mandatory for anyone convinced that justice must be achieved, because persons with moral conscience cannot resign themselves to the eternal return of all things. But the eternal return is an iron circle, unbreakable as long as we fail to perceive the Absolute in the outcry of suffering humanity. Mechanistic materialism and bourgeois nihilism are perfectly interchangeable: Their common denominator—which renders them both ultimately without significance—is the insipid triviality to which they reduce the world when they deny the transcendence of the "other." Nothing but an intervening Absolute can cause the banal circumvolutions of history to stop. Without it, everything will continue to consist of deducible combinations and permutations of either material particles or eternal spiritual essences, but in either case the result is the same: Without this Absolute there can be no *ultimum* which is the achievement of justice in the world.

THE FUTURE GOD

But here we touch upon the problem of the *eschaton*, which will concern us in the following chapter. First we must consider a topic of greater importance: According to the Bible, Yahweh is a future God. The name "Yahweh" etymologically means "he who will be." The God of the Bible defines himself in Exod. 3:14 as the God who will be.

Because of the superficiality and banality we have learned in the West, it seems to us at first impossible that twenty-nine centuries ago a man should have written something of such overwhelming, unprecedented profundity. But hermeneutics would be in difficult straits indeed if it determined by these platitudinarian criteria what an ancient document *can* say and what it *cannot*.

"I will be who I will be," Yahweh says to Moses when Moses asks his name. The force of this name is in the future, for Yahweh goes on to say in the same verse, "Tell the children of Israel, 'I will be' has sent me to you" (Exod. 3:14).

If any interpretation is *a limine* excluded by the context, it is the one proposed by Loisy, who suggests that by the response "I will be who I will be" God evaded Moses' question and concealed his name. Martin Noth quite correctly comments, "The wider context lead[s] us to understand that the name Yahweh is disclosed to Moses as a real divine name."[6] And as Noth and Michel Allard point out, "I will be who I will be" is the etymological explanation of the name "Yahweh."[7] "Yahweh" is the third person imperfect (=future) of the verb "to be," and all those who are not God had to designate God in the third person; on the other hand in "I will be who I will be," it is Yahweh himself who speaks, in the first person.

Allard has shown that the Septuagint, the Vulgate, and other western versions erred when they translated this passage as "I am who I am." As Joüon demonstrates, in Hebrew stative verbs the imperfect always expresses the future, and there is nothing in the context of Exod. 3:14 to suggest that the verb *hayah* ("to be") has ceased to be stative and become active.[8] In fact the Septuagint always translates the first person singular of the imperfect as "I will be" (Greek *esomai*), except in this verse and in Hos. 1:9; in these two passages the translators of the Septuagint are not translating at all but rather propounding the same metaphysical theory that has so fascinated western theologians. As Allard shows, the other two supposed exceptions, Job 7:20 and 2 Sam. 15:34, really are not exceptions, the former because it has a consequential and not a temporal nuance, and the latter because the meaning is clearly preterite.

Yahweh is not, but rather will be. If our ontological categories render us incapable of understanding this, then good hermeneutics demands that we change our ontology, not the biblical message.

To understand this point, let us consider the most futuristic passage of the Old Testament, namely, Jer. 31:31–34 (the new covenant). Here God promises the new humanity that "I will be their God and they shall be my people" and, as a consequence, that all will know Yahweh—everyone, from the youngest to the oldest. The meaning of God's futureness depends on the meaning of "to know Yahweh." This passage, which carries us directly into the New Testament (2 Cor. 6:16, 14; 1 Cor. 11:25; Luke 22:20; Mark 14:24; Matt. 26:28), has occasioned a very serious methodological error in exegesis. Laden with important consequences, this error has consisted in trying to interpret the passage while prescinding from the definition of "to know Yahweh" that Jeremiah himself had formulated nine chapters previously:

He [Josiah] practiced justice and right;
this is good.
He defended the cause of the poor and the needy;
this is good.
Is this not what it means to know me?
It is Yahweh who speaks (Jer. 22:16).

"To know Yahweh" is a technical term, as Mowinckel, Botterweck, and H.W. Wolff have shown[9] and as is made apparent by an examination of Hos. 4:1–2; 6:4–6; 2:22; 5:4; 6:3; Isa. 11:2 (cf. 11:4–5); 1:3 (cf. 11:5–9); Hab. 2:14. "To know Yahweh" is a technical term meaning to do justice and right, to defend the cause of the poor and the needy.

Therefore, when Jer. 31:31–34 says that Yahweh *will be* God, it means that com-passion, solidarity, and justice will reign among people. This is why the God of the Bible is a future God: Because only in the future, at the end of history, will people recognize in the outcry and the otherness of their neighbor the absolute moral imperative that is God. This is what it means to know Yahweh, according to the Bible. In contradistinction to our ontological objects, the God of the Bible does not *be* first, and become known to us later; rather he *is* insofar as he is know to us. He does not allow himself to be changed into an object. He ceases to be God as soon as we break off our moral relationship with our neighbor.

According to western ontology ("a philosophy of injustice," as Levinas says) the object first exists and then it is known, and it exists independently of whether we know it or do not. Like a brick, like a thing, like an . . . object, precisely. Anyone would say that we cannot think of reality in any other way. And yet the biblical authors implacably insist that a god conceived as existing outside the interpersonal summons to justice and love is not the God revealed to them, but rather some idol; moreover the entire Bible is directed toward creating a world in which authentic relationships among people are made possible and become a reality. Only in a world of justice will God be. And if Marxism and existentialism do not find God in the western world, it is because in fact there is no God there, nor can there be.

NOTES

1. Martin Heidegger, *Sein und Zeit* (Tübingen: Niemeyer, 1960), p. 269 [Eng. trans.: *Being and Time*, trans. John Macquarrie and Edward Robinson (New York: Harper & Row, 1962), p. 313].

2. Ibid., p. 229 [Eng. trans.: p. 272].

3. Gerhard von Rad, *Das erste Buch Mose*, 7th ed., ATD 2–4 (Göttingen: Vandenhoeck, 1964) [Eng. trans.: *Genesis: A Commentary*, trans. John H. Marks (London: SCM, 1961)]; "Das theologisch Problem des alttestamentlichen Schöpfungsglaubens," in *Gesammelte Studien zum Alten Testament* (Munich: Kaiser, 1965), pp. 136–47 [Eng. trans.: "The Theological Problem of the Old Testament Doctrine of Creation," in *The Problem of the Hexateuch and Other Essays*, trans. Rev. E.W. Trueman Dicken (New York: McGraw Hill, 1966), pp. 131–43].

4. José Porfirio Miranda, *Marx y la biblia* (Salamanca: Sígueme, 1972), chaps. 2 and 4 [Eng. trans.: *Marx and the Bible*, trans. John Eagleson (Maryknoll, New York: Orbis Books, 1974)].

5. Jean-Paul Sartre, *Critique de la raison dialectique* (Paris: Gallimard, 1960), 1:109.

6. Martin Noth, *Das zweite Buch Mose*, 3rd ed., ATD 5 (Göttingen: Vandenhoeck, 1965), p. 31 [Eng. trans.: *Exodus: A Commentary*, trans. J.S. Bowden (Philadelphia: Westminster, 1969), p. 44].

7. Ibid., p. 31 [Eng. trans.: pp. 43–44]; Michel Allard, "Note sur la formule "ehyeh aser 'ehyeh,'" *Recherches de Science Religieuse* 45 (1957), p. 83.

8. Paul Joüon, *Grammaire de l'hébreu biblique*, 2nd ed. (Rome: Pontificio Istituto Biblico, 1947), no. 113a.

9. Sigmund Mowinckel, *Die Erkenntnis Gottes bei alttestament-lichen Propheten* (Oslo: Universistets-Forlaget, 1941); G. Johannes Botterweck, *"Gott Erkennen" im Sprachgebrauch des Alten Testaments* (Bonn: Peter Hanstein, 1951); Hans Walter Wolff, " 'Wissen um Gott' bei Hosea als Urform von Theologie," *Evangelishche Theologie* 12 (1952–53), pp. 533–34.

Chapter 3

The End of History

As we have said, the conditions of possibility of directly perceptible realities may be detected by the transcendental method. By this method we have established that God, as absolute imperative, is the great condition of possibility of the human conscience. By the same method we also discern that conscience requires another important condition of possibility, related to time; in this chapter we will investigate this additional condition of possibility.

EXISTENTIALISM AND TIME

Time is the touchstone of all philosophy. Contemporary philosophers must not forget that Hegel, Kierkegaard, and Marx were in revolt against Lessing in particular and Greco-Western philosophy in general because these had proved incapable of recognizing the importance of contingent facts. This rebellion failed in Hegel's hands, for he dealt with contingent facts by making them necessary. But the task has been taken up by existentialism, and here we hope to set forth the basic conditions of possibility for existentialism itself.

Heidegger correctly says, "Being cannot be grasped except by taking time into consideration."[1] Sartre summarizes Kierkegaard in the following terms: "The *existent* man cannot be assimilated by a system of ideas; regardless of how much we think or say about suffering, it escapes knowledge to the degree that it is suffered within itself and for itself and knowledge is impotent to transform it."[2] (Sartre continues, "It is noteworthy that Marxism's reproach of Hegel is the same, although from another point of view." One point is striking: To try to deduce real facts from matter or from anything else, merely to assert that they are deducible, is to assert that they are necessary and is therefore to strip of its basis the rebellion of the suffering person and his companions. Thus Kierkegaard's criticism of Hegel is much more radical than Marx's.)

The real person, the one who suffers, is always a contingent reality, that is, he is, but he need not be. Pre-existentialist knowledge, however, was concerned only with the necessary, that is, with what is and could not *not be*. Thus this knowledge misperceived the person and concentrated on essences. Kierkegaard, on the contrary, "made the relationship with a historical fact into something decisive."[3]

The existentialist revolution consists in rendering decisive our relationship with contingent facts. Our ability to transform reality depends entirely on relating to contingent facts in this way. But Kierkegaard discovered this relationship in the particular historical fact called Jesus Christ, and if Heidegger and Sartre consider this irrelevant, then their analysis has been superficial. We are not dealing with a structure that due to the chance of biographical anecdote was linked to the contingent fact called Jesus Christ, a structure which therefore could be disconnected from that fact in order to enrich the atemporal collection of available human experiences. We are rather dealing with the Messiah.

Heidegger discovered that meaningfulness is a condition of possibility for the "world" we actively construct around us, and without which we cannot really exist. He discovered that we cannot articulate a "world" if we are not committed to some meaningfulness. He proceeded one crucial step further when he discovered that meaningfulness either arises from temporality or it does not exist at all. In fact, temporality makes things coeval so that they constitute a world, for without temporality they are absent to each other (past or future, not present). But Heidegger did not consider carefully that temporality draws things together to constitute a meaningful world only to the degree that this temporality itself rests on the sure hope that there will be a messianic time. Time lacks all "sense" if there is no messianic time; temporality cannot give the world a meaningfulness that temporality itself does not have.

Heidegger recognizes that "if the term 'understanding' is taken in a way that is primordially existential, it means *to be projecting toward a potentiality-for-being for the sake of which any person exists*."[4] This potentiality-for-being is the eschatological future of the whole of humankind, not of the isolated individual. Without this potentiality-for-being, nothing has any meaning. Without it, therefore, we cannot understand, for we can understand only something with meaning. We confer meaning on the world by projecting it toward the definitive messianic end. This meaningfulness introduced into the world by the messianic *eschaton* is what gives temporality sense. Because of this meaningfulness time exists.

In a roundabout way, Sartre came to the same conclusion in his thesis on nothingness: "This nothingness that separates human reality from itself is at the origin of time." He goes on to explain, correctly emphasizing the collective dimension lacking in Heidegger: "The for-itself [the human being] is separated from the presence-to-itself which it lacks and which is its own possibility, in one sense separated by Nothing and in another sense by the totality of the existent in the world, inasmuch as the for-itself, lacking or possible, is for-itself as *a presence to a certain state of the world*."[5] This statement is a per-

fectly accurate observation. Our projected presence to
the final state of the world is at the root of time, as the
condition of possibility of time. Without the messianic
eschaton there would be no meaningfulness to the extension of reality into successive past, present, and future moments. Moreover, if the person did not anticipate the presence-to-himself that he lacks, he would not
be for-himself but rather a thing; he would not be conscious of existing; he would not be conscious of himself.
This presence-to-itself is thus the condition of possibility for the very existence of the person as person, of the
person as for-itself, of the person insofar as he is not a
thing. In one sense nothingness separates him from the
eschatological presence-to-itself, which the person can
anticipate and in fact necessarily does anticipate. In
another sense the totality of what exists separates the
person from the eschatological presence-to-itself, since
this future presence-to-itself could not be conscious,
could not be for-itself, if it were not a presence to a whole
world that had been completely transformed.

Thus we can grasp that the messianic *eschaton* is a
condition of possibility for the fundamental consciousness of guilt that we considered in the first chapter.
Sartre expresses it well:

It is only as a lack to *be suppressed* that lack can be internal for
the for-itself, and the for-itself can realize its own lack only by
having to be it; that is, by being a project toward its suppression.[6]

The worker does not represent his sufferings to himself as
unbearable; he adapts himself to them not through resignation but because he lacks the education and reflection necessary for him to conceive of a social state in which these sufferings would not exist.[7]

It is necessary here to reverse common opinion and to acknowledge that it is not the harshness of a situation or the
sufferings that it imposes which are motives for conceiving of
another state of affairs in which things would be better for
everybody. It is only when we can conceive of a different state
of affairs that a new light falls on our troubles and our suffering and that we *decide* that these are unbearable.[8]

That group of living beings called the human race has not been the same since Christ came. Any philosophy that claims to be concrete and yet prescinds from the impact that Christ has had on humankind is a ridiculous contrivance. To ignore Christ's significance requires intellectual acrobatics that only emphasize it and thus establish it all the more conclusively. From the time Christ demonstrated what a person can be, our dissatisfaction with what we are has become torturous. Since Christ came it is worth the trouble to be a person. It matters not if humankind is better or worse since his coming; it is possible that we have lived no more justly and lovingly than before Christ. But humankind itself has changed, for it now has an intolerable sense of lack. A philosophy that ignores this is deliberately playing blindman's bluff. The Messiah is the basis for the world's time in a sense unspeakably deeper than any chronological "A.D." The anguish and guilt that make existing possible are anguish and guilt with respect to the Messiah. For the vindication of all the generations that have died and are now dying—crushed by the heel of oppression and cruelty—depends on our taking the messianic *eschaton* with unrestricted seriousness.

Before going any further, let us summarize three fundamental points: *First:* "Being cannot be grasped except by taking time into consideration";[9] "the central problematic of all ontology is rooted in the phenomenon of time, if rightly seen and rightly explained."[10] This notion was omitted from the whole of the pre-Hegelian philosophical tradition, except Giambattista Vico. In their search for being, the metaphysicians overlooked being because they did not consider time. On the other hand, the anthropologists of time (in Mexico, Octavio Paz and Carlos Fuentes) have not realized that they have touched upon the metaphysical problem par excellence.

Second: Time in general is not the condition of possibility for authentic existence, but rather future time. On the first occasion that time presents itself, it does so as future. The past is past as a function of the future; the present is present because it is not future. And the future is presented as anguish because it demands decision. (As we will see, according to the New Testament the *eschaton* must be made.) The meaning of the past and the present depends on what in the future we will make them to have been.

Third: The future alone is not the condition of possibility for existing, but rather the messianic future; otherwise the future enters into series with the past and the present as interchangeable elements of an eternal return.

THE CONTEMPORANEITY OF CHRIST

In his criticism of Heidegger, Sartre rightly says, "To be in the world is not to escape from the world toward oneself but to escape from the world toward a beyond-the-world which is the future world."[11] But this future world constitutes a beyond only to the degree that it is a solution and an abolition of all our injustices and miseries. If it were not messianic it would suffer from the same dearth of meaningfulness as the past and present.

But, some will object, Christ is in the past.

I will devote the remaining eight chapters of this book to a due consideration of this objection. But let us be well aware that this objection involves the true problem of existentialism—the true problem of time and the true problem of being. In my opinion, this problem has not been resolved. And the reason it has not been resolved is that the New Testament has been read through Greek spectacles.

"Everything I have written," says Kierkegaard, "has tended to bring out the meaning of contemporaneity."[12] "We have to erase eighteen hundred years of Christian history and make ourselves contemporaneous with the moment when God appeared in time."[13] In this idea we find the origin of existentialism, and, as we shall see, existentialism cannot be separated from its origin. But Kierkegaard did not achieve what he intended. On the one hand, we cannot leap nineteen hundred years into the past. On the other, we are not dealing with the timeless, celestial Christ of dogmatic theology—which was devoted to reconstituting the Platonic world with an apparently different content; we are rather dealing with the historical Jesus. I am committed to the Christ who is within time, the Christ we did not understand.

We killed Mozart and Beethoven by starvation and incomprehension, and yet we ornament our lives with their music and call them the honor and glory of the West. But they represent a supreme protest against the West. We do nothing to prevent the same thing from happening again. Van Gogh arrives and is given the same treatment. If a generation were able to prevent such callousness, it would be transformed to such a degree that it could understand Jesus Christ and thereby could begin to make Christianity real.

Let us sum up: On the one hand, we are dealing with the historical Jesus and not the Jesus of some heavenly world nor the Christ of the ecclesiastical Eucharist. On the other, real time does not allow of manipulation. One cannot disdain "vulgar time" in escapist fashion, as Heidegger does. Nor can one—and this amounts to the same thing—consider time as if it were the object of anthropological study: "Unquestionably the conception of time as a fixed present and as pure actuality is more ancient than that of chronometric time, which is not an immediate apprehension of the flow of reality but is instead a rationalization of its passing."[14]

Chronological, dateable time is an inescapable reality; it does not necessarily function as an escapist ruse that enables us to avoid making decisions. It is even more escapist to postulate that time does not exist and that existentially only temporality exists—as Bultmann, following Heidegger, does in reducing the future to futureness, the past to pastness, and the present to presentness. Scholasticism's traditional evasion consists in resorting to a "Christ of faith"—although it may not use this term—a Christ who seemingly remains in a heavenly, Platonic world, outside of time and history. Dogmatic theology could assert contemporaneity with Christ only by assuming a timeless Christ, and this maneuver greatly resembles the Heideggerian disdain for ordinary time.

These and other such conceptual manipulations are symptomatic of an unfulfilled metaphysical need. Contemporaneity with Christ is central to Kierkegaard's thought because Christ is the Messiah; Kierkegaard seeks contemporaneity with the messianic future. Because he fails to attain true contemporaneity, Kierkegaard therefore appears as a "bard of the return" ("*chantre du retour*"), as Wahl says.[15]

Kierkegaard could raise the question of contemporaneity with Christ only because he perceived, though obscurely, the central teaching of the gospel. Our answer must come from a scientific analysis of the New Testament.

THE ETHICAL NATURE OF TIME

The fact that time does not allow of manipulation is indicative of its ethical character; it is indicative of its irreducible otherness with respect to the self. The conscience we spoke of in the first chapter cannot be eliminated by verbal prestidigitation: For our conscience tells us that we have oppressed the other. And in the outcry of the other is the absolute imperative, as we saw in chapter 2.

For centuries the writers of epistemological treatises taught that the sure sign of our touching upon being was that the object of our inquiry was independent of mental considerations. Thanks to Husserl and Scheler, contemporary philosophers have seen that this being of epistemology and ontology is less independent of our intentions and interests than was believed. As Heidegger says: "All ontical experience of entities—both circumspective calculation of what is close at hand, and positive scientific cognition of what can be observed—is based upon projections of the being of the corresponding entities, projections which in every case are more or less transparent. But in these projections there lies hidden the 'toward which' of the projection; and on this, as it were, the understanding of being nourishes itself."[16]

Being, which seemed so demonstrably independent of us, turns out to be unavoidably conditioned by our thought processes. It is constituted as it is because of our plans, our desires, our longings. In other words, far from being independent of the self, being is an extension of the self. It can be manipulated. I am referring to being as it is understood by metaphysics and realism of whatever stripe, not figments of fantasy.

On the other hand, the outcry of the neighbor in need—the only true content of the voice of conscience—absolutely cannot be manipulated. In it there is indeed otherness. It is not a branch office of the self and its world and projections. It cannot be encompassed. It is not neutral; it demands decision. Its otherness cannot be absorbed by the thinker; it remains uncompromisingly exterior to and independent of the thinker. It is truly real and is not at my disposition; nor does it succumb to my powers of affirmation or negation or representation. This outcry alone is imperative. Its demand, insofar as I heed it, increases my responsibility. I am no longer alone. In a word, it is otherness, and manipulation of otherness is impossible.

Time is cut from the same cloth, for it presents exactly the same resistance to the conceptual stratagems and legerdemain by which we try to make the past and the future into the present. It is for this reason that Kierkegaard and the existentialists have failed in their attempt with regard to contemporaneity (although philosophy's greatest success is to have formulated the true problem). Time is ethical, and it can be known only in an ethical resolution. History is made of the outcry of all the oppressed; in this it consists. Neither Kierkegaard nor Heidegger realized this, and therefore their philosophies are individualistic. Kierkegaard never understood that Jesus Christ is the Messiah to the extent that he is the savior of all the poor and the liberator of all the oppressed (see Luke 4:17–21; 7:18–23; Matt. 11:2–6; 12:15–23). On the other hand, Heidegger, with the intention of entertaining no illusions, refuses to look toward the future. His stoic approach of "confronting *the nothingness*" is therefore symptomatic of his failure in his attempt to know *being*. As Sartre says—and this is the fundamental refutation—, "Every negation that did not have beyond itself, in the future, the meaning of an engagement as a possibility which comes to it and toward which it flees, would lose all its significance as negation."[17]

HISTORY AND ESCHATON

With regard to Marx and Sartre, we must explicitly state here that the *eschaton* of the Bible (not that of dogmatic theology) is *in this world*. If we do not state this clearly, there will never be mutual understanding. The biblical *eschaton* is not beyond history, but rather the final and definitive stage of history.

Christ says, "How blest are those of a gentle spirit; they shall have *the earth* for their possession" (Matt. 5:5). No honest person could possibly translate this as locating the *eschaton* in some other world. Christ is speaking of the earth, of this world. Consistent with Old Testament tradition, Christ affirms an end of history in which the just, the gentle, the com-passionate, those in solidarity with their neighbor will be the ones to possess the earth, while the unjust, the hardhearted, the oppressors will be eliminated (or converted).

All this is set forth very clearly in the Old Testament. See for example Ps. 37:28–29, to which Matthew undoubtedly was alluding in the beatitudes cited above:

The unjust will be annihilated,
and the children of the wicked destroyed.
The just shall possess the land
and shall live there forever.

But escapist theologians, posing as guardians of the originality of the New Testament, have ingeniously taught that Christ's message was totally new and that it is therefore superfluous to study Old Testament eschatology. Christ, they say, is the sole authority. But the beatitude quoted above demonstrates that on this point, regardless of what the theologians say, the New Testament reiterates the Old. In the New Testament *eschaton* the com-passionate and the brotherly will conquer this world and no other. Paul denies that those who observe the law "will inherit *the world*," but he assures us that those who through faith become just will do so: "The promise of inheriting the world was not made to Abraham and his descendants on account of the law, but on account of the justice of faith" (Rom. 4:13). Paul of Tarsus has been called a "spiritualistic" writer; but even if the designation were accurate, it does not justify the otherwordly interpretations that have been made of Christ's message.

All biblical scholars without exception have seen that the expression "the kingdom of heaven" means "the kingdom of God" and not a kingdom in the sky, for "heaven" is late Judaism's classical circumlocution for designating God without mentioning his name. Such respect for a name alone might seem excessive to us, but the documentary evidence provided by the Jewish literature of that time is abundantly clear on this point.

Theodor Zahn rightly states, "After the Beatitudes of Matt. 5:3–10, it is obvious that the reward (mentioned in 5:12) will be given to the disciples only in the kingdom that must be established on earth."[18] "Your reward is great in heaven" does not mean that they will be rewarded in heaven, "as if it said *hoti misthon polyn lēpsesthe en tois ouranois* ['you will receive a great reward in heaven']." What it does say is that human actions are in the mind of God, using the word "heaven" instead of "God." To put it figuratively: Human actions ascend to the knowledge of God in heaven and there their reward accumulates like a treasure. This does not say that the reward will be enjoyed in heaven. In Acts 10:4 Luke says, "Your prayers and acts of charity have gone up to heaven to speak for you before God." And this is the precise meaning conveyed by Matt. 5:12; 6:20; Luke 6:23; 12:33; 1 Pet. 1:4–8. This idea already existed in the Old Testament (see Tob. 12:12–15), and the New Testament offers no textual or documentary basis for asserting that it differs from the Old on this point.

The passages in Paul and Luke that speak of extraterrestrial "paradise" (2 Cor. 12:4; Luke 23:43) or a situation called "the bosom of Abraham" (Luke 16:23) or an imminent "being with Christ" (Phil 1:23) have been very carefully studied by the respected Joachim Jeremias and the Catholic Paul Hoffman using all the comparative resources of the Jewish documentation of that period.[19] These passages allude to an entirely provisional situation that will last only until the kingdom of God is established definitively and perfectly on earth.

Objective exegesis has no difficulty in admitting a "heavenly Jerusalem," made up of—as the book of Revelation itself describes it—the apostles, the martyrs, and the just who have died. There is no difficulty *provided* that we understand that this Jerusalem will come down to earth, according to Rev. 21:2, 10. It is therefore identical to the "paradise" referred to by Luke and Paul, an entirely provisional situation having only marginal importance. It is not a place or another world. It consists of persons (cf. Rev. 3:12) whom the book of Revelation considers important, not because of their provisional and passing situation, but because they are destined to "reign upon earth," as Rev. 5:10 expresses it. The description of this kingdom which will have come down to earth (Rev. 21:2, 10) even specifies that there "they shall reign forever and ever" (Rev. 22:5).

In a perhaps not too distant future, when dogmatic theologians become more faithful to the Bible, they will emphatically have to recall that they used to think of the "ultraterrestrial" only as "eternal," with "eternal" understood in a merely negative way as simply an absence of time. This last-mentioned idea is the popular but false conception of eternity (tolerated or even fostered by dogmatic theologians). Upon this popular notion is based the equally false belief that the eternal is of greater value than time and history.

In Matt. 25:34 when Christ says to the just, "Possess the kingdom that has been ready for you," he is speaking of the same kingdom that according to Matt. 12:28 already "has arrived" (*ephthasen*, the aorist, that is, the preterite tense) on earth. And the Evangelist insists that "the field" in which this kingdom is established "is the world" (Matt. 13:38), that Christ will return to this kingdom to root out from it all "those who do iniquity" (Matt. 13:41), and that "the just will then shine as brightly as the sun in the kingdom of their Father. If you have ears, then hear" (Matt. 13:43). The beatitude contains the same idea: "The gentle will possess the earth" (Matt. 5:5). The Bible has been straightforwardly clear on this point from the very beginning, but prescientific exegetes had no ears to hear what it was saying.

Fidelity to the biblical text should not be confused with Protestant fundamentalism. In 1964, after describing modern methods of studying the Gospels, the Pontifical Biblical Commission added: "There remain [in the Gospels] many questions, and these of the gravest moment, in the discussion and elucidation of which the Catholic exegete can and should freely exercise his intelligence and skill."[20] And the Commission expressly states that this is to "prepare the ground for the decisions of the Church's teaching authority." Thus our interpretations should not wait on the pronouncements of ecclesiastical authority; on the contrary, our investigations must move forward. Since the publication of this document, anyone who accuses a serious Catholic student of the Bible of Lutheranism is contradicting the teachings of the Catholic church itself.

To return to our point, the biblical *eschaton* is in this world. It is not beyond history, but is rather the end of history. We must bear this in mind throughout the following chapters, where we will try to make the Fourth Gospel the basis for solving Kierkegaard's problem, which is the problem of existentialism and of all serious philosophy.

THE NECESSARY TELOS

Humanity can become conscious of sin to the degree that it conceives of its situation as able to be changed. Sartre puts it very well: The person "can realize [his] own lack only by having to be it; that is, by being a project toward its suppression."[21] In this chapter we are trying to describe explicitly a condition of possibility of the consciousness of guilt and of the absolute imperative itself.

It seems to me that Sartre makes no sense when he imagines evil to be nothingness inherent in the human being. To think of evil as nothingness, as the negation and lack of being, is the key to Thomas Aquinas's apologetic Aristotelian theodicy, which was inherited by Leibnitz and Hegel: Since God creates only being, then evil cannot be attributed to God. Such a premise naturally concludes in Leibnitzian optimism: "Everything for the best in the best of all possible worlds." But evil is not nothingness. If evil were nothingness, then human finitude would be sufficient cause for the existence of evil. And then there would be no hope.

According to the Bible evil is definitely not the mere absence of being: "It was through one man that sin *entered* the world, and through sin death" (Rom. 5:12). For the Bible, evil and good are equally real: "It was a man who brought death into the world; a man also brought resurrection of the dead" (1 Cor. 15:21).

If evil were not contingent, we would not even be aware of its existence. We become aware of sin to the degree that we affirm an *eschaton* in which sin will be totally abolished—which implies that it is contingent.

Sartre holds that the "future is not *realized*. What is realized is a human being who is *designated* by the future and who is constituted in connection with this future."[22] If Sartre is suggesting that the future is ever reborn and can never be reached, for otherwise it would cease being for-itself and become in-itself, he is in a certain sense correct: The being of human relationships, the being that cannot exist without our decision, is ever reborn and cannot be petrified. The messianic *eschaton* signifies definitive justice; it does not mean people are suddenly frozen into lifeless statues. The otherness of the other is irreducible. Once I have heeded the moral imperative, I am no longer ever alone, and its demand increases to the degree that I obey it. The deepening of interpersonal understanding has no limits. But the future is not a mere structural category of the present, as Bultmann would have it. An *eschaton* consisting of mere warning, of unfulfilled threat directed toward the present destroys itself. If we reduce the future to abstract, repeatable futureness we vaporize history and annihilate time by conceptual decree. We re-establish the eternal return under the guise of the perennially reborn future. At this point Sartrian philosophy becomes the lackey of the bourgeoisie and justifies the tranquillizing bourgeois maxim: "That's the way it's always been." This is pure negation, and in refutation we need only return to Sartre's own words: "Every negation that did not have beyond itself, in the future, the meaning of an engagement as a possibility which comes to it and toward which it flees, would lose all its significance as negation."[23]

This argument also refutes the antiteleology of a certain sector of Marxism, an attitude marked by ingenuousness and superficiality. The denial of an end of history, a *telos*, a goal to the centuries-old strife of humankind, is contradicted by Marx's *Critique of the Gotha Program*, in which Marx describes communist society in terms of two phases of increasing justice—an unequivocal positing of a *telos*. And let us recall that Lenin adopted this description. The workers' dissatisfaction, their rebellion, and the class struggle that Marxism discovers in history (it does not produce them) would be impossible if workers could in no way visualize a goal to their struggle, a society in which the need for profit and for the exploitation of others might cease to exist.

Certain Marxists abhor the idea of *telos* because it represents a finality written into nature, and acknowledging this finality would oblige them to acknowledge a creator who did the writing. They are right about the relationship between *telos* and nature, but that relationship is not the point here. Our point is the *eschaton* that we human beings are writing into nature—a process in which the Marxists themselves participate when they struggle to understand reality and to change it. The workers' struggle, which is our concern here, carries within it a goal to history. And if it is a superficial observation to deny the existence of a *telos* within the workers' struggle, it is even more superficial to deny that there is a *telos* in the act of observing: Those making the denial claim to be merely observing that struggle: But why do they observe? What is science, the best of the sciences, trying to accomplish? Why are certain people determined to make rigorous and methodical observations until they reach conclusions?

Knowing does not consist simply in observing, but in

understanding. We can understand something only if it has meaning. But nothing has meaning unless it is projected toward the messianic end of humankind, toward the real goal of history. Something can be understood only in relation to an end that the whole of history struggles to reach.

By the act of explaining something, the Marxists themselves imply that there is a questioner, an other, and they take a position with regard to that other. They believe that in the end all people will be able to understand each other, and they could not be more correct. But as soon as the otherness of the questioner enters the picture, the whole moral order becomes involved. And this order implies an *eschaton* in which morality is achieved. Positivism is not conscious of its own conditions of possibility. As Levinas says, "The essence of discourse is ethical."[24] And therefore the essence of science is ethical as well. The very words we use to designate things testify that "others" and I participate in them. The very universality of language and concepts has its origin in the moral responsibility that I have in relation to others. Science is to speak of the world to another.

As Levinas notes, critical knowledge can be achieved only "in the face of . . . ";[25] it is possible only with regard to otherness. "If philosophy consists in knowing critically, that is, in seeking a foundation for its freedom, in justifying it, it begins with conscience, to which the other is presented as the Other, and where the movement of thematization is inverted. But this inversion does not amount to 'knowing oneself' as a theme attended to by the Other, but rather in submitting oneself to an exigency, to a morality."[26]

If we are to follow the transcendental method rigorously, we must go even further. Not only is the possibility of philosophy and positive science conditioned by the summons that arises from the otherness of the neighbor. The consciousness *(Bewusstsein)* that every person has of himself is likewise so conditioned. The ability to think of myself in a thematic way depends on conscience *(Gewissen)*, because the self becomes aware of itself only in the presence of the other. But as soon as one is in the presence of the "other," the absolute imperative is fully operative. And the absolute imperative has force only because history has an end, because the *eschaton* is history's *telos*. John says it in other words: Whoever denies the Messiah does not have God.

THE MYTH OF THE GOLDEN AGE

But before dealing with John we must touch upon another point, an appendix to this chapter on the end of history. I am speaking of an error that occurs frequently and more or less explicitly among people of the most diverse cultural levels, namely, the belief that the *eschaton* recreates a past Golden Age from which the course of history should never have departed.

This understanding of history as deviation from ancient perfection often underlies, implicitly or explicitly, the theology of original sin (although not the *biblical* account). In Hegel's *Phenomenology of Spirit* the final achievement of human history is a great return to the original "idea," albeit on a superior and sublimated level (as Urs von Balthasar has approvingly noted). This same understanding of history is operative in the myth of an indemonstrable primitive communism.

More recently and closer to home Octavio Paz posits this notion as the basis for all revolutionary thought: "Every revolution tries to bring back a Golden Age. . . . [This age] prefigured and prophesied the new society which the revolutionary proposes to create. . . . The originality of the Plan of Ayala resides in the fact that this Golden Age was not a simple creation of man's reason or a mere hypothesis."[27] "Thanks to the Revolution, the Mexican wants to reconcile himself with his history and his origins."[28] And Octavio Paz the anthropologist boldly proclaims: "The 'eternal return' is one of the implicit assumptions of almost every revolutionary theory."[29]

If revolution means repeating what has already existed, then frankly our language is leaving us in the lurch. True, the etymology of the term "revolution" implies repetition, but, etymology notwithstanding, "eternal return" is *not* the universally accepted meaning of the term "revolution." So we must disregard Paz's last statement. His other assertions that we have cited attempt to express a diffuse sentiment of return to origins, but in my opinion there is no such sentiment expressed either in the Plan of Ayala or in any other authentic revolution.

Carlos Fuentes is a trustworthy witness for this opinion for he too, following Paz, confesses "the nostalgia for paradise lost."[30] Nevertheless he shows that Zapata and his Plan of Ayala harked back "in appearance only" to documents and situations of the past.[31] Truly, no Golden Age had ever existed, nor did Zapata ever imagine that it had. Revolution has nothing to do with the resurrection of a structure from the past. Revolution is not nourished by myths, but rather by an exact perception of injustice suffered.

If our ideological premises lead us to mourn the loss of some bygone time, if our desire, more or less explicit, is for a grand return, then the logical consequence is to consider "historical change [as] daily more remote and unlikely."[32] Ibargüengoitia rightly criticizes Paz: "We come to the conclusion that we have always been in the same situation and that therefore it is unlikely that we can change."[33]

In his analysis of the Mexican revolution, Paz's observations are more accurate: "The Mexican does not want to be either an Indian or a Spaniard. Nor does he want to be descended from them. He denies them. And he does not affirm himself as a mixture, but rather as an abstraction: he is a man. He becomes the son of Nothingness. His beginnings are in his own self."[34] This indeed is revolution: the destruction of the past in the name of the humanity that has been oppressed. But this is just as irreconcilable with the great return to a Golden Age as it is with the eternal return of an inexorable cycle.

The ability to break with the past is a projection toward a definitively human future—even though, like Fuentes, we may suppose the break to occur instantaneously. The Mexican revolution provides an important example here. It did not imitate anything. It was spontaneous and did not seek to justify itself on the basis of some mythological communist prehistory. The instantaneousness that Fuentes observes in the character of Mexican revolutionaries rather derives from the fact that our revolution was rapidly betrayed and defeated; it consists, even more to the point, in a tacit conviction—habitual among us Mexicans—that a revolutionary outbreak is certainly justified, notwithstanding its eventual defeat; it implies the conviction that "one of these times" the revolution will triumph. I think this is the correct theory of the Mexican revolution. Notwithstanding his theoretical belief in a grand return, Fuentes quite accurately observes that "in Mexico the centuries-old danger, alienation, and violence long since have created in the people the conviction that the end might be just around the corner."[35] The apparent instantaneousness depends, it seems, on this: At any moment justice for all who have been oppressed might be realized. The events of 1968 and 1971 and the later activities of rural and urban guerrillas demonstrate this. Fuentes's thesis that Mexicans are convinced that the end and the future can only be catastrophic seems completely gratuitous to me. If Mexicans believed this, then real revolution would have been impossible. And a real revolution occurred.

Fuentes and Paz are right, however, in believing, as

anthropologists, that the concept of time is of decisive importance in philosophy and that every person, even the most uncultured, has a concept of time. The end of an agricultural year is quite different from the end of a presidential term. Different again are the end of the century, the end of the modern period (or the contemporaneous period, as some writers would term it), or the end of an entire civilization. And these are all different from the end of a whole world or an eon—and the beginning of another, definitive world or eon.

We find the fatalistic natural cycle of the agricultural year not only in the Aztec calendar with its recurrent fiestas, but also in the religious calendar of the "Christian" colonizers. The latter got their calendar, through the church, from the Greco-Roman teachers of the eternal return. Religion, as we have already said, is the natural lubricant of the cycles of the eternal return. To think that the church reduced the dates of Christ's life to integral elements of that lubricant— the Christ who, more than anyone, sought to break the social structures that kept humankind ensnared in vegetal time! Modern lineal time thinly disguises its underlying principle of eternal return with a veneer of entirely superficial "progress," as demonstrated by the current widespread belief that it is impossible for human nature to change. When we see how the Nahuatl, the western, and the post-revolutionary cultures share the same concept of time, we realize that the differences among them are of little significance. The modern Mexican calendar, featuring Benito Juárez and the Virgin of Guadalupe, differs only in externals from the previous religious calendars. It recurs. And it convinces people that no matter what happens, nothing really changes at all.

Fuentes and Paz assert that things will change if we profess the great return to the Golden Age instead of the eternal return. But there never was any such Golden Age. And a myth will not break the chain of fatalism, made of mistrust, cruelty, and injustice among people. The chain can be broken only if we recognize the outcry of the neighbor as absolute.

In his work on Nietzsche, Heidegger correctly states that the importance of the idea of eternal return is matched only by that of the Platonic thesis regarding the world of ideas.[36] But the philosophy of the world of ideas itself was invented to strip time of all its importance: History and the future were reduced to mere applications of universal essences, mere "cases"; only essences had any importance, not the world of their merely fortuitous applications; time was changed into an eternal return of "cases" already implicit in the essences. For long and unhappy centuries "Christian" theologians believed that the idea of eternal return could be separated from the rest of Greek philosophy. Today we are seeing that this conception of time permeates and conditions the whole of Greek philosophy; whatever elements of Greek philosophy are not colored by the notion of the eternal return have no real importance. The Platonic world of ideas was not a philosophic invention independent of the conception of history as eternal return. It was a way of assuring that the human mind reduced history to an eternal return. Christian theology adopted the Platonic world of ideas, stuffing into it other equally nontemporal notions. As a result, theology abandoned the history of real people to its wretched luck.

NOTES

1. Martin Heidegger, *Sein und Zeit* (Tübingen: Niemeyer, 1960), p. 19 [Eng. trans.: *Being and Time*, trans. John Macquarrie and Edward Robinson (New York: Harper & Row, 1962), p. 40].

2. Jean-Paul Sartre, *Critique de la raison dialectique* (Paris: Gallimard, 1960), 1: 19.

3. Jean Wahl, *Études kierkegaardiennes* (Paris: Vrin, 1949), p. 310 note.

4. Heidegger, *Sein und Zeit*, p. 336 [cf. Eng. trans.: *Being and Time*, p. 385].

5. J.-P. Sartre, *L'être et le néant* (Paris: Gallimard, 1943), p. 146 [cf. Eng. trans.: *Being and Nothingness*, trans. Hazel E. Barnes (New York: Citadel, 1968), p. 78].

6. Ibid., p. 249 [Eng. trans.: p. 174].

7. Ibid., p. 510 [Eng. trans.: p. 411].

8. Ibid., p. 510 [cf. Eng. trans.: pp. 410–11]; Sartre's emphasis.

9. Heidegger, *Sein und Zeit*, p. 19 [Eng. trans.: *Being and Time*, p. 40].

10. Ibid., p. 18 [Eng. trans.: p. 40].

11. Sartre, *L'être et le néant*, p. 251 [Eng. trans.: *Being and Nothingness*, p. 176].

12. Wahl, *Études kierkegaardiennes*, p. 296.

13. Ibid., p. 329.

14. Octavio Paz, *El laberinto de la soledad*, 7th ed. (Mexico City: Fondo de Cultura Económica, 1969), p. 189 [Eng. trans.: *The Labyrinth of Solitude*, trans. Lysander Kemp (New York: Grove Press, 1961), p. 210].

15. Wahl, *Études kierkegaardiennes*, p. 251.

16. Heidegger, *Sein und Zeit*, p. 324 [cf. Eng. trans.: *Being and Time*, p. 371].

17. Sartre, *L'être et le néant*, p. 242 [cf. Eng. trans.: *Being and Nothingness*, p. 169].

18. Theodor Zahn, *Das Evangelium des Matthäus*, 3rd. ed. (Leipzig: A. Deichert, 1910), p. 197.

19. Joachim Jeremias, "paradeisos," *TWNT*, 5:766–67 [Eng. trans.: *TDNT*, 5:769–70]; "hades," *TWNT*, 1:148–49 [Eng. trans.: *TDNT*, 1:148–49]; "geenna," *TWNT*, 1:655–56 [Eng. trans.: *TDNT*, 1:657–58]; *The Parables of Jesus* (New York: Scribner's, 1963), p. 185; Paul Hoffman, *Die Toten in Christus* (Münster: Aschendorff, 1966).

20. *Acta Apostolicas Sedis*, 1964, p. 716 [Eng. trans.: *Catholic Biblical Quarterly*, vol. 26, no. 3 (July 1964): 309].

21. Sartre, *L'être et le néant*, p. 249 [Eng. trans.: *Being and Nothingness*, p. 174].

22. Ibid., p. 173 [cf. Eng. trans.: p. 104]; Sartre's emphasis.

23. Ibid., p. 242 [cf. Eng. trans.: p. 169].

24. Emmanuel Levinas, *Totalité et Infini: Essai sur l'extériorité*, 2nd ed. (The Hague: Nijhoff, 1965), p. 191 [Eng. trans.: *Totality and Infinity: An Essay on Exteriority*, trans. Alphonso Lingis (Pittsburgh: Duquesne University Press, 1969), p. 216].

25. Ibid., p. 58 [Eng. trans.: p. 85].

26. Ibid., p. 59 [Eng. trans.: p. 86].

27. Paz, *Laberinto*, p. 129 [Eng. trans.: *Labyrinth*, p. 143]. The Plan of Ayala was promulgated by Emiliano Zapata in 1911; it called for an agrarian reform which, according to Paz, was patterned after the ancient system of land distribution.

28. Ibid., p. 132 [Eng. trans.: p. 147].

29. Ibid., p. 129 [Eng. trans.: p. 143].

30. Carlos Fuentes, *Tiempo mexicano* (Mexico City: Mortiz, 1971), p. 13.

31. Ibid., p. 131.

32. Paz, *Laberinto*, p. 63 [Eng. trans.: *Labyrinth*, p. 70].

33. Jorge Ibargüengoitia, in the Mexico City daily *Excelsior*, February 7, 1972.

34. Paz, *Laberinto*, pp. 78–79 [Eng. trans.: *Labyrinth*, p. 87].

35. Fuentes, *Tiempo mexicano*, p. 13.

36. Martin Heidegger, *Nietzsche* (Pfüllingen: Neske, 1961), 1:257.

Chapter 4

Truths and Imperatives

After reading Kierkegaard we still do not know if we are to seek contemporaneity with Christ by transporting ourselves into the past or by transporting Christ into the present. But even worse, either approach is illegitimate, for philosophy does not consist in wishful thinking. Conceptual prestidigitation and fantasy are of no help, for our task is not to manipulate time with our imaginations. Rather we are concerned with real time, which cannot be manipulated.

If in the final analysis Kierkegaard emerges as a "bard of the return," we must recognize that in this regard he strayed from one of his most basic intentions, namely, to refute Hegel. More important, he strayed from the peculiar realism of existentialist philosophy, which seeks to be and ought to be greater and more implacable than the realism of other philosophies. And in fact it is.

For a philosophy that claims to be concrete, only the present is truly real; the past and the future are ideas. Nothing we have said about the decisive importance of the messianic future can prevent the future from being a mere concept and not a reality for me at the present moment. And notwithstanding all of Kierkegaard's romanticizing about the period in which Christ lived, he is unable to prevent the past from being nothing more than a concept for me at this moment.

Such concepts are very different from the reality that summons me and demands a decision of me, namely, the present. The past and the future are at any given moment categories that form part of the conceptual apparatus of the self. They are integral elements of our selves; they lack otherness, true otherness in the face of the self at the present instant. By contrast, the neighbor who speaks to me at this moment is real. He is not something "thought"; I cannot reassimilate him, making him part of my self.

Thus the experience of contemporaneity with Christ seems unattainable, at least by Kierkegaard's methods. Anticipating objections, I want to point out that existentialists are wrong if they think that they can prescind from this question. We must believe Kierkegaard when he says, "Everything I have written has tended toward describing contemporaneity adequately."[1]

CONTEMPORANEITY IN THE NEW TESTAMENT

But philosophers have not paid sufficient heed to the fact that neither Paul nor John was, strictly speaking, a contemporary of Christ. It is well known that Paul never met Jesus of Nazareth; it has been established that the author of the Fourth Gospel wrote in about 80 or 90 A.D. Nevertheless, the insistence with which both use the adverb "now" clearly identifies their own now with the now of Christ (Rom. 3:21, 26; 5:9, 11; 6:19, 21, 22; 7:6; 8:1, 22; 11:5, 30, 31; 13:11; 16:26; and in John 4:23; 5:25; 11:22; 12:27, 31a, 31b; 13:31, 36; 14:29; 15:22, 24; 16:5, 22, 29, 30; 17:5, 7, 13).

Simply as a historical datum, as a special phenomenon in the history of thought, this contemporaneity with Christ alleged (at least) by authors who were not his physical contemporaries ought to have been considered by *philosophy*—just as today studies are made of Descartes or Nicholas of Cusa or Parmenides. And the philosophers could have ascertained the truth of the allegation more accurately than the faithful, for the scientific mind is better equipped to do so. Philosophy's obligation is all the greater since, as we have seen, the intention of achieving contemporaneity with Christ was at the very origin of existentialism, and all indications are that the solution provided by the New Testament authors to the problem of contemporaneity with Christ is fresher and less imposed by an a priori philosophical system than any solution provided by our sophisticated philosophies of today.

To investigate the matter with scientific rigor, philosophy must employ the historical critical method, which is the method employed by modern exegesis. This method, to be sure, possesses greater scientific control than philosophy itself. Whether or not we adopt the solution that the New Testament authors give to the problem of contemporaneity is a subsequent question, open to resolution by any serious student of philosophy. But objectively to investigate the precise nature of their solution is a task to be carried out on the basis of demonstrable documentary evidence, which is the basis for the exegetical method. For philosophy and exegesis to collaborate in the same study should not constitute a serious objection at this point in the twentieth century. We seek truth by every means; the departmentalization of the sciences is one of the most challenged dogmas of our time. It is defended only by those specialists in one branch of knowledge who fear they might appear incompetent in another branch. The only proviso to our investigation is that methods cannot be mixed: Exegetical questions must be investigated with exegetical methods and philosophical questions resolved by philosophical methods.

BELIEVING AND LOVING

One requirement of exegetical methodology is that we not force biblical authors to deal with issues that were of no concern to them. We must not ask them questions that they did not ask themselves. Rather we must perceive the problems that concerned them and pursue our investigation in that direction. Our procedure must be clear. In this chapter we shall deal with a concrete biblical question that has been seen as such by various exegetes, independently of our philosophical question regarding contemporaneity. The philosophical problem will reappear on its own, only now in the framework of John's mentality and the questions raised by him. We have chosen a concrete problem in the work of John, for Johannine investigations have made the most marked advances in recent decades.

The question is this: Did John perceive a distinction between dogma and ethics or did he consider them to be the same? In other words, are believing and loving two things or one? What is the relationship between truths and imperatives? Two passages from John help us to pose the problem:

Anyone who listens to my word and *believes* in the one who sent me has eternal life and does not come to judgment, but *has already crossed over from death to life* (John 5:24).

We for our part *have crossed over from death to life;* this we know, because we *love* our brothers. The man who does not love is still in death (1 John 3:14).

All commentators have been struck by the occurrence in both passages of the expression "to have crossed over from death to life," *metabebeken (metabebekamen) ek tou thanatou eis ten zoen.* What does John mean by it? Does it consist in loving our neighbor or believing? According to John 5:24 it is believing; according to 1 John 3:14 it is loving our brothers. Which is it?

In his commentary on the Gospel of John, Lagrange emphasizes that John 5:24 "develops the Johannine doctrine par excellence," then he goes on to say, "The same wording occurs in 1 John 3:14, where charity replaces faith. Faith, as it is used in this verse, includes charity."[2]

This approach smacks of harmonism, which consists in juxtaposing, in affirming an "also," "both the one and the other." At least we tend to interpret it harmonistically—given the approaches to interpretation that we have inherited. In this case the harmonists would say that passing from death to life depends both on faith and on love of neighbor. But harmonistic exegesis and theology are always open to suspicion of superficiality: If we cannot see how one proposition relates to another, we simply avoid the issue by asserting both. The danger is that in so doing we may not have understood the meaning of either, for if we did understand them, we could see how they were related. If we do not understand, we can say that anything represents the thinking of John.

Lagrange seems to avoid harmonism and "alsoism," claiming that John includes charity in faith. But if he does not explain how love of neighbor is comprehended and included in faith, this is tantamount to asserting both very strongly, both faith and love, and we return again to alsoism.

The harmonistic interpretation is contradicted by John's wording of these two verses, for he provides clear signals of exclusivity, that is, he gives the clear impression that he does not believe it is a case of "both the one and the other." The exclusivistic, definitional intention is quite clear in 1 John 3:14. After he says that whoever loves his brother has passed from death to life, he adds the starkly illuminating converse: "The man who does not love is still in the realm of death." The strength of the verse lies in its affirmation that *only* he who loves his neighbor has passed from death to life. It is impossible to hold that the author of the text imagined the possibility of some other type of person (for example, "anyone who believes") who had *also* passed from death to life. His intention is clearly exclusionary.

By the same token, John 5:24 is equally definitional: *The one who believes* is the one who has passed from death to life and therefore no longer has to submit to final judgment. The illuminating converse need not be explicitly stated when an author is giving a definition, but in fact one is provided for us later in the same Gospel, in John 8:24b: "If you do not believe that I am what I am, *you will die* in your sins." And in 3:18 John says: "The man who believes in him does not come under judgment; but the one *who does not believe* has already been judged." Although statement and negative counterpart occur in different passages, it is incontrovertible that John is here telling us that passing from death to life consists in believing in Jesus Christ and does not consist in anything else.

But 1 John 3:14 asserts that passing from death to life means loving our brothers and nothing else; a harmonistic interpretation is thereby precluded on an exegetical level, for it does not correspond to the intention of the author whom we are trying to interpret.

This is the concrete biblical question; it exists independently of our philosophical problem of contemporaneity. The solution to this question provides the key to the First Epistle of John. Indeed, our understanding of the entire letter will depend on it. Both Boismard and de la Potterie have seen that according to the Epistle there are—apparently—two prerequisites to divine life: believing in Jesus Christ and loving our neighbor.[3] When John speaks of believing, its absolute importance is emphasized, as if loving did not exist; when he speaks of loving our neighbor, its significance is stressed as if faith did not exist. This juxtaposition recurs throughout the entire letter, and any interpretation which does not take it into account condemns itself to total superficiality.

In my opinion Boismard has taken a systematic analysis further than anyone else. He observes that the common element in eight especially emphatic and definitional passages of the letter (1 John 1:5–7; 2:3–6; 2:8–10; 2:29; 3:5–6; 4:7–8; 4:16; 4:11–12; to which we can add 5:13)

is that they state who are those who truly possess divine
life. This possession of divine life is designated in four
different ways: to be born of God; to abide in God and God
in us; to have communion with God; and to know God.
The four expressions refer to the same reality. But when
it comes to saying *who* possesses this reality, the
letter—in a definitional way—sometimes says that it is
those who love their neighbor and at other times that it
is those who believe in Jesus Christ. The unequivocal
and exclusive sign that someone possesses this divine
and mysterious reality is . . . sometimes love of neighbor
and other times New Testament faith! The reader's
perplexity is thus total.

The question we have been considering is the central
problem of the First Epistle, as shown by Schnackenburg's analysis of the formal structure of the Epistle.
Besides a prologue (1 John 1:1–4) and an epilogue (1 John
5:13–21), the letter has three parts:

> First part: 1:5–2:27
> Second part: 2:28–4:6
> Third part: 4:7–5:12

Keeping in mind that faith is Christological, that is,
that the object of believing is Christ, we notice a striking
pattern: The first part comprises an ethical thesis
(1:5–2:17) and a Christological thesis (2:18–27); the second part likewise contains an ethical thesis (2:28–3:24)
and a Christological one (4:1–6); and the third part, according to Schnackenburg, unites the two theses into
love based on faith (4:7–21) and faith based on love of
neighbor (5:1–12).

The nature of the relationship between Christological
faith and brotherly love is not merely an exegete's question based on John's text; as the structure of the Epistle
demonstrates, John raised the question himself—in
a conscious and thematic way. As Bultmann says,
"This unity of faith and love is the chief theme of 1
John—along with its polemic against false teachings."[4]

But the words "union" or "unity" or "unite" do not

accurately express John's thesis. Only in 1 John 3:23 are love of neighbor and faith mentioned in the same passage. Elsewhere in the Epistle some passages affirm brotherly love to be the sole and exclusive sign of divine life while others state faith in Jesus Christ to be the sole and exclusive sign. Speaking abstractly and formalistically, one is tempted to say that the Epistle's central thesis is that there is only one sign of divine life—whatever that sign may be. What that sign is cannot be resolved by "uniting" belief and love, by "conjoining" dogma and morality; rather it must be resolved by showing that Christological belief is *identical to* the imperative of love of neighbor.

"PURE TRUTHS"

Before attempting this resolution (and only then will the matter of contemporaneity reappear), let us rephrase the question in terms of present-day history.

Today the theologians of liberation are denouncing —from Latin America but for the whole world—the traditional distinction between dogmatic and moral theology. They believe that any truth that is not a moral imperative is alienating, for such a truth provides an alibi behind which people can evade the responsibility of ethical action. These theologians are not simply referring to doctrinal truths or teachings that deny our obligation to follow a particular course of action. They attack all allegedly pure truths, for these are characterized by an alienating idealism that distracts us from our responsibility to transform this world. Such truths are instruments of the status quo, not because they deny moral obligation or justify the world as it is, but because they constitute an ivory tower where the mind takes refuge from the imperative to struggle against the world as it is.

Whether by coincidence or design, the attack unleashed by the Latin American theologians of liberation against all dogmatics separated from ethics resembles Marx's attack on philosophy in his theses on Feuerbach: The point is not to interpret the world, but to change it. To the degree that philosophy attracts human energies toward contemplation of pure truths it serves as a defense of the status quo, for it diverts these energies from combatting the status quo. Even worse, to propound these "pure truths" is to assert an implicit, de facto affirmation that this world of cruelty and injustice is all right, that it is licit to dedicate oneself to contemplating truths, that no nonpostponable obligation exists to struggle to change this world.

The radicalness of Latin American theology undoubtedly seems excessive to European theologians. But the Bible is even more extreme. I second without reservation the denunciation of the separation between dogmatics and ethics. But I add that these "truths" are in fact falsehoods, and that they have been illegitimately deduced from the Bible by "the wisdom of this world" (in its most pejorative sense, as in 1 Cor. 2:6) to prevent the authentic biblical summons from reaching us. I base my rejection of "pure truths" not on Marx's theses on Feuerbach, but rather on the Bible itself, from which these truths are supposed to have been derived.

In reality, I challenge the status of theology itself, both dogmatic and moral. There can be many truths *in se*, millions of them, based on combinations and permutations among themselves. They can be as true as accurate calculations of the distance between Jupiter and Saturn. Theology's task, however, is not to enunciate truths but rather to proclaim the news called gospel. Theology ceases to speak in the name of Christ at the moment and to the degree that its truths or commandments proclaim something other than the great news, the decisive event that is the unique content of biblical evangelizing. Juridical considerations notwithstanding, only the one who proclaims and makes present what Jesus Christ proclaimed is able to be called the representative of Jesus Christ. The content is what matters. All else is excrescence, whose least damaging effect is to distract humankind from the news.

EMPIRICAL THEOLOGY

So-called "empirical theology," however, produces similar damage. It is absolutely true that one of theology's *functions* is empirical criticism, which must be undertaken when theology has understood the testimony of Christ, for Christ throws empirical reality into crisis. But, as Schmithals observes, "anyone who contrasts the empirico-critical *method* with the historico-critical *method* is concealing the fact that he is trying to replace the biblical testimony of Christ (which is the object of *all* theology and *all* method) with some other object," namely, empirical reality. The only legitimate object of Christian theology is the testimony of Jesus Christ. A theology that investigates some other object, for example, its social, economic, or political milieu, ends up being an "ideology no longer controlled by scientific thinking."[5]

I have no doubt that the Holy Spirit is working in the world of today and therefore is present in the reality that surrounds us. But opposing and irreconcilable ideologies invoke this same Spirit. If we do not by verifiable, scientific exegesis ascertain the meaning of the gospel message, then we have only an arbitrary choice between rival theologies; conservative theology has just as much right to call itself Christian as does revolutionary theology. Joachim Jeremias rightly says, "According to the testimony of the New Testament, the Logos made flesh is the revelation of God, only he. ...The thesis of continuous revelation is a gnostic heresy."[6] Only the historical Jesus can judge our differences and be measure of our theologies. And for us this Jesus is to be found in the Bible.

Empirical theology shares the antibiblical approach of European dogmatic theology, and it is equally escapist—though unwittingly—for it obscures the immeasurably subversive message of the gospel. Therefore our social revolutions are destined to engender new oppressions, for without the God of the Bible exploitation recurs spontaneously, even within the struggles undertaken to abolish it. Hugo Assmann is correct in recognizing that the theology of liberation is immensely deficient in Christology and in methodology.[7] But the result of both deficiencies is the same: to prescind from Jesus of Nazareth.

THE CONTINGENT CHRIST

The essential need to identify dogma with morality, truth with imperative, has its origin in the very preaching of Jesus, as we shall see. In the First Epistle of John this identification is obvious, even in the very structure of the letter. And this identification of truth with imperative is the basis of the new being discovered by existentialism,[8] the new field of being that demands our decision in order to be. Bearing in mind that New Testament "truths" are historical facts, we see the antecedent for the Marxist rejection of a separate treatment of morality and the Marxist insistence on facts.

It is significant that the two best known Catholic commentaries on the moral teaching of the New Testament, those of Spicq and Schnackenburg, each devote an entire first chapter to the sacred writers' awareness that they lived in the *eschaton*, the *ultimum*, the end of human history.[9] Spicq and Schnackenburg feel that this eschatological consciousness profoundly affects the moral teaching of the New Testament, although they fail to discover what effect it has. At first glance the following statement by Schnackenburg appears accurate:

Then the question is raised what the enduring lesson of this intense eschatological awareness of the early Church is for Christian morality. It cannot be simply set aside as a phenomenon due to temporary conditions or even as a dangerous apocalyptic tendency.[10]

Of course the eschatological consciousness found in the New Testament has been and continues to be considered or ignored by orthodoxy as a dangerous apocalyptic tendency. And there are no exceptions. Schnackenburg and Spicq unwittingly indicate the totally dependent relationship (or better yet, identification) between New Testament moral teaching and the only "truth" believed in the New Testament, namely, that with Jesus the *eschaton* has arrived. But their efforts fail because of their Greco-western presuppositions. In the paragraph cited above Schnackenburg attempts to extract "the enduring lesson," that is, the *nontemporal* lesson; and he supposes that "Christian morality" is a nontemporal set of ethical affirmations. As it is customarily posed, his question is tantamount to asking what remains, as a nontemporal and eternal residue, from a historical, contingent, tumultuous situation, localized in concrete time. What remains, Schnackenburg and Spicq answer (in order to avoid that nothing remain), is a consciousness of a *status viatoris*. It is a consciousness that we are not in heaven, a suitable state of mind to accompany moral actions in any period or circumstance, one more praiseworthy sentiment, a beautiful attitude contributed by the early Christian community to the eternal list of moral virtues and worthy sentiments. It is difficult to imagine a more complete castration of the New Testament message.

The contingency of revelation has always been repugnant to rationalism, the heir to the eternal truths and immutable essences of Greek philosophy. If the Greek intellectual heritage had been completely faithful to itself, it could have never called itself Christian, that is, it could never have accepted as norm the historical event called Jesus Christ. But it devised a stratagem whereby it could be at the same time Greek and (allegedly) Christian: It detemporalized Christ; it invoked a heavenly, dehistoricized, eternal Christ—a Christ who was very much God, as much as possible. From Christ's contingent life it extracted only nontemporal examples, eternal commandments, and detemporalized truths. Once this maneuver was accomplished, history lost its importance, for it lost its effect on the content of revelation or belief. The historical Jesus was reduced to an irrelevant incident, almost a shadow, as Plato would have considered him. What mattered were the eternal truths—whose number Jesus incidently increased. Orthodox theology does not deny the historical humanity of Christ (to do so would be formal docetism); it simply disregards it. Orthodox theology is concerned with Christ's eternal "human nature," but not with the contingent event of Christ in the world, nor with the fact that Christ belongs totally to history. They do not realize that this is a docetism much more extreme than formal docetism.

On the other hand, the sole object of John's faith, its sole "truth," is the contingent fact called Jesus Christ. Only this conviction breaks the eternal return of all things, and it is precisely this conviction that we find in every New Testament author. But it is reduced to nothingness if we situate Christ outside history as a nontemporal being called "the Christ of faith." Paradoxically, the higher we raise Christ in his heaven and minimize the contingent facts of his life and death at a specific historical moment, the less chance we have of revolutionizing human history. For by removing Christ from history we condemn history again to its natural pattern of the eternal return of all things. This is why conservatives show no interest in the Bible, a lack of interest very ill-advisedly shared by the theologians of liberation. For without the Bible there is absolutely no basis for an identification of dogma with ethics, of truth with imperative.

THE KINGDOM HAS ARRIVED

John's moral teaching is a messianic morality, a morality of the *eschaton*, of the kingdom of God already achieved on earth. At the end of the Fourth Gospel, John says that the whole book was written "that you may believe that Jesus is the Messiah" (John 20:31). Note his description of the sole heresy: "Who is the liar? Who but he that denies that Jesus is the Messiah" (1 John 2:22). And in contrast: "Everyone who believes that Jesus is the Messiah is born of God" (1 John 5:1). Such is the content and object of faith: not a nontemporal truth or a doctrine, but rather *a fact*, namely, that Jesus of Nazareth, that man among men, is the very same Messiah anxiously awaited for generations. The first time he mentions this fact (John 1:41–45), John feels obliged to stress its contingency, indeed he takes delight in stressing it: "Can anything good come from Nazareth?" (John 1:46).

As Bultmann has noted, the primordial meaning of "to believe" is *to believe that* . . . , not *to believe in* (though the latter is preferred by nineteenth-century romanticism). We see this in the Fourth Gospel itself. John uses the term "to believe in" *(pisteuein eis)* thirty-four times, and yet he concludes by saying that the whole Gospel was written so that we might *believe that.* . . . The latter wording is appropriate for focusing on a historic fact as an object of belief: to believe that something happened. Bultmann correctly concludes, " 'To believe in . . . ' is thus to be regarded as an abbreviation which in the language of the mission became formal."[11] "To believe in Jesus Christ" is an abbreviated way of saying "to believe that Jesus is the Messiah."

Therefore, in the nine instances in John's First Epistle and in the ninety-eight instances in the Fourth Gospel in which the verb "to believe" occurs, the historical fact that Jesus is the Messiah is the sole object and content of that belief.

In the following chapters we shall explore the imperative sense of this truth-in-fact: that Jesus is the Messiah. For on this the whole problem of contemporaneity depends.

When Jesus himself spoke of "believing that . . . , " the object or truth to be believed was "that the time has been completed and the kingdom of God has arrived" (Mark 1:15). Jesus refers to the same fact as John, but John specifies that the coming of the kingdom is identical to the coming of Jesus as the Messiah. Elsewhere Jesus himself made this same identification: When John the Baptist sent disciples to ask if Jesus was the one to come or if they should continue to wait for another (Matt. 11:3; Luke 7:19), Jesus, describing his own works, repeated point for point the description of the kingdom found in innumerable passages of the Old Testament—including the resurrection of the dead (Matt. 11:4–6 and Luke 7:22–23).

The fact is the coming of the messianic kingdom, and for Mark the "good news," the gospel, consists in proclaiming this fact:

Jesus came into Galilee proclaiming the gospel of God: "The time has been completed; the kingdom of God has arrived; be converted and believe in the gospel" (Mark 1:14–15).

The wording is very careful, very deliberate. First he explicitly states the content, the meaning itself of the message called the great news or gospel (of God, of course, not of Jesus). Then he adds, "Be converted and believe in this message whose content I have just indicated." What grammatically seems to be a case of *believing in* turns out to be one of *believing that*, for he is referring to the fact that the time is completed and the kingdom has arrived. This is possibly the only instance in which Jesus himself uses the *verb* "to believe."

As Friedrich has shown, the Hebrew word corresponding to "gospel" or "good news" is a noun of action.[12] The term does not refer to the content of the news, but rather to the very fact of announcing it, of pronouncing it, of proclaiming it—to the act of evangelizing. Hearers of the proclamation had long known what the good news would be. They knew what the kingdom would be and what the gospel would be. Jesus' response to John the Baptist's question shows that people had no doubt about this. And the Baptist's very question asks only "already?" or "not yet?" The only important point was *the fact that* the kingdom should arrive, *the fact that* the arrival of the kingdom should be proclaimed. Not *what* it is, but *that* it is. As Friedrich says,

A new message is not expected with the dawn of God's kingdom. What will be proclaimed has been known from the time of Deutero-Isaiah. The longing is that it should be proclaimed. Hence [in contemporary literature], the messenger and the act of proclamation are much more important than the message. The new feature is not the content of the message, but the eschatological event.... Because all the emphasis is on the action, on the proclamation, on the utterance of the Word which ushers in the new age, *besorah* [message] is less prominent than *mebasser* [messenger, announcer, evangelizer] and *bisser* [to announce, to evangelize].[13]

Not *what*, but *that*.... According to Jesus and the New Testament authors this *fact that* the kingdom is arriving is the truth believed, the object of faith. Everyone knew that there was going to be a kingdom of God. Everyone knew that there had to be an *eschaton*. No one doubted that there had to be a Messiah. All that was easy to accept, for it belongs to the unreal realm of concepts. But that all this was really happening, that it was becoming present reality—that is what the Pharisees, the conservatives, the establishment refused to accept. Not *what*, but *that*. ... The gospel's only content is a *that*... , not a *what*.

THE GOSPEL AS NEWS

Neither the theologians nor the exegetes are sufficiently aware that the gospel is news or it is nothing and that for the Greek mind there can be no news. News, *the* news, has no meaning at all for the Platonic mind. For such a mentality, "messianism" is not only an absurdity, but something worse: It is a word that it thinks it understands but in fact does not. The Platonic mind necessarily reduces the word "messiah" to an attribute, a nontemporal predicate among the other titles or names ascribed to Christ. The Greek mind turns a historical fact into an eternal truth. And then, of course, it is not an imperative. (Likewise, since the being of western ontology was nontemporal, Kant could distinguish between pure reason and practical reason.)

Thus Aristotle and the Scholastics had to have a "basis" for their moral teaching; they had to "demonstrate" the imperative, to deduce it from premises. But if the premises are an indicative statement, then the conclusion cannot be an imperative—without some intervening sophistry. And if a premise is an imperative, then it includes the imperative grounded in itself; it cannot be demonstrated because it is obligatory in and of itself.

Heidegger's words are especially applicable here: "The object we have taken as our theme is *artificially and dogmatically curtailed* if 'in the first instance' we restrict ourselves to a 'theoretical subject,' in order that we may then round it out 'on the practical side' by tacking on an 'ethic.' "[14] This existentialistic rejection of the distinction between truth and imperative derives precisely from the gospel, which proclaims *that* ... , not *what*.

Let us consider the imperative sense of the truth-in-fact that Jesus is the Messiah. For on this the whole problem of contemporaneity depends. The "truth" announced by the gospel is a historical fact: the fact that the kingdom has arrived, the fact that Jesus of Nazareth is the Messiah. And if the messianic kingdom consists in justice being done to all the poor of the earth, then this fact is the most commanding and urgent imperative imaginable. There is not the slightest difference between love of neighbor and New Testament faith—provided that we take this love of neighbor with unreserved seriousness. The news is grammatically in the indicative, but it is an indicative saying that the time has come to enact the imperative of love of neighbor on a worldwide scale.

The Greek incapacity to accept any real news has contaminated even exegesis, as we see in the tendency to neutralize the verb *engiken* in Mark 1:15; Matt. 3:2; 4:17; 10:7; and Luke 10:9, 11. Above we translated this as "has arrived," while the neutralizers would translate it as "has drawn near." There are three arguments against this evasive postponement.

First, Matthew Black's detailed linguistic study has vindicated the philologist Joüon, who as early as 1927 with perfect security translated the term as "has arrived."[15] Mark 1:15 has a surprising parallel in Lam. 4:18: "Our end has arrived *(engiken-karab)*, our days have been completed because our time has come *(parestin-ba)*." Black rightly observes that the term must mean arrival, not approach. The elements common to both of the passages, he notes, are—in addition to *engiken*—the substantive *kairos* and the verb *pleroo* in the passive voice ("to be filled," "to be completed"). A similar idea is similarly expressed in Ezek. 7:6–7. The neutralizers forget that the construction of Mark 1:15—"The time has been completed and the kingdom of God has arrived"—implies that the events described are either synonymous or consecutive (in other words the "and" is either epexegetical or consecutive). In either case, the "approach" of the kingdom is incompatible with "the time has been completed." The paired clauses preclude interpreting *engiken* as "approach."

Second, although the procrastinators of the kingdom would eliminate Mark 1:15, nevertheless Matt. 12:28 and Luke 11:20 say the same thing using the verb *ephthasen;* the latter cannot be interpreted as approach, but rather must be translated as "the kingdom *has arrived* to you." Why, then this great resistance to Mark 1:15?

The third reason is conclusive and central. Mark 1:15 explicitly intends to give us the text and formulation itself of *the news.* It was not news to say that the *eschaton* had drawn near. Abel could have said it, comparing his own time to Adam's; any generation was nearer than its predecessors to the *eschaton.* The ordinary passage of time accounted for the drawing near of the *eschaton.* The neutralizers would make Jesus into a madman, for their translation has him proclaiming the most common knowledge as great news—and proclaiming it with a passion unique in history. They thereby show that they are not really concerned about the historical Jesus.

Behind the neutralist exegesis is the desire to postpone the *eschaton* indefinitely. The Pharisee, says Oscar Schmitz, takes upon himself the task of preventing anything, even the Messiah, from becoming real. And he does this while scrupulously accepting all of the dogmas—provided that they remain as concepts, that is, provided that they are not realized.

Not every historical fact constitutes a "truth" that can be identified with imperative, only the historical fact of the *eschaton.* The new being discovered by existentialism ceases to demand decision and resembles the neutral being of ontology the moment it is divorced from the historical fact called Jesus Christ. The historical facts that Marx invokes could not unseat idealistic, Platonic morality if they were not messianic. Only eschatological time summons us with a "that...." Other times do not constitute news; they are times with no special importance: They are simply any time. When the *eschaton* is denied, time becomes "any time," and history reverts to the eternal return.

NOTES

1. Cited by Jean Wahl, *Études kierkergaardiennes* (Paris: Vrin, 1949), p. 296.

2. M.-J. Lagrange, *Évangile selon Saint Jean*, 3rd ed. (Paris: Gabalda, 1927), p. 146.

3. M.-E. Boismard, "La connaissance de Dieu dans l'Alliance Nouvelle d'après la première lettre de Saint Jean," *Revue Biblique* 56, no. 3 (July 1949): 365–91; Ignace de la Potterie, *Adnotationes in exegesim Primae Epistulae s. Ioannis*, 2nd ed. (Rome: Pontificio Istituto Biblico, 1966–67), mimeographed.

4. Rudolf Bultmann, *Theologie des Neuen Testaments*, 2nd ed. (Tübingen: Mohr, 1954), p. 428 [Eng. trans.: *Theology of the New Testament*, trans. Kendrick Grobel (New York: Scribner's, 1970), 2:81].

5. Walter Schmithals, *Evangelische Kommentare* 8 (1969), pp. 451–52.

6. Cited by Ernst Käsemann in *Evangelische Versuche und Gesinnungen*, 5th ed. (Göttingen: Vandenhoeck, 1967), 2:38.

7. Hugo Assmann, *Teología desde la praxis de la liberación* (Salamanca: Sígueme, 1973), pp. 100–02 [in English see *Theology for a Nomad Church* (Maryknoll, New York: Orbis Books, 1976), pp. 103–05].

8. See above, chap. 1.

9. Ceslaus Spicq, *Théologie morale du nouveau testament* (Paris: Gabalda, 1965); Rudolf Schnackenburg, *The Moral Teaching of the New Testament* (New York: Herder and Herder, 1964).

10. Schnackenburg, ibid., p. 195.

11. Bultmann, "pistis," *TWNT*, 6:204 [cf. Eng. trans.: *TDNT*, 6:203–04].

12. Gerhard Friedrich, "euangelizomai," *TWNT*, 2:705–35 [Eng. trans.: *TDNT*, 2:707–37].

13. Ibid., *TWNT*, p. 723 [cf. Eng. trans.: *TDNT*, p. 726].

14. Martin Heidegger, *Sein und Zeit* (Tübingen: Niemeyer, 1960), p. 316 [Eng. trans.: *Being and Time*, trans. John Macquarrie and Edward Robinson (New York: Harper & Row, 1962), pp. 363–64].

15. Matthew Black, *An Aramaic Approach to the Gospels and Acts*, 3rd ed. (Oxford: Clarendon, 1967), pp. 208–11; Paul Joüon, "Notes philologiques sur les Evangiles," *Recherches de Science Religieuse* 17 (1927), pp. 537–40.

Chapter 5

The Gospel Genre

At the Last Supper the "new commandment" was for-mulated as love of neighbor (see John 13:34). The First Epistle of John says of it:

It is a new commandment that I am giving you, . . . *because* the darkness is passing and the true light already shines (1 John 2:8).

In this passage John declares the presence of the *eschaton* to be the reason for the commandment. As Bultmann observes, the fact that the true light already shines "serves as the basis for the commandment."[1] The Catholic commentators Michl, Schnackenburg, and de la Potterie, as well as the Protestants Bultmann and Schneider, indeed all the renditions I have seen, trans-late the word *hoti* as "because."[2] De la Potterie states explicitly that *hoti* is causal. It is also grammatically possible for *hoti* to be recitative, in which case the re-mainder of the sentence would state the content of the commandment. But Schnackenburg correctly rejects this possibility, pointing out that the remainder of the sentence "has nothing to do with commandment."[3]

But then we are faced with a very important datum: The reason for the commandment in which God reveals himself is precisely that the messianic *eschaton* has al-ready arrived. The unavoidable implication is that except for the historical, contingent event of Christ there would be no reason for the commandment of love of neighbor, that without Jesus of Nazareth God could not reveal himself. The fact or historical truth that we considered in the last chapter turns out to be the sole basis of the imperative.

In spite of the mental jugglery of those having no respect for real time, everything leads us to believe that we can be contemporaneous with Christ only in the *eschaton*. (An eternal, *non*temporary point, cannot be *con*temporary to anyone.)

The problem we have been considering is this: How and why can the author of the Fourth Gospel and the First Epistle of John feel that he is—and indeed be—contemporary with Christ, since he knew as well as we that he was writing a half century after Christ's crucifixion and death? The problem is an exegetical one, thus involving questions much broader and partially different than those that are today customarily asked in philosophy. This may seem to be a disadvantage. But, on the one hand, there are the obvious advantages of objectivity and verifiability in analyzing thinking that has already been done and documented, that is not subject to our preconceptions and therefore can tell us something we did not already know. And, on the other hand, since we are dealing with time and being itself, which are the most basic questions in philosophy, we are more than justified in again posing our problem of contemporaneity in terms very different and much broader than those to which philosophy is accustomed. For it is possible that precisely these new dimensions will provide us with the elements needed for the solution.

With regard to exegesis itself, we have already seen that the meaning of John's entire message is involved in this question of contemporaneity. Therefore, as we come to understand contemporaneity, other particular exegetical problems may be answered for us as well.

To broaden the dimensions of the problem of John's

contemporaneity with Christ, we will deal with a datum from John's prologue that seems heretofore to have been insufficiently emphasized. Then we shall consider the implications of the very existence of a prologue, which is the key to understanding the literary genre of gospel. In the Gospel of John the prologue has special importance.

"BORN OF GOD"

John's prologue differentiates between those who did not receive or accept the word (John 1:11) and those who did indeed receive it and "believed in his name" (John 1:12). The latter, it goes on to explain, are "those not born of any human stock, or by the fleshly desire of a human father, but they who had been born of God" (John 1:13). In his thorough monograph on the prologue, Feuillet comments, "Only those who have been born of God are able to take this step and so believe in the Logos."[4]

The importance of John 1:13 lies in this: In the prologue, before the detailed, scene-by-scene narration of the rejection of Christ by the majority of Israelites and acceptance by the few, the Gospel attempts—in thesis form—to explain why some believed and others did not. Authors of closely reasoned, difficult works frequently write the prologue last. Feuillet even suggests that the Gospel prologue was written after John's First Epistle.[5] The entire prologue, and John 1:13 in particular, seems to be a subsequent reflection on the events described in the Gospel, an attempt to grasp and explain the true meaning and scope of those events. Therefore the theme of this verse and the question raised above in our chapter 4 must be closely connected.

If, according to John, some believe in Jesus Christ and some do not because the former have been born of God, then it is incumbent on us to ask what it means "to be born of God." Moreover, the passage suggests that being "born of God" was a notion more familiar than "accepting Christ," for John uses the former term to clarify the meaning of the latter. If "born of God" was not a recognized theological term, then it was at least an expression well known among those to whom the Gospel was addressed.

In fact, "to be born of God" and "to be children of God" (interchangeable expressions, as we see in 1 John 3:9–10; 1 John 2:29–3:1; and the pericope 1 John 5:1–2) have a specific meaning for John and throughout the New Testament. If this specific meaning explains the historical enigma of *why* some have believed in Jesus Christ and some have not, then John 1:12, 13 becomes one of the most important theses in the Bible. Although overlooked by theology and tradition, it becomes a crucially important explanation of historical events. Therefore, before we evaluate John's thesis and consider what "the word" might mean, we must exegetically define "to be born of God" or "to be children of God" or "to be of (*ek*) God" (the preposition *ek* designates origin: to proceed from God).

Everyone who does justice is born of God (1 John 2:29).

Everyone who loves is born of God (1 John 4:7).

That is the distinction between the children of God and the children of the devil: Anyone who does not do justice is not of God, nor is anyone who does not love his brother (1 John 3:10).

My dear friend, do not imitate bad examples, but good ones; the one who does good is of (*ek*) God (3 John 11).

Clearly, John's intention in these expressions is to define. To love one's neighbor and to do justice are not acts that might be incidentally performed by one who is "born of God." They are acts that distinguish one who is born of God from one who is not. The author's intention is to demarcate, to define.

Note that John—like all other biblical authors[6]— identifies loving one's neighbor with doing justice. Love of neighbor had not yet degenerated into the romantic and allegedly impartial sentiment that the West made of it, a love that under the guise of universality claims to embrace rich and poor equally. John's love is love of the deprived, the poor, the needy. Therefore it is identified with justice, an identification demonstrated in 1 John 3:17–18:

If a man has enough to live on, and yet when he sees his brother in need shuts up his heart against him, how can it be said that the love of God dwells in him? My children, love must not be a matter of words or talk; it must be genuine, and show itself in action.

Jesus himself defined precisely what it means "to be children of God": After telling us to "love your enemies" (Luke 6:35), he says in apodosis: "and you will be children of the Most High, because he himself is kind to the ungrateful and the wicked" (Luke 6:35b). And he goes on to recapitulate: "Be compassionate as your Father is compassionate" (Luke 6:36). That is what it means to be children of God. Matthew understood this thought perfectly: "Love your enemies and pray for your persecutors; only so can you be children of your heavenly Father" (Matt. 5:44–45). "Blessed are the peacemakers, for they shall be called children of God" (Matt. 5:9).[7] Keeping in mind that "good works" is a technical term, we find the same teaching in Matt. 5:16: "And you, like the lamp, must shed light among your fellows, so that, when they see the good works you do, they may glorify your Father in heaven." The sense of this passage is reduplicative: It means that when they see your good works your fellows will recognize God as your Father, they will know that you are children of God.

This definition of "to be born of God" or "to be children of God" did not, as we have seen, originate with John but was well known in his time. It makes John's explanation of the historical fact that some believed in Jesus Christ and others did not (John 1:12–13) particularly unsettling: Only those who loved their neighbor, who hungered and thirsted for justice, were able to understand "the word."

GOOD WORKS AND EVIL WORKS

If a thesis of such vast import appears in the prologue, then it should reappear in some form throughout the Gospel itself; otherwise the prologue is not really a prologue. We must demonstrate that the thesis does so recur.

John records the following passage—John 3:18–21—as Jesus' own words:

(18) Anyone who believes in him does not come under judgement. Anyone who does not believe has already been judged, for he has not believed in the name of God's only Son. (19) And this is the judgment: The light has come into the world but men loved darkness more than the light, *because their works were evil.* (20) For anyone who *does evil* hates the light and avoids it so that his works might not be denounced; (21) but anyone who does the truth comes to the light so that it may be clearly seen that his works are done in God.

This passage comes at the end of Jesus' conversation with Nicodemus. If these words are related to the preceding conversation, Jesus was simply explaining to Nicodemus that the teachers and Pharisees were typical of those whose evil works prevented their belief in him. If, on the other hand, this is a "free-floating" kerygmatic passage, as Schnackenburg holds,[8] then it has the same universal scope as John 1:12–13.

The most remarkable statement in John 3:18–21 is, of course, the assertion—repeated several times in the Fourth Gospel—that the Last Judgment takes place during the temporal lifetime of the historical Jesus and in relation to Jesus himself. But in the present context our first concern is to know why those people who had "already been judged" refused to believe in Jesus Christ. John tells us why explicitly: because their works were evil. In our traditional escapist fashion we tend to interpret this phrase generally, nonspecifically, making it into a catch-all for whatever behavior western morality deems bad. But there is clear and abundant biblical and extrabiblical evidence that, in the cultural milieu of the New Testament, "good works" (*kala erga, agatha erga*) and "evil works" (*phaula erga, ponera erga*) were specialized, definitional terms with precise and limited meanings.

Walter Grundmann, one of the scholars who has most adequately dealt with this matter, tells us:

> Good works are actions of mercy on behalf of all those in need of them, and they are works of peacemaking that eliminate discord among people. This is sufficiently documented by Matt. 25:31–46 and Matt. 5:38–48; it is confirmed by the concept of "good works" in Jewish literature.[9]

Strack and Billerbeck, who have also dealt exhaustively with this subject,[10] have shown conclusively that "good works" and "evil works" are strict technical terms in biblical and extrabiblical Jewish literature (see, for example, Isa. 58:6–7; 1 Tim. 5:10, 25; 6:18; Tit. 2:7, 14; 3:8, 14; 1 Tim. 3:1; 2:10; 5:10a, 10b, 25; 6:18; 2 Tim. 2:21; 3:17; Eph. 2:10; Col. 1:10; 2 Thess. 2:17; Matt. 5:16; Mark 3:4; Acts 10:38; Tit. 1:16; 2:14; 3:1, 8, 14; 2 Cor. 9:8; Rom. 13:3; Mic. 6:8; etc.). Perhaps the most interesting analysis is that of Joachim Jeremias.[11] He shows that the "good works" are most specifically defined—by examples—in Matt. 25:31–46: "Good works" consist in giving food to the hungry, drink to the thirsty, etc. Burying the dead, customarily included in the list, is surprisingly omitted by Matthew, perhaps because he is concerned exclusively with the living or perhaps because Jesus had said: "Leave the dead to bury their dead" (Matt. 8:22).

Matt. 25:31–46 is the only description of the Last Judgment in the New Testament, and in this passage the only criterion of judgment is stated to be good or evil works. We can assume that this criterion was accepted by all New Testament authors; there is much evidence to corroborate our assumption (Rom. 2:5–12, for example), and none to contradict it.[12] Therefore it is not extraordinary that John (3:18–21) employs the same criterion. John says that this judgment is realized during the historical lifetime of Jesus and in relation to him, but the decision depends on the human disposition to do "good works" or not do them. John supposes and utilizes the only criterion for who is to be saved and who is to be condemned that we find in the New Testament.

The unsettling thesis of the prologue (John 1:13) is restated with full force in the main body of the Gospel (John 3:18–21). Bultmann says of this passage, "In the decision of faith or unbelief it becomes apparent what man really is."[13] Bultmann is right: John is not dealing with the question of pure exteriority of works (cf. 1 Cor. 13:3); rather "what man really is" depends on the disposition (or lack of it) to do "good works," to do good to one's neighbor. John believes that this disposition is what defines a person's being, and that this being is what becomes manifest in the presence of Christ. In other words, one's disposition to do "good works" determines what one "really is," and this in turn determines whether one accepts or rejects Christ.

There is another passage in the main body of the Gospel in which the thesis introduced in John 1:13 reappears. This is John 7:1–9, from which we transcribe only Jesus' answer to his relatives who were urging him to go up to Jerusalem for the feast:

(6) My time [kairos] has not yet come, but your time is always at hand. (7) The world cannot hate you; but it hates me *because I give testimony that its works are evil*. (8) Go to the festival yourselves; I am not going up to this festival because my time has not yet come.

In John 3:20 we were told that anyone who does evil works hates the light. In 7:7 John uses for the second time the verb *misein* ("abhor," "hate") to tell us of the hatred that "the world" has for Christ. We hear it repeated in Christ's conversation during the Last Supper (John 15:18, 19, 23, 24, 25; 17:14). John 7:7 is important because it explicitly tells us *why* the world hates Christ: "because I give testimony that its works are evil." The world did not believe in Jesus Christ because it hates him, and it hates him because he testifies that its actions are antithetical to giving food to the hungry, drink to the thirsty, clothes to the naked, a home to the homeless. Most of us find it more comfortable to attribute the world's rejection of Christ to "irreligiosity," "worldliness," "sin," "immorality"—all taken in the broadest, vaguest, and most undetermined possible sense. But "good works" and "evil works" are technical terms with a highly exact meaning.

Western theology occasionally (although grudgingly) recognizes that the God of the Old Testament is anything but neutral toward social injustices, that, on the contrary, he is terribly partial toward the poor and the needy. But theologians often attribute this to some alleged imperfection inherent in the revelation of the Old Testament. Yet John, the most "spiritual" of the New Testament authors, explains the world's incredulity toward Jesus Christ by its denial of food to the hungry and drink to the thirsty.

If the world's inability to believe in Jesus Christ proceeds, as John says it does, from its "evil works" (understood in the strict sense of the technical term), then the purpose of Christ's mission in history is completely different from what we have for centuries believed. Christ's mission is not "related to" good works; rather it consists in good works, which is a very different matter.

Recent discoveries, such as the Qumran scrolls, have emphasized dramatically how antithetical John's message is to "religious" Christianity, how it opposes and challenges it. As early as 1954 Bultmann, despite his well-known antipathy toward Qumranic parallels,

wrote: " 'Walking in the light' gets a more precise definition in 1 John 2:9–11; it is 'to love one's brother.' "[14] And
in 1961 Boismard made explicit the implications of the
similarity between John and the Qumran scrolls. Commenting on John 3:18–21, he said, "This dualism is distinguished from gnostic dualism by the fact that it is not
physical, but rather essentially moral: the dominion of
light and truth is that of good works, accomplished in
accord with the will of God; the dominion of darkness
and evil is that of evil works."[15] The antithesis between
"religious" Christianity and Christ's purpose was plain
without the Qumran scrolls, but we were prevented
from seeing it by the world's desperate denial of the true
meanings of "good works" and "evil works."

The whole Gospel of John, considered as a unified
literary composition, corroborates the thesis stated in
the prologue: that it was those "born of God" who could
accept Christ. At the same time, our study of John 1:13,
John 3:18–21, and John 7:6–8 has enlarged and clarified
for us what it means to be "born of God."

THE WORLD

Verse 10 of the prologue, as well as John 3:18–21 and
John 7:6–8, speaks of "the world" as subject of the ignorance, hatred, and rejection whose object is Jesus. What
is "the world"? Of whom does it consist? As various
commentators have pointed out, "the world" is used by
John in three different senses.[16]

First and least significantly, "the world" means more
or less what we call the universe, the sum total of everything that exists. For example, "before the creation of
the world" (John 17:24) or "the world could not hold the
books that would be written" (John 21:25).

Second, "the world" is the stage on which human history is enacted, the earth as humanity's habitation. For
example, "they are still in the world, and I am on my way

to you" (John 17:11) or "the goods of this world" (1 John
3:17); see also John 16:21; 13:1.

The third meaning of "the world" is humankind. When
John speaks of the world's covetousness (1 John 2:17) or
says that the world hates (John 15:18–19) or affirms that
Christ came to save the world (John 3:16–17), he is using
the world to mean humankind.[17]

But this third meaning contains an apparent contradiction or ambiguity, hitherto overlooked by scholars,
that we must clarify. Using "the world" to denote
humankind, John presents two series of affirmations
that seem mutually contradictory:

Series A: John 1:10c; 7:7; 12:31; 14:17, 30; 15:18–19;
16:11, 33; 17:14; 1 John 2:15–17; 3:13; 5:4–5, 19.

Series B: John 1:29; 3:16–17, 19; 4:42; 6:33, 51; 8:12; 9:5;
12:46–47; 1 John 2:2; 4:14.

The world of Series A is to be vanquished; it is evil,
characterized by passions like hatred and covetousness;
it must end. As van den Bussche says, "The world is not,
according to John, an impersonal reality; it is diabolical.
It is the incarnation of Satan (John 12:31; 14:30;
16:11)."[18]

But "the world" of Series B must and will be saved. Sin
will be "taken away" from "the world" (John 1:29).

I see no way of resolving this contradiction except by
making the following assumption: that the humankind
of Series A statements is characterized, both in each
individual and in societal relations, by an organization
and structure from which it has been liberated in Series
B statements. As Barrett says, *"ho kosmos outos* is the
whole organized state of human society, secular and
religious."[19]

The modern word "civilization" provides a rough
equivalent of John's pejorative use of "the world": both
refer to the sum total of the ways in which people function within and among themselves. John's pejorative
"world," like the "civilization" of Freud and Marcuse, is

neither an abstraction nor a universal but a supra-individual and eminently concrete reality that clearly refers to all of civilization and not only to any one civilization in particular.

Bultmann concludes exegetically that the term refers to "the way men are closed against God—a closure indeed that becomes a power ruling the individual, precisely as the 'world' to which every man intrinsically belongs and which he jointly constitutes in his individual closure."[20] Unless we understand "the world" in the pejorative sense (Series A) as civilization, it is impossible to reconcile the affirmations in Series A that the world must be overcome and end with the affirmations in Series B that the world must be saved. "The world" in Series B is humankind liberated from sinful civilization.

THE HOUR OF DEATH

Having discovered what is meant by "the world," we can begin to analyze what is meant by Jesus' saying that the world hates him "because I give testimony that its works are evil" (John 7:6–8). Clearly this is an important thesis, for it is reiterated throughout the Gospel of John, not merely by isolated passages, but by the whole Gospel as a compositional unity.

Barrett points out that "my time," in the phrase "my time [*kairos*] has not yet come " (John 7:8), cannot be distinguished from the more common Johannine expression "my hour."[21] The parallel with "my hour has not yet come" (John 2:4) is particularly clear: In both scenes (2:1–11 and 7:1–10) Jesus uses the phrase to reject a request or suggestion made to him by relatives, and in both scenes, after rejecting the petition, he in fact proceeds to do what was suggested (John 2:7–11 and 7:10). The common structure of the two scenes is striking. As van den Bussche has emphatically pointed out, Jesus' hour—first imminent and then present—is the unifying thread of the Fourth Gospel (John 2:4; 4:21, 23; 5:25, 28–29; 7:6, 8, 30; 8:20; 12:23, 27; 13:1; 16:25, 32; 17:1).

The Gospel makes abundantly clear that Jesus' "hour" is the hour of his death. Twice John tells us that the Jews wished to seize Jesus in order to kill him (John 7:19, 25) and then he expressly states, "They tried to seize him, but no one laid a hand on him because his hour had not yet come" (John 7:30). We find the same meaning in John 8:20: "These words were spoken by Jesus in the treasury as he taught in the temple. Yet no one arrested him, because his hour had not yet come." And when the narrative reaches the time of Jesus' passion, John 13:1 calls it "his hour": "Jesus knew that his hour had come and he must leave this world and go to the Father." Likewise John 17:1: "Father, the hour has come. Glorify your Son, that your Son may glorify thee." "The hour" is used in the same sense in Jesus' premonition (John 12:23–24), which in the Fourth Gospel replaces the prayer in the garden of the Synoptic Gospels:

The hour has come for the Son of man to be glorified. In truth, in very truth I tell you, a grain of wheat remains a solitary grain unless it falls into the ground and dies; but if it dies, it bears a rich harvest.

Only if Christ's "hour" or *kairos* is the hour of his death does his explanation (John 7:1–9) of his reluctance to go up to Jerusalem make sense: "My *kairos* has still not come." If *kairos* does not mean "hour of death," then the causal connections stated in John 7:6–9 are in fact meaningless.

"My hour," then, means "the hour of my death" wherever it appears in the Fourth Gospel. Therefore, when Jesus at Cana replied to his mother, "What do you want with me, woman? My hour has not yet come" (John 2:4), he must even then have been referring to the hour of his death, regardless of the fact that it was still far in the future. Barrett says, "It is unthinkable that in this verse 'hour' should have a different meaning,"[22] and his opinion is especially convincing because in his commentary he is not ready to extract the brutal consequences of this interpretation for the Fourth Gospel as a whole.

If such is the meaning of "hour," then it was Jesus' miracles or "good works" that provoked the aggressive hatred of the world incarnate in the Jews. His testimony that the world's works are evil consists of his own "good works." This interpretation is irrefutably reinforced by John 10:32: "I have set before you many good deeds, done by my Father's power; for which of these would you stone me?"

All of Jesus' miracles are "good works" in the sense of the term we have indicated. If these good works put Jesus in danger of death, then we can understand his reluctance to grant his mother's petition at Cana to do the first miracle in the series that would lead to the cross. John emphasizes that this was Jesus' very first miracle (John 2:11); with it Jesus kindled the world's murderous hatred. It is hardly strange that he was loathe to begin that fatal concatenation. That is the explanation of John 2:4, which has always been a *crux interpretum*.

Our explanation is corroborated by the first part of Jesus' answer to his mother: *ti emoi kai soi*, meaning "What do you want with me?" or "What do you have against me?" This same formula is spoken repeatedly in the Old and New Testaments (Judg. 11:12; 2 Sam. 16:10; 19:23; 1 Kings 17:18; 2 Kings 3:13; 2 Chron. 35:21; Mark 1:24; 5:7; Matt. 8:29; Luke 4:34; 8:28), and is invariably addressed to someone who represents a threat or a danger to the speaker. In the Synoptics the formula is used only by evil spirits threatened by the presence of Jesus. In Judg. 11:12 Jephthah sends a mission to the king of Ammon to ask, "What do you have against me that makes you come to attack me in my own country?" David (2 Sam. 19:23) asks: "What do you have against me, sons of Zeruiah, that you have today become my adversaries?" (Compare this with 2 Sam. 16:10.) In 1

Kings 17:18 the woman of Zarephath says to Elijah: "What do you have against me, you man of God? Have you come here to bring my sins to light and kill my son?" In 2 Kings it is clear that Elisha has much to fear from the son of Ahab and Jezebel, the implacable enemies of his teacher Elijah. In 2 Chronicles Necho addresses the formula to Josiah, who comes to wage war on him at Carchemish.

The second part of Jesus' reply to his mother, the aloof vocative "woman," sustains the tone of the first part. Schnackenburg comments that it is "impossible to deny that Jesus holds himself aloof from his mother (and her request) to some extent."[23] After so many centuries of tiresome, convoluted mariological equivocations,[24] such an admission by a Catholic exegete is valuable indeed, especially considering that Schnackenburg himself does not provide an interpretation of the verse that really explains this aloofness. In the context of our understanding—that the formula "What do you want with me?" is spoken only to someone who is wittingly or unwittingly endangering the speaker—the aloof vocative "woman" is understandable and perfectly appropriate.

After recounting the miracle at Cana, which initiated the series of "good works" that aroused the world's hatred and led to the cross, John deliberately reminds us that this was Jesus' first miracle. Therefore it is not surprising that John should also tell us explicitly that the last miracle (the resuscitation of Lazarus, John 11) resulted in the Jews' definitive decision to kill Jesus (John 11:45–54): "From that day on they plotted his death" (v. 53).

Thus Barrett is correct when he describes Jesus' reaction to Lazarus' death as "shaking with anger" (the verb *embrimasthai* in John 11:33 and 38). Barrett refers to Dan. 11:30, Lam. 2:6, Mark 1:43, and Matt. 9:30, where the same word unequivocally means "to shake with anger." Barrett comments on Jesus' reactions: "This miracle it will be impossible to hide (cf. vv. 28, 30); and this miracle, Jesus perceives, will be the immediate occasion of his death (vv. 49–53)."[25] Such an interpretation is confirmed by the expression "he was in turmoil" (*etaraxen heauton*), which in John 11:33, as well as in John 14:1, 27; 12:27; and 13:21, always describes turmoil due to fear, and in the last two passages cited means turmoil due to fear specifically of death.

The verb *embrimasthai* (John 11:33, 38) is also used by Mark (1:43) and Matthew (9:30) in recounting Jesus' puzzling prohibition against making his miracles known. This prohibition, the famous "messianic secret," according to Wrede and Minette de Tillesse, constitutes the interpretive key to Mark's Gospel.[26] The reason for this otherwise inexplicable prohibition (expressed in Mark 1:25, 34, 44; 3:12; 5:43; 7:24, 36; 8:30; 9:9, 30; and parallel passages) is supplied by John's thesis that Jesus' "good works" aroused the murderous hatred of the Jews and that Jesus knew it. That is the reason Jesus wished to keep his "good works" from becoming common knowledge; the "messianic secret" resulted from his fear of death. Even when he accepted his death, Jesus did all he could to avoid being killed before faith had taken root in the world. The "messianic secret" was a wholly human response to fear of death.

Lest this explanation of Mark's Gospel by the use of John's seem arbitrary and unwarranted, note the first time that the term "to do good" (a definitional term equivalent to "good work") appears in Mark:

On another occasion when he went to synagogue, there was a man in the congregation who had a withered arm; and they were watching to see whether Jesus would cure him on the Sabbath, so that they could bring a charge against him. He said to the man with the withered arm, "Come and stand out here." Then he turned to them: "Is it permitted to do good rather than evil on the Sabbath, to save life rather than kill?" They had nothing to say; and, looking round at them with anger and sorrow at the hardness of their hearts, he said to the man, "Stretch out your arm." He stretched it out and his arm was restored. But the Pharisees, on leaving the synagogue, began plotting against him with the partisans of Herod to see how they could kill him (Mark 3:1–6).

Mark's intention is clearly to contrast "to do good" and "to do evil" and then immediately to emphasize that the Jews decided to kill Jesus for "doing good." It is crucial to recall that this miracle occurs early in Mark's redaction just as the miracle at Cana does in John's. It occurs in Mark after seventy-nine verses; in John after sixty-two. Taylor comments that the Marcan passage "has dramatic appropriateness at so early a point. Like a dark cloud the death of Jesus hangs over the further course of His ministry."[27] Cranfield hypothesizes that "it is intrinsically likely that the intention of his opponents to bring about his death developed quite early in the course of [his ministry]."[28] The reluctance of some exegetes to admit that "my hour" in John 2:4 is the hour of death derives from their failure to grasp the essence of the literary genre of Gospel.

THE COMPOSITIONAL UNITY OF THE GOSPEL GENRE

Let us keep in mind that the creator of this genre was Mark, and that, according to Kahler's analysis, Mark's Gospel consists in a long introduction followed by the passion and death of Jesus. Structurally, Kahler's thesis may be exaggerated, but it contains a more accurate intuition into the idea that generated the Marcan work than might be supposed. It indicates that the very genesis of Mark's Gospel—as well as that of its three imitations or amplifications, the Gospels of Matthew, Luke, and John—is the idea of causal connection between Jesus' life of "good works" and his death. Without this originative conception the account of Jesus' life and the account of his death are linked only incidentally by their subject; the second is not a necessary sequel to the first.

Jesus's life, consisting in "good works," is intrinsically linked to his death by the world's hate-filled reaction, which he anticipated, to those "good works." John had more time than Mark to consider his purposes in writing; perhaps that is why his work expresses more clearly and explicitly this germinal and central idea of the literary genre that has come to us as gospel.

As van den Bussche has observed, the narrative structure of John 2–12 is a perfect arch. What follows John 12 is the hour of the passion and death. As we have indicated, John's account of Jesus' life is structured by frequent premonitions of "the hour" and by reflections on the nature and meaning of "good works" (John 1:13, 3:18–21, 7:6–8, and 10:32). The relationship between Jesus' "good works" and his death is the thematic mainspring of John's narrative.

Remember, though, that Jesus' miracles were not simply what we call "good deeds"; they were messianic "good works." They implied the terrifyingly revolutionary thesis that this world of contempt and oppression can be changed into a world of complete selflessness and unrestricted mutual assistance. Jesus created an intolerable situation; his behavior and his words were a constant goad to "the world"; they inescapably demanded a collective decision.

The "good works" of the Messiah did not consist in giving what was left over, in distributing the surplus of a civilization that in itself remains untouched by the distribution. They were not works of supererogation. Had they been no more than that, Christ would not have been afraid nor would he have died as he did. On the contrary, society acclaims and venerates charitable works. No status *feels* challenged by the works of the Red Cross; rather, the exploiter needs the charities as much or more than the charities need the exploiter. But Jesus' words and deeds proclaim to the world "that its works are evil" (John 7:7). They challenge the very right to exist of "the world"—meaning the overall organization of society. They insist that "the world" *must* be converted into a world of goodness and selflessness, which means that it must completely transform itself,

which means that it must abolish its present self.
"Be converted, for the kingdom of God has arrived" (Matt. 4:17).

Nietzsche says that in the presence of the hero everything turns into tragedy. Jesus transcended the heroic:
He was the Messiah, calling upon the world immediately
to transform itself.

The writings that have come down to us as Gospels are
consistent with the meaning that the word "gospel" has
on the lips of Jesus (see our chapter 4 above). They are
messianic; they proclaim the *eschaton.* If the "good
works" recounted in their opening chapters were not
messianic, if they did not attack this world at its very
foundations, they would not have caused Christ's death
as recounted in their closing chapters. They would then
be like the good deeds of the worldwide charitable organization of the North American or Roman churches
—perfectly acceptable to the world of the oppressors.
The "good works" described in the Gospels have to be
the object of "the world's" hatred; otherwise there is no
gospel, there is no news. Like the Messiah they are
welcome only to "those who have been born of God"
(John 1:13), that is, to those who are dedicated to love of
neighbor and the achievement of justice. As Matthew
says in his fourth beatitude, only those who hunger and
thirst for justice will be filled when the kingdom arrives
(Matt. 5:6). The coming kingdom belongs only to the poor
(Matt. 5:3)[29] and to those who "suffer persecution for
justice' sake" (Matt. 5:10). It cannot be acceptable to the
exploiters of the poor and the persecutors of those who
seek justice.

NOTES

1. Rudolf Bultmann, *Die drei Johannesbriefe* (Göttingen: Vandenhoeck, 1967), p. 22 [Eng. trans.: *The Johannine Epistles*, trans. R.
Philip O'Hara et al. (Philadelphia: Fortress, 1973), p. 16].

2. Johann Michl, *Die Katholischen Briefe*, RNT 8/2, 2nd ed. (Regensburg: Pustet, 1968), ad loc.; Rudolf Schnackenburg, *Die Johannesbriefe*, 3rd ed. (Freiburg: Herder, 1965), p. 112; Ignace de la Potterie,
Adnotationes in exegesim Primae Epistulae s. Ioannis, 2nd ed. (Rome:

Pontificio Istituto Biblico, 1966–67), mimeographed, ad loc.; Bultmann, *Johannesbriefe*, p. 22 [Eng. trans.: *Johannine Epistles*, p. 16]; Johannes Schneider, *Die Kirchenbriefe*, NTD 10 (Göttingen: Vandenhoeck, 1967), p. 140.

3. Schnackenburg, *Johannesbriefe*, p. 112.

4. André Feuillet, *Le prologue du quatrième évangile* (Paris: Desclée, 1968), p. 82. Josef Schmid ("Joh. 1, 13," *Biblische Zeitschrift* 1 [1957], pp. 118–25) has shown that it should be translated as "they had been born" and not in the singular "he had been born," as Mollat and de la Potterie propose. See also Raymond E. Brown, *The Gospel according to John (i–xii)*, Anchor Bible 29 (New York: Doubleday, 1966), pp. 11–12; and likewise Rudolf Schnackenburg, *Das Johannesevangelium* (Freiburg: Herder, 1965), 1:240–41 [Eng. trans.: *The Gospel according to St. John*, trans. Kevin Smyth (New York: Herder and Herder, 1968), 1:264–65].

5. Feuillet, *Prologue*, p. 216.

6. Cf. José Porfirio Miranda, *Marx y la biblia* (Salamanca: Sígueme, 1972) [Eng. trans.: *Marx and the Bible*, trans. John Eagleson (Maryknoll, New York: Orbis Books, 1974)].

7. This is the messianic peace, listed among the characteristics of the kingdom of God in Old and New Testament descriptions. It is necessarily based on justice: "The work of justice will be peace" (Isa. 32:17). Matthew is referring to peacemakers for the entire world.

8. Schnackenburg, *Johannesevangelium*, 1:374–77 [Eng. trans.: *Gospel according to John*, 1:360–63].

9. Walter Grundmann, *Das Evangelium nach Matthäus*, 3rd ed., THKNT 1 (Berlin: Evangelische Verlagsanstalt, 1968), p. 140. Grundmann is also the author of the article "kalos," *TWNT*, 3:539–53 [Eng. trans.: *TDNT*, 3:536–50].

10. Herman L. Strack and Paul Billerbeck, *Kommentar zum Neuen Testament aus Talmud und Midrasch*, 6 vols. (Munich: C. H. Beck, 1922–63), 4:536–58 and 559–610.

11. Joachim Jeremias, "Die Salbungsgeschichte Mk 14, 3–9," *Zeitschrift für die neutestamentliche Wissenschaft* 35 (1936), pp. 77ff.

12. See *Marx y la biblia*, chapter 4, section 1 [Eng. trans.: *Marx and the Bible*, pp. 111–37].

13. Rudolf Bultmann, *Das Evangelium des Johannes* (Göttingen: Vandenhoeck, 1941), p. 115 [Eng. trans.: *The Gospel of John: A Commentary*, trans. G. R. Beasley-Murray et al. (Philadelphia: Westminster, 1971), p. 159].

14. Rudolf Bultmann, *Theologie des Neuen Testaments*, 2nd ed. (Tübingen: Mohr, 1954), p. 427 [Eng. trans.: *Theology of the New Testament*, trans. Kendrick Grobel (New York: Scribner's, 1970), p. 81].

15. M. E. Boismard, "L'évolution du thème eschatologique dans les traditions johanniques," *Revue Biblique* 68 (1961), p. 511.

16. Herman Sasse, "kosmeo," *TWNT*, 3:867–98 [Eng. trans.: *TDNT*, 3:867–98]; Rudolf Bultmann, *Glauben und Verstehen* (Tübingen: Mohr, 1933), 1:135–39 [Eng. trans.: *Faith and Understanding*, trans. Louise Pettibone-Smith (New York: Harper & Row, 1969), pp. 166–70]; Bultmann, *Theologie des Neuen Testaments*, pp. 361–67 [Eng. trans.: *Theology of the New Testament*, pp. 254–59]; C. K. Barrett, *The Gospel according to St. John* (London: SPCK, 1955), pp. 355 and passim; Schnackenburg, *Johannesbriefe*, pp. 133–37; Henri van den Bussche, *Jean* (Paris: Desclée, 1967), pp. 456 and passim; Brown, *Gospel according to John (i–xii)*, pp. 508–10.

17. In several passages there is a mixing of the second and third meanings; the word seems to designate humankind together with the earthly stage on which it enacts its history (1 John 4:9; 2:15–17; John 3:17; 10:36; 11:27; 12:46–47; 16:28; 17:18; 18:37).

18. Van den Bussche, *Jean*, p. 456.

19. Barrett, *Gospel according to St. John*, p. 355.

20. Bultmann, *Johannesbriefe*, p. 23 [Eng. trans.: *Johannine Epistles*, p. 17].

21. Barrett, *Gospel according to St. John*, p. 257. Note that the two expressions are interchangeable in Matt. 26:18 and 45; this is the hour of death, the *kairos* of death, as in Rom. 5:6.

22. Ibid., p. 159.

23. Schnackenburg, *Johannesevangelium*, 1:333 [Eng. trans.: *Gospel according to St. John*, 1:328].

24. Some of the more recent examples include those of Peinador, Quirant, and Delatte, briefly described in Feuillet's "L'heure de Jésus et le signe de Cana," *Ephemerides Theologicae Lovanienses* 36 (1960), pp. 5–22 [Eng. trans.: "The Hour of Jesus and the Sign of Cana," *Johannine Studies* (Staten Island, New York: Alba House, 1965), pp. 17–37].

25. Barrett, *Gospel according to St. John*, p. 332.

26. William Wrede, *Das Messiasgeheimnis in den Evangelien, zugleich ein Beitrag zum Verständis des Markusevangeliums* (Göttingen: Vandenhoeck, 1901) [Eng. trans.: *The Messianic Secret*, trans. J. C. G. Greig (Cambridge: Clarke, 1971)]; G. Minnette de Tillesse, *Le secret messianique dans l'évangile de Marc* (Paris: Cerf, 1968).

27. Vincent Taylor, *The Gospel according to St. Mark*, 2nd ed. (London: Macmillan, 1957), p. 224.

28. C. E. B. Cranfield, *The Gospel according to St. Mark* (Cambridge: University Press, 1959), p. 122.

29. Jacques Dupont has shown that the addition of the words "in spirit" does not mean that the phrase does not refer to the needy and indigent; see *Les béatitudes*, 2nd ed. (Paris: Gabalda, 1969), 2:98, 13–15, and 19–51.

Chapter 6

The Word

What is the content of this "word" of John's prologue? In what does this "word" consist if only those who love their neighbor and do justice are capable of understanding it?

John could have begun his Gospel as the Synoptics did, with a description of "the word's" activity after it became flesh (John 1:14). If he chooses to begin instead with a prologue comprising an entire thesis on "the word" that "was in the beginning," it is because he has something decisive to tell us, something that cannot be conveyed simply by narrating the life and death of the word made flesh. John's very decision to begin with a discussion of the word as such leads us to believe that his intention was unusually profound. Hermeneutically speaking, there is no justification for supposing that the prologue represents the ingenuous thinking we are accustomed to attribute to a mere raconteur. Under the circumstances, it would be surprising if John's thinking were not surprising. Since John's initiative in speaking about the word quite forcefully demonstrates his philosophical insight, no idea we find in his prologue can seem too profound or philosophical.

To understand John we must rid ourselves of the a priori progressivist prejudice that human history is progress and later periods are in all ways inevitably better than earlier ones. This prejudice would lead us into the fallacious assumption that anything seeming to us profoundly original and superior cannot possibly derive from ancient times but only from modernity or the incipient future.

Applied to biblical exegesis, such progressivism is revealed as absurd, the negation of hermeneutics. It is tantamount to saying that we already know more than the Bible can tell us. Such a belief, far more prevalent than is generally admitted among Catholics, besides being patently ridiculous is irreconcilable with the pontifical directive of 1964, which states that in our understanding of the Bible "there remain many questions, and these of the gravest moment."[1]

For example, does not Paul's assertion that "men impede truth with injustice" (Rom. 1:18) seem philosophically revolutionary? Had he said that ignorance or false premises or faulty logic or self-serving deceit impedes truth, we would find his statement acceptable and thoroughly ordinary. Had he said that the whole condition of human immorality prevents us from knowing truth, we would credit him with Pascalian profundity. But Paul's assertion is more trenchant than the former and more specific than the latter: It is by their *adikia*, their injustice, described in terms of interpersonal relationships (Rom. 1:28–32), that people suppress the knowledge of truth within themselves. Paul's thesis strikingly resembles Marx's theory of the origin of ideological alienation, and because of our progressivist prejudices it seems to us exceedingly "modern." But it was written in 58 A.D. Should it surprise us, then, that John, writing in the same philosophic tradition some thirty or forty years later, speaks of "the word" with equal trenchancy, subtlety, and insight?

Schnackenburg identifies a specific instance in which John is thinking existentially and must be so interpreted, no matter how anachronistically modern that might seem. He refers to John 3:33: "To accept his

[Christ's] testimony is to acknowledge the truth of God's words." Schnackenburg says, "the very similar passage in 1 Jn 5:9–12 shows that this 'existential' understanding of the text is both possible and necessary."[2] Indeed, by accepting Christ's witness, which is God's, one makes God truthful, that is, one brings about the fulfillment of God's promise. If there is to be eternal life, this acceptance must occur (see John 5:24). God testified that he had given us life in Christ (see 1 John 5:11); therefore, when we have achieved that life, God is then truthful. The thesis of John 3:33 and 1 John 5:10 does not seem to me exceptionally profound, but it certainly is unambiguously existentialist regardless of its authorship some eighteen centuries ago. I cite this instance, not for its own sake, but to demonstrate the inapplicability of our customary progressivist criteria to hermeneutics. Surely, if the narrative portion of John's Gospel contains statements that startle by their modernity, we should not be surprised to find even more powerfully original ideas in the prologue, which is obviously an attempt to extract the theological meaning of the narrative.

THE WORD AS WORD

In the body of the Gospel itself there are several passages that deal with the word as word and not specifically as the word of God. The word insofar as it is word is the very fact that someone is being spoken to, the very fact of summons, of that irreducible otherness that we perceive only to the degree that it is being exercised. One of these passages is John 8:25:

They said to him, "Who are you?"
Jesus said to them, "Absolutely, that I speak to you."

Many exegetes have been baffled by this verse, but Barrett notes that the difficulty of Jesus' answer "has perhaps been exaggerated. It must be observed at the outset that *(ten) archen* is used quite frequently in

Greek adverbially."[3] He refers to the lexicon of Lidell and Scott, which abundantly documents the adverbial use of *(ten) archen*, translated above as "absolutely." Westcott and Brown suggest the adverbial translation "at all";[4] several German exegetes propose *überhaupt* ("at all" or, better, "absolutely"). Barrett prefers "at first," which fits the English translation well. Whichever of these translations one prefers, the meaning of the rest of the phrase remains unchanged: "that I speak to you."

In any case, the passage cannot mean "I am the beginning, who speaks to you." There is nothing to warrant translating an accusative term that is normally used adverbially as though it were nominative and predicate nominative. Nor can the passage mean, "What from the beginning I have told you." This translation could be correct only if *ten archen* modified the verb, and here it does not.

Another attempt at translation divides the recitative particle *hoti*, changing it into the interrogative *ho ti*. Thus Jesus' response becomes an evasion: "How is it that I speak to you at all?" But Brown notes that the interrogative *ho ti* occurs rarely[5] (and I think it may even have been invented in support of this translation). Furthermore, such a translation implies that Jesus interrupted the conversation at this point, which in fact he did not.

As a grammatical parallel to Jesus' response in John 8:25, Lagrange, over half a century ago, perceptively cited the Hellenist passage in Achilles Tatius 6:20 *ouk agapas hoti soi kai lalo*. He translated this as "N'es-tu pas ravie que je veuille bien parler avec toi?"[6] "Aren't you delighted that I even speak with you?" Actually *kai* has no modern equivalent. It is the emphatic-pleonastic, found in the Greek text of Heb. 7:25; 11:19; Acts 10:29; 2 Cor. 2:9 (and similar to Rom. 4:22; John 12:18; Heb. 13:12; 1 Pet. 4:19; Luke 1:35; 11:49). But its usage here is exactly the same as in John 8:25: *ten archen, hoti kai lalo hymin*. Lagrange's discovery of the grammatical parallel is our most valuable key to this passage. And Brown considers the correct translation to be indeed possible: "That I speak to you at all." This might be better phrased as "In the first place, that I am speaking to you."

In any case, the Hellenist parallel drawn by Lagrange makes the recitative "that" inescapable: "that I speak to you." The power of Jesus' answer lies in the word "that." The Jews were anticipating a predicate or an attribute, something reducible to a concept. Reduction to a concept is our most useful device for suppressing the otherness of the one who speaks to us, for enclosing ourselves in ourselves by use of categories that are not "other" but merely different beads from the same string of our selves. But the only time, according to John, that the Jews asked Jesus, "Who are you?" he answered, not with a predicate or an attribute, but "That I am speaking to you." He is the word as word.

Jesus deliberately refused to supply another predicate ("God" would be a predicate like any other), another category whose combinations and permutations the self could employ to close in upon itself and avoid the summons of the "other." The other, who is not I, exists only in the word as such. Jesus Christ is the fact that I am being spoken to. He is the word.

The second passage in the Gospel narrative that refers to the word as such—the conversation with the Samaritan woman in John 4:10—is less clear. Eduard Schweizer inchoately perceived its significance.[7] Van den Bussche grasped it more fully and accurately by detecting a synonymic parallel and an epexegetical or explicative *kai* in this passage:

If you knew God's gift and who it is that is saying to you, "Give me a drink."

In fact this is a synonymic parallel, as frequently found both in the Psalms and in modern everyday usage. The gift or favor of God is explained ("and") by the synonymic expression that follows. Van den Bussche comments: "The parallelism clearly indicates that the gift to which Jesus refers is precisely this word that he is directing to her; it is the fact that he is speaking to her."[8]

The third and last passage we shall consider has a double aspect. The observation of F. M. Braun enables us to see how for John the word as word takes on significance, the word as the very fact of one person addressing another: "Controlled by the same verb, the three terms *logos, remata, phone* ['word,' 'terms,' and 'voice,' respectively] are, more or less, synonymous."[9] By saying that having life depends on listening to Jesus' word (John 5:24 and passim) or his terms (John 6:63, 68) or his voice (John 5:25; 10:27–28), John indicates that neither the content of the word nor its divine source is of primary importance. What is important is the address, the allocution, the fact that one person is being spoken to by another: word, terms, voice.

With that in mind we see that the last passage in John's narrative to treat the word as word, namely, John 8:43, does so in two ways:

Why do you not understand my language?
Because you cannot listen to my word.

Most commentators have ignored this passage, which the Evangelist attributes to Jesus, finding in it no special significance. But it is worthy of note that John distinguishes quite clearly between *lalia* and *logos*; obviously they are not synonymous, for if they were, Jesus' question and answer would make no sense at all. *Lalia* means "language," "idiom," "audible speech" (Barrett), "*Sprache*" (Bultmann). *Logos* means "word." In our linguistic tradition *lalia* means the actual sounds that are uttered, while *logos* means the conceptual content of those sounds. But, while people customarily "listen to" or "hear" sounds (*lalia*), and "understand" or "know" content (*logos*), Jesus has here made the opposite connection, linking understanding to sound and hearing to content. Why? Because what the Jews could not listen to was the fact of the word; what they could not tolerate was the fact of being summoned. Since they could not stand the very fact of being summoned, they could not understand his language.

Independently, however, of the exact meaning of the passage and the distinction between *lalia* and *logos*, one thing is clear about John 8:43: John is here focusing on the question of the word as word, and not specifically as the word of God.

THE PRE-EXISTENT WORD

Most exegetes agree that the opening words of the prologue—"In the beginning..." (John 1:1)—and the thesis that "everything was made through it [the word] and without it nothing came to be" (John 1:3) undoubtedly allude to the first verse of Genesis—"In the beginning God created heaven and earth"—and to the entire first chapter of the Bible. Genesis resounds ten times with the words "God *said*... and it was done" (Gen. 1:3, 6, 9, 11, 14, 20, 24, 26, 28, 29), emphasizing the power of the word (of God) alone. In corroboration, Genesis 1 enumerates everything that was made through the word and stresses that without it nothing came to be. There is no doubt that "the word" of John's prologue is the word of God; the fact that John ignores this and speaks only of the word alone must, therefore, be deliberate. That is the most important fact of the entire prologue, and exegesis has not yet paid it sufficient heed.

I am not laboring to break down an unlocked door. Both Protestant and Catholic Christology customarily and exclusively fasten upon the fact that John hypostatizes the word, that is, the fact that in John's Gospel the word is a person. Consequently we read the substantive "the word" as if it were a proper name serving only to designate the person called Christ, as if it were merely an appellative, a code word with no meaning except as a synonym for Jesus. Who cares that "Graciela" is the diminutive of "grace"? What matters is that the name points out, like a finger, Graciela and not Patricia. She could just as easily be called Antoinette, for the function of the name is simply to distinguish one person from another. According to traditional Christology, John could easily have said "wisdom" or "omnipotence" or "the wisdom of God," for the conceptual significance of any word disappears when it is used only to designate a concrete person. When we understand "the word" simply as a reference to Christ, everything John wants to tell us escapes us. We are left with a series of affirmations that are true in themselves but are not what John wants to tell us.

This "Christocentric" exegesis, based solely on the hypostatization of the word and the person of Christ, truncates the gospel message to the point of making it unrecognizable. It makes a new gospel out of John's words. John does not even state that the word is Christ until 1:14, and although from verse 14 on, John very much personifies "the word," his really important point is that it continues to be the word. The contrast between John's treatment of the pre-existent word and biblical and rabbinic speculation on the pre-existence of the law and of wisdom (greatly emphasized by Feuillet, Schnackenburg, and Brown) cannot be explained by personification alone. If John intended simply a personification, he could have affirmed the pre-existence of Christ by asserting that the wisdom (or the law) existing from the beginning—a concept familiar and acceptable to the Jews—became incarnate in Christ. If he does not choose to personify that concept, it is because he is concerned with "the word" itself. If the word that existed from the beginning later became flesh, for John the important aspect of this incarnation was that the person continued to be word.

Why this emphasis on the word? Schnackenburg, who does not have the answer, poses the question accurately. After comparing John's use of "the word" with its closest parallels, Wisd. 9:1–2 and the *Slavonic Enoch* 30:8 and 33:4, he says,

When, therefore, the Logos-hymn describes the sovereign action of the Word in terms of Wisdom, particularly in relation to men, this constitutes a later stage of development, and it is not clear why the author then recurs again to the term 'word', and not the 'word of God' but to the term 'the Logos', used absolutely. Thus the Wisdom speculation provides the aptest parallels in thought, but leaves the term chosen by the Christian hymn unexplained.[10]

Some commentators proffer the ridiculous explanation that John reverted to the masculine term *logos* because it was more appropriate than the feminine *sophia* ("wisdom") to designate the male Jesus of Nazareth, but this answer is unworthy of the question. John's main concern in the prologue is not simply Jesus' pre-existence, nor is it the word of God; it is simply "the word." The exegetes' problem is: Why?

THE WORD'S INTERLOCUTOR

The key to the question lies in the first verse of the prologue. John's philosophical and theological maturation led him to affirm the pre-existence of the word as such, that is, as summons, as otherness that "is addressed to..., " that "speaks to another." But the primordial objection to this definition was that "in the beginning" there existed neither people nor the world to be addressed, to be spoken to. Therefore, after the first verse says that "in the beginning was the word," John must add, "and the word was addressed to God," and further, "the word itself was God."

F. C. Burkitt understands clearly that "the word was

addressed to God,"[11] and L. M. Dewailly translates the phrase as "et la parole s'addressait à Dieu."[12] More recently C. Masson rendered it as "la parole parlait à Dieu."[13]

Kai ho logos en pros ton theon (John 1:1b) can be translated only as "and the word was addressed to God." As de la Potterie has shown, it is groundless to suppose that John's use of the Greek prepositions *eis, en,* and *pros* is colloquially ungrammatical or careless. The validity of de la Potterie's careful study is attested in several ways, including his very failure to realize that *ho logos* continues to mean the word, that the word continues to be word. De la Potterie says, "Simply to invoke 'Hellenistic usage' to give *eis* the meaning of *en,* as is often done, is quite unconvincing, for we are trying to discover precisely whether or not John conforms to this usage. And until now we do not have the least indication that such is the case."[14] He makes the same point about John's use of *pros:* There is no basis for assuming that John confused these prepositions with each other and failed to perceive the exact nuance of each. Therefore, we are obliged to translate *pros ton theon* as "addressed to God." De la Potterie has definitively proved wrong the customary translation "and the word was with God" (or "near God"), citing the following four reasons:

1. There is no other text in John in which *pros* with the accusative means "with" or "near."

2. The sapiential texts describe Wisdom as "near God" or "with God," but they do so according to the classical usage, that is, using the preposition *para* (Prov. 8:30) or the preposition *meta* (Sir. 1:1)—never *pros.*

3. Whenever John wants to express the presence or proximity of one person to another, he uses *para* (1:39; 4:40; 14:17, 25; 19:25; cf. 14:23) or *meta* (3:22, 25, 26). In particular, when he speaks of the proximity or presence of the Son to the Father he always says *para soi* (17:5), *para to patri* (8:38).

4. Even with verbs other than verbs of motion,

whenever John says *pros ton theon* (or *pros ton patera*) he always clearly suggests the idea of "direction toward . . . ," of "orientation toward. . . ." Thus *parakleton echomen pros ton patera* (1 John 2:1) does not mean simply "in his presence," but "turned toward him," "addressing himself to him," "summoning him." Westcott says:" "Not simply in His presence, but turned toward Him, addressing Him with continual pleadings."[15] The same connotation exists in 1 John 3:21 and 5:14.

De la Potterie's conclusion from these findings is to translate John 1:1b as "Le Logos était *tourné vers* Dieu." Because he forgets that *logos* means "word," he does not see that the sentence must mean "the word was addressed to God," "the word's interlocutor was God." Given that the word existed from the beginning, this translation is unavoidable, for without an other to address, there is no word.

To de la Potterie's proofs of the meaning of *pros* we can add this point: of the twenty-eight examples in the Fourth Gospel of non-motion verbs used with *pros*, twenty-two of those verbs mean "to say to . . . " (2:3; 3:4; 4:15, 33, 48, 49; 5:45; 6:5b, 28, 34; 7:3, 35, 50; 8:31, 33, 57; 10:35; 11:21; 12:19; 13:28; 16:17; 19:24). The most significant of these examples occurs in John 10:35, because this is the only verse in John besides 1:1b, 2 where *pros* appears with a non-motion verb and with *logos* as subject "to those to whom the word was addressed" (*pro hous ho logos egeneto*). This expression, containing the noun *logos*, the verb *ginomai* and the preposition *pros*, appears in the Septuagint some 110 times, as far as I can determine, and invariably means "the word was addressed to . . . " or an equivalent phrase. In the Hebrew text, the verb in every one of these 110 cases is "to be," as it is in John 1:1, 2. The Septuagint uses *ginomai* to assist in the translation, but uses it in a colorless way, almost as a simple copulative. The meaning is entirely conveyed by *logos* and *pros*, as in John 1:1, 2.

Logos with *pros*—with the verb "to be" understood —occurs in 1 Kings 2:14, 2 Kings 9:5; Zech. 4:6; Jer. 9:12 (11), always meaning "addressed to. . . . " In these four passages the verb "to be" can be understood because the tense is present. But in John 1:1b, 2 the verb must be explicitly stated because it is in the preterite tense.

Comparative analysis of this kind is the only method we have to determine what John 1:1 means. To clarify and emphasize his meaning, John restates in the second verse the ideas introduced in the first:

(1) In the beginning existed the word,
and the word was addressed to God,
and the word was God.
(2) It was in the beginning addressed to God.

For the word to be word, it must be addressed to someone, and if it existed from the beginning it could have been addressed only to God. And John's first message, immediately restated, is that it did exist from the beginning: His prologue does not speak of the pre-existence of Christ, but rather of the pre-existence of the word. What existed from the beginning was the word. It was the word as such that later became flesh, became a human being, became tangible and visible to us.

GOD AS WORD

We hold that the word was a person from the beginning, but John does not focus his attention on this. His clear reference in John 1:3 to the phrase from Genesis, "he *said* . . . and it was done," shows that he is not considering the word as person but as word. Otherwise he would have said "wisdom" or "the word of God" instead.

"The word," used without qualification, appears frequently throughout the New Testament (Mark 2:2; 4:14, 33; Matt. 13:19, 21–23; Luke 5:1; 9:28; Mark 8:32; Acts 4:4, 29, 31; 6:2, 4, 7; 8:4, 14, 25; 10:36, 44; 11:1, 19; 13:5, 7, 49; 16:6, 32; 19:20; Eph. 1:13; Col. 1:5; etc.). We know that the sacred writers (and Jesus himself) mean "the word of God," but it is most significant that they call it simply "the word." It was inevitable that a genius of John's philosophic turn of mind should be led to consider the word as such, that nonresorbable otherness that, as we shall see, exists only in the great news of the gospel.

Note John's penultimate step in chapter 17 of his Gospel. After Jesus said that he had given the word of God to his disciples (v. 14), he added, "As you sent me into the world, so too I have sent them into the world" (v. 18). He was not concerned only about his disciples, but also about those who would come to believe through their word (v. 20). The word passes from bearer to bearer; the important thing is that the world should continue to be addressed by the word. John understood that God consisted in this very fact of addressing, in the very event of the word. Therefore he asserts: What existed at the beginning was the word, and the word was addressed to God, and the word itself was God. He also saw that Jesus' entire life and death were characterized by this unparalleled fact: He was the word, he was the incarnation of the word. That insight is summed up in the Johannine Christ's best definition of himself: "Above all, that I am speaking to you" (John 8:25).

NOTES

1. *Acta Apostolicae Sedis*, 1964, p. 716 [Eng. trans.: *Catholic Biblical Quarterly*, vol. 26, no. 3 (July 1964): 309].

2. Rudolf Schnackenburg, *Das Johannesevangelium* (Freiburg: Herder, 1965), 1:399, 398 [Eng. trans.: *The Gospel according to St. John*, trans. Kevin Smyth (New York: Herder and Herder, 1968), 1:386, 385].

3. C. K. Barrett, *The Gospel according to St. John* (London: SPCK, 1955), p. 283.

4. Brooke Foss Westcott, *The Gospel according to St. John* (London: Clarke, 1958; the first edition appeared in 1880), p. 131; Raymond E. Brown, *The Gospel according to John (i–xii)*, Anchor Bible 29 (Garden City, New York: Doubleday, 1966), p. 348.

5. Brown, *Gospel according to John (i–xii)*, pp. 347–48.

6. M. J. Lagrange, *Evangile selon saint Jean*, 8th ed. (Paris: Gabalda, 1948), p. 238.

7. Eduard Schweizer, *"Ego eimi,"* Forschungen zur Religion und Literatur des Alten und Neuen Testaments 56 (Göttingen: Vandenhoeck, 1939), p. 161.

8. Henri van den Bussche, *Jean* (Paris: Desclée, 1967), p. 187.

9. F. M. Braun, *Jean le théologien* (Paris: Gabalda, 1966), 3:103.

10. Schnackenburg, *Johannesevangelium*, 1:260 [Eng. trans.: *Gospel according to St. John*, 1:484].

11. Francis Crawford Burkitt, *Church and Gnosis* (Cambridge, Eng.: The University Press, 1932), p. 95.

12. L. M. Dewailly, *Jésus-Christ, parole de Dieu* (Paris: Cerf, 1945), p. 17.

13. C. Masson, cited by André Feuillet in *Le prologue du quatrième évangile* (Paris: Desclée, 1968), p. 267.

14. I. de la Potterie, "L'emploi dynamique de *eis* dans Saint Jean et ses incidences théologiques," *Biblica* 43 (1962), p. 377.

15. Westcott, cited by de la Potterie, ibid., p. 379.

Chapter 7

The Word of Which God Consists

Till now we have dealt with passages that focus on "the word" as such, which consists in the summons, that otherness that the self cannot assimilate because it is ever the "other" that cannot be identified with the self. The word is not a medium; it is not an instrument of information that is dispensable once the data are transmitted and the information is registered by the subject, that is, once the subject is reintegrated into its solitude. On the contrary, the word is—always and essentially—a rupture of the solitude and immanence of the self, the only possible rupture, the only possible negation of idealism and solipsism.

Heteronomy and otherness, combated by Kant with a determination worthy of a better cause, are in reality the imprescindable condition of possibility of the absolute imperative, the only possible basis for unconditional injunction. On the other hand, Marxism, which conceives of the word as an instrument of the ends and needs of the self, as an extension or "long arm" of the self's utilitarianism, remains encapsulated in idealism. It cannot transcend its idealistic, solipsistic little habitation, designed by the self for itself, in which the neighbor is a mere means to the "enriching" ends of the self. But the word is gratuitous. The self in no way needs it, nor is anyone able to utilize it as an instrument. So

126

much we have demonstrated. But what basis does John have for saying that the word existed from the beginning?

Could the word exist from the beginning except by virtue of its specific, unique content? For notwithstanding our necessary prior emphasis on the word as word, as summons, the word *says* something. We must now ask whether the existence of the word as summons does not result from its content. Could the otherness exist and remain nonassimilable except by virtue of *what* the word *says*?

THE WORD OF LOVE

We considered an extremely important datum in our chapter 5: According to John 1:13 only those who love their neighbor and do justice can understand and embrace the word. The masculine accusative *auton* in verses 10, 11, and 12 has only one masculine antecedent, namely, *ho logos*, "the word." It is saying, therefore, that the world did not know *it*, that its own did not receive *it*, that all those who received *it* were born of God, that is, lovers of their neighbor and doers of justice. This means that the content of the word is related to justice and love of neighbor and that the word could not exist as summons if it were not because of its content. This content is thus the condition of possibility of the word as summons.

We must relate what we said in chapter 6 to the theme of chapter 5, that is, the world's hatred of "good works." We see that good works are the content of "the word" in John 17:14:

I gave them your word and the world hated them.

In this verse the "and" is clearly consecutive and causal: I gave them your word *and therefore* the world hated them. The laconic, paratactical phrasing of the following passage from John's First Epistle lends to the same meaning an even greater emphasis:

My brothers, do not be surprised if the world hates you. We know that we have crossed over from death to life, in that we love the brothers (1 John 3:13–14).

By omitting the particles that explicitly relate one clause to the other, John compels the reader to furnish them. That is the purpose of the parataxis. The meaning of the verses is that, since John and the believers are already accomplishing "the word" of love of neighbor, they must expect the world's hatred. As far as I know, no modern commentator separates these two verses. But it is also necessary to point out the logical relationship between them: otherwise verse 13 seems like an erratic segment, unrelated to the preceding and following verses, almost like a marginal gloss. The world's hatred (v. 13) is not occasioned by the "crossing over from death to life" (v. 14), but by the love of one's brothers that is the visible sign of this passage from death to life, because this visibility is really the thesis of verse 14. The axis of verse 14 is love of neighbor; thus it is this axis which must be related with the admonition not to wonder if the world hates you. The same connection occurs in John 17:14 ("I gave them your word, and therefore the world hated them") and in John 10:32 ("I have set before you many good works, done by my Father's power; for which of these would you stone me?"). In our chapter 5 we emphasized that the world hates all who proclaim the imperative of good works, implying that the whole social system must be transformed into a world of goodness and solidarity. 1 John 3:13–14 shows us the same hatred directed against whoever confronts the world and history with the fulfilled imperative of loving one's neighbor. In John 17:14 we find the world reacting identically to the bearer of "the word." The content of the word in these passages seems unequivocally implied; there seems no question about what the word *says*.

According to Westcott, whose stylistic analysis is meticulously accurate, we find the same idea in John 15:17–18:

(17) These things I command you: that you love one another. (18) If the world hates you, bear in mind that it hated me before you.

These two verses are frequently considered independently of one another. But Westcott points out that verse 17 "must be taken as the introduction of a new line of thought. ... On this point the usage in St. John is conclusive against the received arrangement."[1] As proof he cites John 14:25; 15:11; 16:1, 25, 33; and John 16:4b also proves his point. In fact, whenever the Johannine Jesus says "*tauta*" ("these things"), it is to initiate a new subject or a new aspect of the preceding subject. Therefore John 15:17 cannot be separated from John 15:18; the paratactical relationship between them is consecutive and causal, like that between 1 John 3:13 and 14. Westcott rightly concludes that Christian love is "the antidote to and the occasion of the world's hatred."[2]

The challenging assertion in John 8:37—"You want to kill me *because* my word makes no headway with you"—explicitly affirms the causal connection we found in John 17:14: "I gave them your word and the world hated them." All these passages point to one conclusion: The content of the word is the commandment or imperative to love our neighbor.

This conclusion is confirmed by the formulation of John 8:31: "If you abide in my word, truly *you will be my disciples*." For John uses the italicized phrase only once more, in John 13:35, where he defines it thus: "By this all will know that *you are my disciples*: that you love one another." A comparison of these two verses seems to demand a univocal conclusion: To abide in the word is to love one's neighbor. This means that the content of the word is "love one another."

A recent commentator on the Fourth Gospel has seen that "for John 'word' and 'commandment' are virtually interchangeable."[3] Love of neighbor, rightly understood as the imperative of justice and not as a form of solipsistic romantic delusion (see chapter 5), is certainly the content that gives the word life as nonresorbable otherness. If John believed that "the commandment" existed from the beginning, then he could affirm that the word existed from the beginning.

AN OLD COMMAND

Two passages from John's First Epistle are fundamental to any discussion of the word's pre-existence. They further document that "the word" of the Gospel prologue is the commandment to love one another.

Dear friends, I give you no new command. It is the old command which you have had from the beginning; *this old command is the word which you heard.* And yet again, I am giving you a new command—which is made true in him [Christ] and in you—because the darkness is passing and the true light already shines (1 John 2:7–8).

The causal conjunction "because" (v. 8, above) has been discussed at the beginning of our chapter 5. The historical, temporal nature of the word of which God truly consists has been demonstrated in chapters 6 and the present one, which will establish the premises on which the following three chapters will be based.

All scholars recognize that the words "in him" (v. 8, above) refer to Christ. The "command" is to love one's neighbor, as proven by the following verses (1 John 2:9–11) and by 2 John 5. Moreover, the entire passage obviously alludes to John 13:34, in which the Johannine Christ designates the command to love one another a "new commandment." 1 John 2:7–8 appears to be a reflection on the newness or oldness of the imperative that Jesus called "a new commandment." The italicized hemistych in 1 John 2:7 expressly asserts that that commandment is identical to "the word" we have heard. In the previous sentence John affirms that we have had that commandment from the beginning. Because he is convinced that word and commandment are identical, and convinced that the commandment existed from the beginning, John can assert in his Gospel's prologue that the word existed from the beginning.

What does John mean by "from the beginning"? In this passage, "from the beginning" cannot mean from the beginning of the preaching of the gospel, as Bultmann holds, for then there would be no difference between the affirmation that the commandment is old (v. 7) and the affirmation that it is new (v. 8). The expression "from the beginning" must mean from the beginning of time, as it does in 1 John 2:13 and 14: "You have known the one who was [or is] from the beginning [ton apharches]."

Comparing verse 7 (an "old" command) with verse 8 (a "new" command), Günther Klein correctly observes: "It is not by chance that the Christological dimension does not enter into the picture with reference to 'oldness'; rather it does so only with reference to the 'newness' of the commandment."[4] Verse 8 undoubtedly refers to the historical epoch inaugurated by Christ, which is the *eschaton*. Therefore "the old commandment which you have had from the beginning" (v. 7) is an imperative that antedated Christ's entry into the world. With Christ's advent the "old commandment" becomes new in a sense that John wishes to examine. Whatever John may mean by "new" and "old," in verse 7 he undeniably says that the commandment existed before Christ came into the world and in verse 8 that the commandment was new in the epoch of Jesus Christ. He is making a chronological contrast.

To deny that this chronological contrast is stated by the text itself is to deny the nonmanipulable reality of time, to deny that John is speaking of time. Bultmann makes this denial: He claims that verse 8 does not refer to a historical period but rather to an "eschatological reality."[5] Of course the epoch of Christ is eschatological, but this does not mean that it is not historical. The dehistorifying of the *eschaton* is the principal flaw in

Bultmannian interpretation. This flaw derives from Heidegger's scorn for "vulgar time" (see our chapter 3) and from the mistaken belief that a nontemporal "eschatological reality" is the only valid alternative to the precocious Catholicism of "salvation history," which has enabled the church to establish itself in western history as the official religion of the great civilization of oppression. But to detemporalize the *eschaton* is even more perniciously "Catholic" than to categorize salvation as past history. In fact, this detemporalization has been the principal tool of the theology that tranquillizes consciences and legitimates crimes committed in the name of "imperishable Christian values." The detemporalizing of the *eschaton*—rejuvenated by Bultmann—strips the *eschaton* of the only real meaning it could possibly have.

Günther Klein, although believing with Bultmann that eschatological time is nontemporal, nevertheless declares Bultmann's interpretation of 1 John 2:7–8 to be untenable: "In the process of linguistic apocalypticization, the eschatological 'hour' has lost its original ontological independence of the chronological hours constituting the temporal continuum. Eschatological time itself has become a chronological dimension, that is, the last link of the temporal continuum."[6] "In the First Epistle, the *eschaton* acquires the character of an epoch."[7]

But Klein's interpretation is equally indefensible: "The commandment is 'old' because the history of the church has already lasted quite some time. It is 'new' because taken as a whole the history of the church marks a new phase in the history of the world."[8] This is indefensible because verse 8 does not say simply "which is made true in you"; rather it says "which is made true *in him* and in you." The period referred to in verse 8 is a unit of time in which Christ and the readers of John's Epistle are both present simultaneously; it is the period marked out by the person and life of Jesus of Nazareth.

And if the commandment is "new" by virtue of being given in Jesus' lifetime, then it can be "old" only by virtue of having existed prior to Jesus' lifetime. Therefore the expression "from the beginning," with which verse 7 describes the commandment's oldness, cannot mean from the beginning of Christian preaching, but rather from the beginning of time.

It is conceivable that the Epistle was addressed to converted Jews and that "old" in verse 7 refers to Israelite legislation promulgated before Christ: "Love your neighbor as yourself" (Lev. 19:18). But the formula "from the beginning" is never used in that way. It means either from the beginning of time or from the beginning of Christ's preaching. These are the only meanings that can be documented, and the second is proved inapplicable to 1 John 2:7–8 by the wording itself.

Therefore 1 John 2:7–8 affirms that the commandment of love of neighbor is identical to "the word" and that it existed from the beginning of time.

THE WORD OF LIFE

Before 1 John 2:7, the expression "from the beginning" is used only once in the Epistle. It occurs in 1 John 1:1, the second passage that is fundamental to our understanding of the word's pre-existence:

What was from the beginning,
what we heard,
what we saw with our eyes,
what we looked upon and our hands touched,
our theme is the word of life.

"Life," as the Epistle itself tells us later on, consists in love of neighbor ("We know that we have crossed over from death to life, in that we love the brothers"—1 John 3:14). This being the case, then "the word of life" must be the word regarding love of neighbor. And 1 John 1:1 says that this word "was from the beginning."

Extra-exegetical reasons prompt Bultmann to deny that John is speaking here of "the pre-existent Logos"[9] and of a time previous to the incarnation. In a "more precise interpretation" Bultmann himself has shown that "the beginning of the Epistle means substantially the same thing as the prologue of the Gospel."[10] To the overwhelming majority of exegetes, *en arche* in John 1:1 and *ap' arches* in 1 John 1:1 both refer to the pre-existence of the *logos*.[11] Conzelmann and Herbert Braun point out that the beginning of the Epistle connotes an object and is neuter, that it is less hypostatic and personal than the Gospel prologue.[12] In fact, the Epistle deals with the content of "the word" from the first verse. The observations of both scholars derive from our common distortion of the Gospel prologue: making "the word" into a proper noun designating Christ, and completely forgetting its conceptual meaning. For John, as we emphasized in chapter 6, the word did not cease to be word when it became flesh. The point of his prologue is that precisely the word as such—that which existed from the beginning as the summons of otherness —became a human being; the life of Christ about to be recounted to us has meaning insofar as "it" addresses us as "the word." Christ's works themselves are *verba visibilia*, as Bultmann shows in another context.

The beginning of the Epistle undoubtedly emphasizes the element of message, of content, in the word ("what" repeated four times and again in v. 3, always in the neuter gender). That message or content is "the word of life." As we shall soon see, the Gospel prologue also indicates of what "the word" is "full." The Epistle also tells us that some*thing* became flesh: "what we saw with our eyes, what we looked upon and our hands touched." This formulation obliges us to recognize that the beginning of the Epistle and the prologue of the Gospel contain the same message. It is our interpretation that must change, our centuries-old inclination to distort the prologue by forgetting that *ho logos* means "the word."

The "it" through which all things were made is no more a person than "what was from the beginning." And "the word" that was addressed to God is as neuter in gender as "what existed from the beginning."

"In the word was life" (John 1:4) is another way of referring to "the word of life" (1 John 1:1). Note that John finds it necessary to add, "And the life [of which I speak] was the light of men, and the light shines in the darkness, and the darkness did not receive it" (John 1:4b–5). The summoning that is implicit in the term "light," which Bultmann rightly perceives at the beginning of the Epistle (1 John 1:5–6), is clearly manifest in the Gospel prologue in the allusion to people's free response to the light, whether *katelaben* is translated as "they received" or as "they overcame." The word that bears life can be accepted or rejected. It is a demand, an imperative.

WORD AND COMMANDMENT

In these two passages of the Epistle (1 John 1:1 and 2:7–8) "the word" is identical to the commandment of love of neighbor. As Brown has shown, "for John 'word' and 'commandment' are virtually interchangeable," in the body of the Gospel as well.[13] Note this parallel:

If you love me, you will keep my commandments (John 14:15).

If anyone loves me, he will keep my word (John 14:23).

Only eight verses separate these two statements. Jesus was saying that his word is his commandments and nothing else. Even more meaningful for us, his commandments (*entolai*) are reduced to one (*entole*), as Brown observes.[14] Jesus' conversion of plural into singular reflects neither casual speech nor careless redaction. Likewise, the plural "my words" in John 15:7 is made progressively more specific through John 15:7–11 until it is intentionally defined as singular in "This is my commandment: that you love one another" (John 15:12). As Barrett comments: "The commandment [becomes] singular, summarizing all commandments."[15] Herbert Braun agrees: "The change of number indicates from the beginning on that we cannot hold the author to the plural, as if his were an atomistic ethics; 'the commandments' are 'the commandment,' 'the word.' "[16]

This Johannine pattern must be intentional, for it reappears in 1 John 2:3-7 and in 2 John 6. Lagrange observes that the whole of Jesus' message is expressed in this verse: *"These things* I command you, that you love one another" (John 15:17). And he comments: "The plural 'these things' is surprising for a single commandment; but this only makes the expression the more provocative: This is all that I command you; it is reduced to the precept of fraternal charity."[17]

An additional concept, even more significant than the synthesis of all commandments into one, is contained in John 14:15 ("If you love me, you will keep my commandments") and John 14:23 ("If anyone loves me, he will keep my word"). Bultmann has pointed it out: It is the concept that love of God consists in keeping his commandments, his "word."

The intention of the conditional clauses in vv. 15, 23 ("If you love me, then . . . ") is not to state that when love for Jesus is present in the disciples, then the result must be the keeping of the commandments; the intention rather is to define the nature of love, as is made plain in the definition-sentence in v. 21 ["Anyone who holds my commandments and keeps them, he is the one who loves me"]: To love is simply to keep the commandments. The question therefore which activates the section vv.15-24 is this: What is this love, which is directed to Jesus? The clear presupposition of vv. 15, 21, 23f. is that the believer must love Jesus, indeed that he wants to do so, and this presupposition implies that love is a personal relationship; that is to say, a false conception of the relationship to the Revealer, to the divinity, is presupposed here, one that is characteristic of man: man desires to "love" the divinity, i.e. to achieve a personal, direct, relationship to it . . . . Over against this, a new understanding of love is unfolded: the love that is directed to the Revealer can only be a keeping of his commandments, of his word.[18]

This understanding is not new. Although Bultmann does not say so, it is the sole message of the Old Testament as has been demonstrated by the North American Jesuits William L. Moran and Matthew J. O'Connell.[19] Neither they nor Bultmann note that in order for the commandment to be the sole revelation of the true God its content must be justice and love of neighbor, but the authors of the Old and New Testament considered this point absolutely essential. The New Testament is not new with regard to the content of God's word, regardless of what Bultmann says, but this does not diminish the merit of his analysis of John 14:15–24. Bultmann is the first commentator, as far as I know, to perceive the true revelatory intention in John 14:15–24.

The defining characteristic of the God of the Bible is the fact that he cannot be known or loved directly; rather, to love God and to know him means to love one's neighbor and to do one's neighbor justice. This is what makes the God of the Bible different from all other gods; by overlooking this one biblical teaching "Christian" theology has fallen into a protracted idolatry. I affirmed above in chapter 2 that religion is incompatible with real Christianity, because religion is the desire for a direct relationship with divinity; the confines of the self, however, cannot be transcended without the real otherness of the neighbor who seeks justice. Those who desire a direct relationship with God wish to prescind from the "other"; they may practice a religion of the multitudes, but they have enclosed themselves in solipsism and in the irremediable immanence of solitude.

KNOWING THE TRUE GOD

That this revelation is absolutely central for John is strikingly manifested by his affirmation (John 7:28d; 8:19; and 8:55a) that the Jews, the people of Israel, did not know the true God. The reader must contemplate deeply so stupendous an affirmation. Textual analysis alone is inadequate to penetrate its meaning.

One would think that if any people on the earth at the time of Christ knew the true God, it would have been the people of Israel. If they did not, then who did? According to the common conception, all other peoples were atheists or idolators; the people of Israel alone indeed knew the true God.

John denies this, with an insistence that should make us reconsider all our presuppositions. If the thesis that "the world" does not know the true God (John 15:21; 16:3) seems obvious, if pagans' not knowing God seems self-evident, if the statement in the prologue that "the word was in the world . . . and the world did not know it" (John 1:10) seems very easily comprehensible, then we are understanding with a superficiality tantamount to misunderstanding. For John holds that the Jewish people did not know God either (John 7:28d, 8:19, and 8:55a).

We Christians customarily interpret those Gospel passages as contrast and comparison with ourselves. We customarily take them to mean that the pagans lack something—a knowledge of God—that we have. That is not what John means. Our claim to know the true God is no better than the Jews'.

In denying that the Jews knew God, John is not accusing them of pride or arrogance, or of worshipping Jupiter or Aphrodite or Osiris. John is saying that they have not known God because they have not understood in what God consists: "It is my Father who glorifies me, he who you say is your God, and you do not know him" (John 8:54–55).

John is not expressing hyperbolically the conviction that the Jews have achieved a partial or less-than-perfect knowledge of the true God. He is saying that they have failed absolutely to know God. "The time is coming when anyone who kills you will suppose that he is rendering a service to God " (John 16:2). The accusation is absolute, not relative.

When the Johannine Jesus says that his Jewish contemporaries do not know the only true God, the issue is of the utmost seriousness. It is impossible to trivialize it with our clichés that would reduce to a devaluation what John wants to designate as a negation. Such a procedure is not exegesis but rather an accommodation of the biblical assertions to our preconceived theological system.

The clue to understanding the accusation lies in John's affirmation that "the word" is the light "that enlightens *every man*" and that nevertheless "the world did not know it" (John 1:9–10). The word of Old Testament revelation enlightens only the Israelites, but "the word" of which John speaks enlightens every human being, both Israelite and Gentile. Like Paul, who holds that the pagans "know God" (Rom. 1:21) though they "refuse to acknowledge God" (Rom. 1:28), John is defining the knowledge that all people have of God as the moral imperative of justice and love of neighbor. John asserts that this imperative is "the word" and that "the word was God." Knowing the content of the word, knowing that it is identical to "the commandment," we can understand John's affirmation that the word existed from the beginning. As Brown has shown, John, like the Old Testament authors, uses "word" and "commandment" as virtual synonyms (see Exod. 20:1; Deut. 5:5, 22; Ps. 119:4, 25, 28; and especially Deut. 4:12–13).

In his commentary on John 15:22–25, Brown correctly observes, "When in John 15:21 and again in 16:3 Jesus says that those who persecute his disciples have not known the Father (nor himself), there is no suggestion that such ignorance lessens culpability. Rather, the ignorance itself is culpable."[20] In other words, when John says that the world's criminal behavior is due to ignorance of the true God, he clearly does not consider that the ignorance excuses this criminality; on the contrary, he is affirming that this ignorance is itself the crime. So we can understand why he is not content to hold that the world did not know God but must add that the people of Israel itself did not know him. There can be only one ignorance or lack of knowledge that is culpable in itself: a willful ignorance—a refusal to acknowledge—the moral imperative. Bultmann correctly discerns that the Johannine "truth" is "the reality of God," but there he stops. He fails to perceive that the "reality of God" is the summons, the word that calls for love and justice.

It is this ethical essence that the Jews refuse to know, while supposing that they adore the true God in contra-distinction to other gods. They delude themselves. They confuse God with a mental construct, a non-material idol. This is what the Johannine Jesus means by telling them that they do not know God. John is identifying ignorance of God with the culpable attitude of inter-personal enmity by which we voluntarily separate our-selves from the word that summons us. In this word, and only in this word, is God God.

GOD AND GOOD WORKS

In the following three chapters it will be seen that to reject Christ is to reject his summons to justice and love which is God. But before that we must obviate an objec-tion. In John's account of the Jews' rejection of Christ we encounter an apparent contradiction. Throughout the Gospel John insists that the world's hatred is pro-voked by good works and the fulfillment of the word. Yet when Jesus, with revelatory intent, asked the Jews for which of his good works they wished to stone him (John 10:32), John has the Jews reply, "We are not going to stone you for any good work, but for blasphemy: You, a mere man, make yourself God" (John 10:33).

We could interpret this response as mere rationalization, common then as it is now: The masters of this world have always convinced themselves that they are persecuting people, not for deeds of love and justice, but for attacks on "holy religion." The fact that John 10:33 is spoken, not by Jesus or by the author, but by the Jews, would seem to bear out such an interpretation. But in John 5:18 it is John himself who tells us: "This made the Jews still more determined to kill him, because he was not only breaking the Sabbath, but, by calling God his own Father, he claimed equality with God."

The contradiction between blasphemy and good works as the reason for rejecting Christ is apparent. But it cannot be resolved by resorting to harmonism ("both the one and the other") nor by suggesting that John was a careless author, unaware of or unperturbed by self-contradictions. A careful reading of the Johannine passages we have just cited shows that John considers good works and blasphemy each to be an exclusive cause of the Jews' hatred. To resolve the contradiction we must show how the two theses are identical.

John 5:16–30 (and especially John 5:18) points out the path to a solution. We must bear in mind that the entire controversy recounted here revolves around the "good work" described in John 5:1–15. (The intentional link is clear if we compare verses 16 and 18 with verses 9 and 10.) Lagrange is convinced that in John 5:18ff. "God is compared to a craftsman who works, and his Son, when he performs cures, works in the same way, even on the Sabbath."[21] Dodd has discovered, by comparing these verses with the Palestinian and Hellenistic customs of the period, a heretofore unnoticed parable.[22] In John 5:19—"The son can do nothing by himself; he does only what he sees the father doing"—the article before "son" and before "father" is the generic article, as in Mark 3:27, 4:3, and 4:21. Following this article, the words "son" and "father" designate neither God the

Son nor God the Father. The parable is simply saying
that an artisan teaches his son the skills of his trade.
Dodd comments:

> It is a significant detail that the apprentice *watches* his father
> at work.... The detail is not made use of in the theological
> exposition which follows; it is not a feature dictated by the
> requirements of the deeper meaning which is to be conveyed.
> It is integral to the scene as realistically conceived. It is pre-
> cisely at this point that the difference between the parable and
> the allegory reveals itself most clearly.[23]

In the controversy Jesus brandishes the fact that his
activity is identical to his Father's, just as any artisan's
work is the same as his father's; he indicates thereby the
unmistakable nature of his "works," of his "good
works." His powerful thesis is already expressed in its
entirety in John 5:17: "My Father is still working now,
and so too I also am working." Bultmann correctly observes that this response "contains not only the assertion of the *equality* of Jesus' work with God's work, but
this equality, which is described in verses 19f. with regard to the content of the work, is regarded in verse 17 in
terms of its *constancy*."[24] Verse 17 implies what is to
follow, for the times and hours of an artisan's work are
equal to the times and hours of his father's work. Commenting on this verse, Brown remarks, "That the implications of this argument were immediately apparent is
witnessed by the violence of the reaction."[25] Indeed in
the very next verse (5:18) John tells us that the issue of
the Sabbath was of small concern; rather, they tried to
kill him because he called God his own father.

This is sonship by virtue of engaging in identical activity, performing the same good works. To say so is not to
deny or doubt Christ's divinity, but rather to try to
understand what for John is much more important than
the divinity of Christ. Our obsession with Christ's divinity (pro or con) is constantly distracting us and preventing us from hearing what John is trying to tell us.

The evangelist must attribute great importance to

the identical nature of these works, for he again speaks of it before narrating the detailed account of the miracle in chapter 9: "Neither this man nor his parents sinned. He was born blind so that *the works of God* might be displayed in curing him. We must carry out *the works of him who sent me*" (John 9:3–4). And in chapter 10 the emphasis becomes even stronger: "If I am not doing *the works of my Father*, do not believe me. But if I am doing them, even though you do not believe me, *believe the works*" (John 10:37–38). It is difficult to imagine a more powerful theological thesis than this: Even if you do not believe me, believe the works. It appears again as the absolute core of revelation at the Last Supper: "Believe me when I say that I am in the Father and the Father in me. Or else believe it *because of the works themselves*. In truth I tell you: He who believes in me, the *works* that I do, he also will do them, and greater than these because I am going to the Father" (John 14:11–12). These events provide more than enough opportunity for the narrator to affirm Christ's divinity; and clearly John is not loath to affirm it, for in the first verse of his Gospel he tells us that "the word was God." If he does not repeat it when Jesus speaks of his works and God's, it is because he is more concerned that the qualitative identity of their works be revealed.

The Catholic exegete Feuillet shows that in all these passages the intention is clearly to teach more than the messiahship of Jesus; nevertheless the Johannine thesis is in no case what we understand as the divinity of Christ.[26] Structurally speaking, we should expect to find a revelation of paramount importance in chapters 5 through 10 of the Gospel. Following van den Bussche, we see that in the long section John 1:19–10:42, the first unit (1:19–4:54) is devoted to the proclamation of the messianic event, and the second unit (5:1–10:42) is intended to express something further. But it is hermeneutical error to presuppose that this something can be only the divinity of Christ. This theological prejudice prevents revelation; we close every door on what the Gospel says, preferring to hear what we already know.

Could there be something more important for John than the divinity of Christ? Yes: the divinity of God. And this, according to John, is what the chosen people has shown itself incapable of accepting.

John 1:19–10:42 (the section analyzed by van den Bussche) is closed by a quotation from Psalm 82, which Jesus employs with all the profundity intended by its ancient author—a profundity that modern exegesis has only begun to glimpse.[27] This very ancient psalm, apparently ingenuous, compares Yahweh with all the other gods, challenging them to save the orphan and the widow, to liberate the weak and the needy from the hand of the unjust. The gods show themselves incapable of performing these truly good works. And *this is how it is shown* that they are not the true God, but rather mortals like ourselves. Only Yahweh is the true God, judge of all nations. Thus we can understand why Jesus adds, after quoting the psalm, "If I am not doing the works of my Father, do not believe me. But if I am doing them, even though you do not believe me, believe the works" (John 10:37–38).

It is totally unimportant to John (in this context) whether Jesus Christ is God. What matters to him is that God is in the historical fact called Jesus Christ. What matters to him is that God is revealed in Jesus: "Even though you do not believe me, believe the works, so that you may recognize and know that the Father is in me and I in the Father" (John 10:37–38).

The unmistakable quality of these works, which as historical fact reveal God, is Jesus' sole claim. The congruence of John 5 with John 10 (two piers of a perfect arch) is all the more significant since the two discourses use entirely different compositional means to state that Yahweh is revealed in works: chapter 5 using the parable of the artisan and his son and chapter 10 the theology of Psalm 82. The link between the chapters seems intentional: In 10:36 the Jews are reproached for interpreting Jesus' claim of sonship as blasphemy; this claim of sonship is not formally introduced in 10:33, but in 5:18. The argument of Psalm 82 is that the "judgment" consists in the "good works"; this argument, however, is not presented thematically in John 10:32–39, but in John 5:20–22.

John has an underlying intent in depicting the Jews' reaction to Jesus' blasphemous audacity. In making himself God or equal to God or the Son of God, the Johannine Jesus takes it upon himself to show that this divinity or equality or sonship consists in the good works that reveal the one true God in the historical and contingent fact before them. So the "blasphemy" by which they claim to be infuriated is in fact the unpostponable imperative of good works in which God consists. Their murderous hatred is directed toward the God of Israel, whom they claim to worship, but do not know. What really angers them is "the word"—the commandment of love and justice. "You want to kill me because my word makes no headway with you" (John 8:37).

THE UNSEEN GOD

Let us now return to John's prologue. If we read it as a whole and do not divide it in two, then, even without reference to the First Epistle, it will reveal the content of "the word." Lagrange notes that John 1:18 "refers us back to the first verse by a kind of *inclusio* or bracketing."[28] Regardless of the diverse literary or theological origins of the elements articulated by John in his prologue, we must now read it as a unit to see its message clearly.

The prologue focuses on "the word" (which essentially is indirect communication, that is, injunction across a distance that, fortunately, is insuperable). Since John's purpose is to teach us that God is only in the word, the prologue's conclusion—"no one has ever seen God"—fits his purpose perfectly. Therefore those exegetes who prefer to deny that God is only in the word find it imperative to ignore or misinterpret this verse.

Modern exegesis—even the most conservative (see, for example, Wickenhauser[29])—unanimously precludes misinterpreting the phrase "no one has seen God" according to the Greek, Scholastic thesis that God cannot be known by the corporal senses but only by spiritual understanding. John was not concerned with this question.

That misinterpretation has been abandoned, but there is another. Some say that "no one has seen [*heoraken*] God" refers to the past, that the statement constitutes a denial of past facts without prejudice to the future and without asserting a nontemporal thesis about the absolute impossibility of seeing God. According to this misinterpretation John is saying that no one has seen God "yet," not that God absolutely cannot be seen. But John could very well have used the adverbial "not yet" if that were what he meant. He does so in John 7:39 (twice), 7:46, 19:41, and 20:9—a total of five times, more than any other New Testament author. When he wants to point out the absence in the past of something that in the present or the future is no longer absent, John is sufficiently skillful to say "not yet" or "still not" or "never before" (compare the *oudepote* of 7:46 with the *oudeis popote* of 1:18). The question whether God can be seen or not is too important to John for him to omit the "yet" if that were what he meant. This misinterpretation allows John no possibility of saying that God absolutely cannot be seen. If John has used the axiomatic present ("no one sees God") it would say that John is referring to the present—without prejudice to the future.

This misinterpretation is conclusively refuted by the fact that *heoraken* is in the gnomic or axiomatic perfect tense,[30] whose force is specifically nontemporal. (Other examples of this axiomatic perfect occur in Matt. 13:46

and James 1:24.) This same perfect *heoraken*, in its negative form, appears again in the Third Epistle:

The one who "does good" is of God;
the one who "does evil" *did not see* God (3 John 11).

The axiomatic character of the passage is obvious, and the verb is the same negative form of *heoraken* that we find in John 1:18.

The passage in which the meaning of "no one has ever seen God" is finally beyond dispute occurs in the First Epistle. Here John uses the perfect tense of the verb *theaomai*, which, like *horao* (perfect tense, *heoraken*), means "to see":

No one has ever seen God;
if we love one another, God dwells in us,
and his love is brought to perfection in us (1 John 4:12).

Here the axiomatic character of the verb, its validity for all times, is revealed by the passage itself. God is not to be *seen*—now or ever. If we love one another, God is already in us, and everything that constitutes loving God is already perfectly fulfilled in us; loving God is only this. The same thesis is repeated in John 14:15, 21, 23: There is no direct knowledge of the true God; unlike all other gods, the God of the Bible is known only in the imperative of love of neighbor. Herein lies the unprecedented profundity of the prologue: God is not seen (John 1:18) because God is the word (John 1:1).

A careful reading of the text adds further proof that John 1:18a cannot refer to the past. John 14:9 uses the same verb *heoraken* to say that God has already been seen: "Whoever has seen me has seen the Father." And in 3 John 11c this same past fact is implicitly but clearly affirmed: "Whoever does evil has not seen God" (implying that whoever "does good" *has* seen God). The "visibility" of God asserted in John 14:9 and 3 John 11 is indirect. Indeed, John 14:9 is a clear rejection of Philip's request to see God directly: "Have I been all this time with you, Philip, and you still do not know me? Anyone who has seen me has seen the Father. Then how can you say, 'Show us the Father'?" In saying "no one has seen God," John is not telling us that no one has seen God *till now*, nor is he telling us that no one has seen God *with his eyes*. He is telling us that no one ever has or ever will know God (cf. "has not known God" in 1 John 4:7–8) except indirectly, in the fulfillment of the command to love one another.

"COMPASSION AND GOODNESS"

The transcendence of God must be a being-summoned by the word, otherwise it simply becomes a thought, an immanent epithet conceived by the self, a part of the self that does not transcend the self, regardless of one's intention. Without the word, otherness disappears, becomes subsumed by the thinker, and loses its power of summons as external being. The glorious impossibility of assimilating the one who speaks to me is the very life of moral conscience. Only because of it am I not alone; only because of it is immanence sundered.

The essential link between John 1:18 and John 1:1 forces us to specify the content of the word, for when John proclaims his controversial thesis that "no one has ever seen God," he does so to make us understand that only in love of neighbor can we know God (1 John 4:12, 20, 7). The presence of this thesis in the prologue makes sense only insofar as "the word" is identical to the imperative of loving one another.

Thus we can understand why John's prologue about the word includes an attack on Moses:

The law was given through Moses, compassion and goodness came to be through Jesus Christ (John 1:17).

According to Exod. 33:18 Moses asked "to see" the glory of Yahweh, but according to Exod. 34:6 all that was granted him was Yahweh passing before him as the God rich in "compassion and goodness." John uses this same hendiadys to describe the content of the *glory* of the word made flesh (John 1:14), only to state, immediately, that no one has seen God but that "compassion and goodness" came to be through Jesus Christ.

"Came to be" is a singular verb: *egeneto*. Use of the singular verb with two non-neuter subjects indicates that "compassion and goodness" is a hendiadys ("one by means of two"). The Johannine term *charis kai aletheia* is an attempt to translate into Greek the famous Hebrew hendiadys *hesed we'emet*, which Tit. 3:4 renders, more accurately than John, as "goodness and philanthropy." It is a single idea expressed by means of two terms.

As early as 1880 Westcott realized that *charis kai aletheia* is John's translation of the common Old Testament hendiadys *hesed we'emet*.[31] In 1912 Joüon, noted for his philological sensitivity, came to the same conclusion.[32] Bultmann's Old Testament allergies have not impressed modern scholars: Schnackenburg, Wickenhauser, Zerwick, Barrett, Brown, and van den Bussche, among others, all maintain that John 1:14 and 1:17 refer to *hesed we'emet*.[33] Schnackenburg's testimony is especially convincing. He disputes Chrysostom, Thomas Aquinas, Theophylactus, Bede, Maldonatus, and Calmes with regard to John 1:13, vehemently denying the moral sense of "to be born of God" (see our chapter 5) and arguing that such a sense is foreign to the context. Nevertheless he is forced to recognize that John 1:14 and 1:17 refer to *hesed we'emet*, which is pure moral teaching.[34]

Bultmann's misreading results primarily from his failure to note that John 1:17 has a singular verb and the subject therefore demands to be translated as a hendiadys.[35] Besides Bultmann translates *'emet* as "faithfulness," which does not fit the Johannine context. An analysis of the series of Old Testament passages in which *hesed we'emet* occurs, published by Quell in 1933, showed that the translation of *'emet* as " 'faithfulness' nowhere commends itself"[36] and to translate it in this way "always implies a measure of refining and retouching,"[37] but Bultmann ignored this conclusion. We must realize that Quell was one of the first to break a centuries-long tradition of arbitrariness and caprice in interpreting the Bible, a tradition that "finds" in the Old Testament exactly what the interpretor wishes to find there. But it is not for the exegete to decide what the Bible is saying or why it was written; the Bible's authors themselves have already done that.

The hendiadys *hesed we'emet* appears in the following passages: Gen. 24:12, 14, 27, 49; 32:11; 47:29; Exod. 34:6; Josh. 2:14; 2 Sam. 2:6; 15:20; Prov. 3:3; 14:22; 16:6; 20:28; Ps. 25:10; 40:11, 12; 57:3; 61:7; 85:11; 86:15; 89:15; 115:1. The equivalent hendiadys *hesed we'emunah* should also be kept in mind; it occurs in Hos. 2:22; Ps. 36:6; 88:12; 89:2, 3, 24, 49; 92:2; 98:3; 100:5. There are, finally, nine instances in which *hesed* occurs in synonymic parallel with *'emet*: Ps. 26:3; 57:10; 69:13; 108:4; 117:2; Isa. 16:5; Hos. 4:1; Mic. 7:20; Zech. 7:9. There are forty-two passages in all. A careful reading of these passages leads us to conclude that *hesed we'emet* (or *hesed we'emunah*) is a hendiadys with a univocal meaning. Many spiritualistic exegetes, however, manage to avoid that conclusion by adopting an erroneous method. They choose as normative those passages in which, because the contexts are insufficiently determinative, the expression could be assigned various meanings. They then attribute to the term in question whatever meaning they wish, so long as it is not absolutely excluded by the context. This definition they then adopt as the sole correct meaning of the expression in all contexts. For example, in translating *hesed we'emet*, these pious interpreters cite Exod. 34:6, where Yahweh is described as a God rich in *hesed we'emet*. In this verse the context is not definitional, and escapist exegetes take advantage of this fact: They decree that the hendiadys means loyalty and faithfulness to the covenant or the promise, and then they impose this same meaning on all the other occurrences of *hesed we'emet* that we have listed. If the subject is God, then the term refers to God's faithfulness to the covenant; if the subject is human beings, then it refers to human beings' faithfulness to the covenant. The method is fallacious, but the conclusions are satisfactory for those who wish to think them so.

Provided we abjure this absurd method, a careful review of the passages we have listed leads to a univocal and objectively established meaning. We will cite several examples, the first a passage from the book of Samuel, which is recognized as the most classic part of the Hebrew Bible. When David was anointed king, he was notified that the inhabitants of Jabesh had given Saul a proper burial. David sent word to them: "May Yahweh bless you for having mercy (*hesed*, 'compassion') on Saul your lord and giving him burial" (2 Sam. 2:5). David's message continues:

May Yahweh in his turn have *compassion and goodness* on you, and I too "will do good" to you for what you have done (2 Sam. 2:6).

The hendiadys *hesed we'emet* receives great emphasis. It clearly refers to good works as we defined them in chapter 5: works of mercy (such as burying the dead), of solidarity, of compassion and goodness. David thanks the Jabeshites for their work of mercy, he hopes that Yahweh will reward them in kind, and promises that he will do the same. In this passage the context of *hesed we'emet* is a promise, and *hesed we'emet* is what the promiser promises to do; but he could have also promised to wreak vengeance or to tap dance. In no way does *hesed we'emet* mean faithfulness to the promise; it is the content or object of the promise, and its only meaning is compassion and goodness.

The same meaning is evident in Prov. 16:6: "With compassion and goodness sin is expiated." The teaching of Tob. 12:9 is the same: "Almsgiving . . . purifies of all sin."

We should keep in mind that the Septuagint always translates *hesed* as *eleos* ("compassion"). There is no better one-word translation of *hesed*, in spite of the degeneration into paternalism that the term "compassion" has suffered over the last twenty centuries. It is less equivocal than "love" or "faithfulness." Using the latter terms, some interpreters have tried to outdo the Septuagint: They would make *hesed* signify a vertical "religious" relationship, a direct God-man relationship. This meaning, however, is completely foreign to the term. (To have "compassion" on God is an idea too bizarre even for the spiritualized theologies.)

Hesed is linked with justice (*sedakah*) and/or right (*mispat*) by means of hendiadys or synonymic parallel in Jer. 9:24; Isa. 16:5; Mic. 6:8; Hos. 2:21–22; 6:6; 10:12; 12:7; Zech. 7:9; Ps. 25:9–10; 33:5; 36:6–7; 36:10; 40:11; 85:11; 88:12–13; 89:15; 98:2–3; 103:17; 119:62–64. In these passages *hesed* is compassion closely linked to a sense of justice; it is compassion-on-the-poor-and-the-oppressed, identical to indignation over the violation of the rights of the weak. Because of this compassion Yahweh assails the oppressors "with raised hand and outstretched arm" (see Deut. 4:34; 5:15; 7:19; 26:8; Exod. 6:6; Ps. 136:12); because of this compassion "he breaks the teeth in the mouths" of the unjust (see Ps. 58:6; 3:7).

The paternalistic sense of compassion is foreign to both the Old Testament and the New. In Matthew 23 Jesus of Nazareth denounces the scribes and the Pharisees seven times as "hypocrites!" (vv. 13, 14, 15, 23, 25, 27, 29), five times as "blind!" (vv. 16, 17, 19, 24, 26), and once as "stupid!" (v. 17)—and yet in the same passage he teaches "justice, compassion, and goodness" (v. 23). Biblical compassion is not condescension; it is unreserved commitment to the weak, the poor, and the oppressed. It acknowledges their rights; it is identical to an absolute sense of justice.

In this light we can understand John 1:17. John takes for granted that *charis kai aletheia* is an extremely well-known term: It is the *hesed we'emet* spoken of so often in the Old Testament and used in Exod. 34:6 to define the true God. Moses did not see God, because God is not seen. As for compassion and goodness, the law given by Moses had commanded it but not brought it about. Compassion and goodness came to exist in this world through Jesus Christ. This is the difference between the work of Jesus Christ and the work of Moses: The era of compassion and goodness began in the world thanks only to Jesus Christ; the laws of Moses had not achieved it.

John 1:14 (without which the prologue is no prologue) tells us the content of the word, the word that was made flesh, as the same verse also tells us. In fact, it has always been thought that the whole point of this verse is the fact that the word made flesh, whose glory we saw, was full of compassion and goodness (irrespective of whether or not *pleres*, "full," refers to the word itself, to the only-begotten Son who is identical to the word, or to the glory of the Son; the last alternative is the most likely—see Exod. 33:18 and 34:6). In relating to us the life of Christ, all four evangelists are in fact recounting a life full of compassion and goodness. It is John who tells us (at the very outset) that this is "the word."

NOTES

1. B. F. Westcott, *The Gospel according to St. John* (London: John Murray, 1908), p. 222.
2. Ibid.
3. Raymond E. Brown, *The Gospel according to John (xiii–xxi)*, Anchor Bible 29A (Garden City, New York: Doubleday, 1970), p. 765.
4. Günther Klein, "Das wahre Licht scheint schon," *Zeitschrift für Theologie und Kirche* 68 (1971), p. 305 n. 186.
5. Rudolf Bultmann, *Die drei Johannesbriefe* (Göttingen: Vandenhoeck, 1967), p. 33 [Eng. trans.: *The Johannine Epistles*, trans. R. Philip O'Hara et al. (Philadelphia: Fortress Press, 1973), p. 27].
6. Klein, "Wahre Licht," p. 301. To say that the *eschaton* originally was ontologically independent of real time is a gratuitous Bultmannian affirmation.
7. Ibid., p. 302. It does not "acquire" the character of an epoch be-

cause it always had it. Nevertheless Klein's testimony is valuable because his Bultmannian prejudice does not keep him from recognizing what John says.

8. Ibid., p. 305.

9. Bultmann, *Johannesbriefe*, p. 15 [Eng. trans.: *Johannine Epistles*, p. 9].

10. Rudolf Bultmann, *Theologie des Neuen Testaments*, p. 380 [cf. Eng. trans.: *Theology of the New Testament*, trans. Kendrick Grobel (New York: Charles Scribner's Sons, 1951), 2:33].

11. Johann Michl, *Die Katholischen Briefe*, RNT 8/2, 2nd ed. (Regensburg: Pustet, 1968), p. 200; Johannes Schneider, *Die Kirchenbriefe*, NTD 10 (Göttingen: Vandenhoeck, 1967), p. 134; A. E. Brooke, *The Johannine Epistles*, International Critical Commentary 38 (Edinburgh: T. & T. Clark, 1912), p. 2; Rudolf Schnackenburg, *Die Johannesbriefe*, 3rd ed. (Freiburg: Herder, 1965), pp. 58–59; G. Delling, "archo," *TWNT*, 1:480 [Eng. trans.: *TDNT*, 1:481–82]; etc.

12. Hans Conzelmann, "Was von Anfang war," in *Neutestamentliche Studien für R. Bultmann, Beiheft zur Zeitschrift für die neutestamentliche Wissenschaft* 21 (Berlin: Töpelmann, 1954), p. 196; Herbert Braun, *Gesammelte Studien zum Neuen Testament und seiner Umwelt* (Tübingen: Mohr-Siebeck, 1962), p. 232.

13. Brown, *Gospel according to John (xiii–xxi)*, p. 765.

14. Ibid., pp. 638 and 663.

15. C. K. Barrett, *The Gospel according to St. John* (London: SPCK, 1955), p. 397.

16. Braun, *Gesammelte Studien*, p. 220.

17. M. J. Lagrange, *Evangile selon Saint Jean* (Paris: Gabalda, 1948), p. 409.

18. Rudolf Bultmann, *Das Evangelium des Johannes* (Göttingen: Vandenhoeck, 1964), pp. 473–74 [cf. Eng. trans.: *The Gospel of John*, trans. G. R. Beasley-Murray et al. (Philadelphia: Westminster Press, 1971), pp. 612–13].

19. William L. Moran, S. J., "The Ancient Near Eastern Background of the Love of God in Deuteronomy," *Catholic Biblical Quarterly* 25, no. 1 (January 1963):77–87; Matthew J. O'Connell, S. J., "The Concept of Commandment in the Old Testament," *Theological Studies* 21, no. 3 (September 1960): 351–403.

20. Brown, *Gospel according to John (xiii–xxi)*, p. 697.

21. Lagrange, *Evangile selon Saint Jean*, p. 141.

22. C. H. Dodd, *More New Testament Studies* (Grand Rapids: Eerdmans, 1968), pp. 30–40.

23. Ibid., p. 39.

24. Bultmann, *Evangelium des Johannes*, p. 183 [cf. Eng. trans.: *Gospel of John*, p. 245].

25. Brown, *Gospel according to John (i–xii)*, p. 217.

26. André Feuillet, "Les *ego eimi* christologiques du quatrième évangile," *Recherches de Science Religieuse* 54, no. 2 (April–June 1966): 236.

27. See A. González, "Le Psaume LXXXII," *Vetus Testamentum* 13, no. 3 (July 1963):293–309; F. Charles Fensham, "Widow, Orphan, and the Poor in Ancient Near Eastern Legal and Wisdom Literature," *Journal of Near Eastern Studies* 21, no. 2 (April 1962):129–39.

28. Lagrange, *Evangile selon Saint Jean*, ad John 1:18.

29. Alfred Wickenhauser, *Das Evangelium nach Johannes*, RNT 4, 2nd ed. (Regensburg: Pustet, 1957), p. 50.

30. F. Blass and A. Debrunner, *A Greek Grammar of the New Testament*, 3rd ed., trans. Robert W. Funk (Chicago: University of Chicago Press, 1967), no. 344.

31. Westcott, *Gospel according to St. John*, p. 13.

32. Paul Joüon, "Notes de lexicographie hébraique," *Mélanges de la Faculté Orientale* 5 (1911–12), p. 407.

33. Rudolf Schnackenburg, *Das Johannesevangelium* (Freiburg: Herder, 1965), 1:248 [Eng. trans.: *The Gospel according to St. John*, trans. Kevin Smyth (New York: Herder and Herder, 1968), 1:272]; Wickenhauser, *Evangelium nach Johannes*, p. 49; Max Zerwick, *Analysis philologica novi testamenti graeci*, 2nd ed. (Rome: Pontificio Istituto Biblico, 1960), p. 212; Barrett, *Gospel according to St. John*, p. 139; Brown, *Gospel According to John (i–xii)*, p. 14; Henri van den Bussche, *Jean* (Paris: Desclée, 1967), p. 102.

34. Schnackenburg, *Johannesevangelium*, 1:238–39 and 248 [Eng. trans.: *Gospel according to St. John*, 1:262 and 272].

35. Bultmann, *Evangelium des Johannes*, pp. 49–50 n. 3 [Eng. trans.: *Gospel of John*, pp. 74 n. 2]. In *TWNT*, 1:247 he holds that it is "possible, but not very likely" [Eng. trans.: *TDNT*, 1:246].

36. Gottfried Quell, "aletheia," *TWNT*, 1:233 n. 2 [Eng. trans.: *TDNT*, 1:233 n. 2].

37. Ibid., *TWNT*, 1:237 n. 12 [Eng. trans.: *TDNT*, 1:236 n. 12].

Chapter 8

The Mistake Known as Christianity

John's thinking on the subject of the word, the commandment, the summons, is of decisive importance as preamble to his ultimate message. That message—the thesis of this book—is presented in our chapters 8, 9, and 10, but to understand it we must first have grasped the importance of the word. It remains now to resolve the question of Kierkegaardian contemporaneity, which heretofore we have only touched on. It remains to demonstrate why Hegel and Marx were correct to replace nontemporal moral teaching with historical facts. Here we must again consider that truth and imperative are identical. We must describe the new field of being that requires our decision in order to be; it is existentialism's task to discover this new being and humankind's to bring it about.

It was not a late dogmatism that caused the Christian churches to affirm that without Christ there is no God; but it has become clear to us that the churches themselves did not genuinely understand their own affirmation. They based their tenet on some positive decree of God, as if God in an authoritarian, extrinsic way punished those who rejected his emissary by depriving them of their knowledge of God. But we know that such arbitrary authoritarianism would be profoundly immoral and whoever acted in this way would not be God but a superhuman despot against whom we should be morally obligated to rebel. According to the Bible, such a one would not be God but an idol.

Christianity has been characterized by two inveterate errors. We have already presented the first in chapters 6 and 7: It consists in religion, in misconceiving the true God as one who can be directly known, loved, and invoked, that is, it consists in changing God from the God of Jesus Christ into a mental idol.

The second error is even deeper and more tragic, for it refers to Christ himself, and the churches have taken it upon themselves to maintain that Christ—the Christ who would differentiate the Christian churches from Israel—is necessary for salvation. Ironically, the error has to do with the very word "Christ" (=messiah), in which the term "Christian" originates. This second error is dealt with in chapters 8, 9, and 10.

JESUS IS THE MESSIAH

To interpret extrinsically the New Testament thesis that "anyone who denies the Son does not have the Father either" (1 John 2:23) is to misinterpret it. We have already seen that the commandment is new "*because* the darkness is passing and the true light is already shining" (1 John 2:8). This means that the commandment would not be a commandment, it would not summon as irreducible otherness, if the historical fact called Jesus of Nazareth did not exist.

That van den Bussche glimpsed this is evident in his perceptive commentary on John 1:14: "Regardless of the importance of the state of incarnation in Johannine thought, it is of less significance than the hour of Jesus; for it is the latter that indeed is the definitive revelation and the total realization of salvation."[1] This commentary on the thesis that "the word was made flesh" constitutes the greatest advance in Johannine exegesis since 1941, the year that Bultmann published his book on the Fourth Gospel. But it is lamentable that van den Bussche saw a contrast between the hour and the flesh. "Flesh" (*sarx=basar*) means much more than "the entire human being who acts in community, who is visible and tangible to those around him."[2] It means a bit of contingent human history. What John says is that the word became flesh in a historical fact called Jesus of Nazareth.

The term "flesh" as used in John 1:14 and 1 John 4:2 has no antispiritualist connotations; John's purpose is not to refute those who abominate matter and deny the corporeality of the Son of God. For centuries we have too readily assumed that John's thesis, as well as the antithesis he combated, was nontemporal. For centuries we have projected onto the New Testament our Scholastic quarrels about the union or separation of spirit and matter. But John's purpose is infinitely more important than to differentiate between a materialistic and a spiritualistic worldview, both of which in the last analysis remain enclosed in immanence. The passage that speaks of "flesh" in the Epistle reads:

Every spirit that confesses that Jesus is the Messiah who has come in the flesh is from God. And every spirit that does not confess Jesus is not from God. This is the spirit of the Antichrist (1 John 4:2–3).

In 1912 Brooke, breaking with a long, enslaving interpretative tradition, commented, "The error which the writer condemns seems to have been the rejection of the identy of the historical man Jesus with the pre-existent Christ."[3] This is well expressed, except that what preexisted was not precisely the Messiah but the word. Brooke's commentary, however, definitively supersedes the antidocetist interpretation, according to which John is refuting the belief that Jesus' flesh was a phantasmic phenomenon. "There is nothing in the Epistle which compels us to suppose that the author is combatting pure Docetism."[4] In the quoted passage we can see that *homologein Iesoun Christon en sarki eleythota* is the same as *homologein ton Iesoun,* to confess something about Jesus as such, not about Jesus Christ as such. And the Antichrist is precisely anti-Christ; he denies that Jesus *is* the Christ, he denies that he *is* the Messiah. The exact point in 1 John 4:2 at which the understood verb "to be" should be inserted is made clear by the other passage in which the Epistle defines the Antichrist: "Who is the liar? Who but he that denies that Jesus is the Messiah [*christos*]? He is the Antichrist" (1 John 2:22). In both passages John is defining Antichrist. The last part of 1 John 4:3 would be better translated "this is the substance of the Antichrist." The translation "this is the spirit of the Antichrist" also conveys John's definitional intention.

In addition, 1 John 5:1 expresses the verb "to be" in exactly the same context in which it is left understood in 1 John 4:2–3 and stated in 1 John 2:22: "Anyone who believes that Jesus is the Messiah has been born of God." The verb "to be" comes between "Jesus" and "Christ." We find the same idea in John 9:22: "The Jews had already agreed that anyone who confessed him as Messiah should be banned from the synagogue" *(ean tis auton homologese christon).* There is no basis for the antidocetist interpretation that would render 1 John 4:2 as "confesses that Jesus Christ has come in the flesh." In all the related passages "Jesus" is the subject and "Messiah" is the predicate. The verb "to be" is either expressed between the two terms (1 John 2:22 and 5:1) or, as often occurs in the classical languages, it is implied there (John 9:22: "confessed Jesus to be the Messiah"). Therefore in 1 John 4:2 and 2 John 7, which, like John 9:22, are constructed with the governing verb "to confess," the verb "to be" must be understood between the subject "Jesus" and the predicate "Messiah." "Come in the flesh" is in apposition to "Messiah"; it describes the "Messiah."

JOHN'S ADVERSARIES

Van den Bussche notes that the "heretics" combated in 1 John 4:2–3; 2:22–23; and 2 John 7 "do not deny the man Jesus; they deny in this man the Christ," that is, the Messiah.[5] And with regard to John 1:14 he asks, "Was the apostle thinking of the Docetists, who denied the reality of the body of Christ, in which they recognized only the appearance of a body? This does not seem certain to us."[6]

Note that the Jews accepted and earnestly professed a future Messiah, and many even professed a pre-existent Messiah. Jews and Christians could not doubt this unreal Messiah. Nor could denying such a Messiah mean being anti-Christ. What the adversaries referred to in the Epistle deny is "that *Jesus* is the Messiah." What they deny is that in this man the Messiah has come to the world. What they refuse to allow is that the messianic kingdom should become real history. What they deny is the reality of the *eschaton*. Van den Bussche's contribution—although he does not draw out its consequences—is to have understood that for John the decisive point is Jesus' "hour," not his human nature (see John 2:4; 4:21, 23; 5:25, 28; 7:6, 30; 8:20; 12:23, 27; 13:1; 16:4, 21, 25; 1 John 2:18; 2:8; 4:3). The "flesh" of John 1:14, 1 John 4:2, and 2 John 7 is a concrete episode of real, chronological human history, an "hour," the hour of Jesus. It is the historical fact called Jesus of Nazareth.

That understanding is necessary if we are to see how the whole argument of the First Epistle relates to its central affirmation: "that the true light is already shining" (1 John 2:8). In sum, this is what John's adversaries deny: that the true light is already shining. There is a literary link between this affirmation and the Antichrist's denial of Jesus' messiahship in 1 John 4:3; the link is provided by the adverb "already," which occurs only in these two instances. John even recasts his argument, neatly and elegantly employing the traditional belief that when the Antichrist had arrived the *eschaton* would have arrived as well: "You were told that the Antichrist was to come; now many Antichrists have appeared. By this we know that this is the last hour" (1 John 2:18). He bases his argument on the fact that the Antichrist is—etymologically—the one who opposes the existence of a Messiah and an *eschaton*.

Since "Antichrist" is so powerfully charged a word, it is surprising that exegesis, which has so often tried —unsuccessfully—to identify the "adversaries" of the First Epistle, has paid it so little attention. In fact this lack of attention seems so inexplicable that one is obliged to suspect the exegetes of a subconscious block.

The adversaries John has in mind lie—or err—by denying that Jesus is the Messiah. But of the many who denied it, whom in particular does John mean? Bultmann correctly doubts Schnackenburg's conviction that John is referring to the Gnostics.[7] To deny that Jesus is the Messiah pertains to time, to history, whereas gnosis is a nontemporal belief. Moreover, in the Gospel everything, absolutely everything, is said to depend on our knowing God and Jesus Christ; so if John says that Israel itself does not know the true God, then sound methodology requires us to search the First Epistle for an elaboration of this message and not for the refutation of a heresy specifically related to knowledge. Only failure to understand or accurately to gauge the importance of John's Gospel message could cause us to misconstrue his First Epistle.

Even the terms "heresy," "erroneous doctrine," and "error," which the commentators customarily employ, lead to misunderstandings. The Johannine Jesus, as we have seen, was not accusing the Jews precisely of doctrinal errors when he said to them, "The one who you say is your God, and you do not know him" (John 8:54–55).

Here we must turn again to John 8, observing with Dodd: "It is possible for others beside first-century

'Judaizers' to think that they 'believe,' to boast of their 'freedom,' to say with conviction (as Christians say every day), 'We have God for our Father'—and yet not to 'listen to the words of God.' John would have his readers consider such possibilities and face the consequences."[8]

The intraecclesial intention of John 8 is clear; without it verse 37 leads to an exegetical dead end. In verse 30 John tells us that while Jesus spoke, many believed in him; in verse 31 he emphasizes that Jesus is addressing these believers ("Jesus, then, said *to the Jews who had believed in him*"). But in verse 37 Jesus says to those very Jews who had believed in him: "You want to kill me."

With typical British understatement Barrett comments, "These words follow oddly after v. 31": those who had believed in him.[9] He suggests two alternative explanations of the problem: "Either John is writing very carelessly or he means that the faith of these Jews was very deficient."[10] The first explanation is unacceptable, because John 8:30–40 forms a clear intentional and redactional unit. Even Bultmann—who dismembers John 8, attributing phrases and even whole verses to different discourses and thus turning the chapter into a puzzle—leaves this unit intact.[11] And if Bultmann leaves the passage intact, it has passed the test of fire, as those familiar with Johannine or Synoptic exegesis well know.

The unity is clear. Since they already believed in Jesus Christ (v. 30), the theme of "abiding in his word" (v. 31) can be introduced. Abiding in Jesus' word means "knowing the truth." This leads to "the truth will make you free" (v. 32). But Jesus' interlocutors object that, as sons of Abraham, they have never been enslaved and therefore require no freeing (v. 33). To this Jesus replies by explaining the nature of true liberty (vv. 34–36). He concludes: I know that you are sons of Abraham, but you want to kill me (v. 37).

The concatenation of ideas may seem inappropriate for a treatise, but there is indeed a strict concatenation, from the "believing" of verses 30–31 to the "wanting to kill him" of verse 37. For John it is precisely those who have believed in Jesus Christ who want to kill him. John clearly has an underlying intent here.

Barrett's alternative explanation—that the Jews' faith was deficient faith—was proven by events to be objectively true, but it cannot explain the narrator's intention in John 8:30–40, because the formula *pisteuein eis*, which sets the entire pericope in motion ("many *believed in him*" in verse 30), is the most characteristic Johannine expression for the highest level of Christian faith. This formula has the same connotation throughout the New Testament. The supreme exhortations to adopt the Christian faith are exhortations to *pisteuein eis*. If John distinguishes among various types or levels of faith—and it has not yet been proven that he does— he is certainly not concerned with such distinctions in this pericope.

Barrett himself chooses a third explanation that points us toward the only possible interpretation: "These references to 'many' believers must be taken like the 'you shall know' of v. 28, to refer to a time other than that of the ministry of Jesus."[12] The references Barrett cites are John 2:23; 7:31; 8:30; 10:42; 12:11, 42, ranging over the entire first part of the Gospel. They occur even in the most anecdotal portions of John's narratives, like John 8:30. The "other" time to which Barrett alludes is the time of the church, during which John's Gospel was written. It is John's literary devise to report Jesus' exchange with the Jews; the audience for whom Jesus' words are really intended is John's Christian contemporaries, and John is asserting that in spite of being Christian (that is, without becoming "heretics") they are betraying Jesus Christ.

If that is John's intention in the Gospel, where he is not directly addressing Christians but is formally narrating the deeds and words of Jesus addressed to the Jews, then he is all the more likely to speak similarly in the Epistle.

CHRISTIAN ANTICHRISTS

We must consider the possibility that the First Epistle is reproving the Christians themselves and not any particular doctrinal error or heresy. The Gospel does this very thing by its incisive definitions of knowing the true God; therefore it is all the more likely that John's intent in the Epistle, when he examines the meaning of believing that Jesus is the Messiah, is the same. Some may object to me: Those who do not believe that Jesus is the Messiah are automatically not Christians, so John could not be addressing Christians. I respond: Those who do not know the true God are less so, yet John addresses them. The Jews too could say that those who do not know the true God were automatically not Israelites; but all this evades the true issue. Jesus does not mean heresy or doctrinal error when he says, "He who you say is your God, and you do not know him" (John 8:54–55). The thesis of the Epistle, that the Christians do not believe that Jesus is the Messiah, acquires a profundity and a revolutionary power worthy only of the author John and the evangelizing Jesus of Nazareth. The very affirmation that the word was made flesh means something completely different from the antidocetism we have so placidly attributed to it.

John's Gospel was written for John's Christian contemporaries. Note the end of chapter 2 and the beginning of chapter 3. After recounting the expulsion of the merchants from the temple (John 2:13–22), John says that during this first stay of Jesus in Jerusalem "many believed in his name" (John 2:23). But he immediately adds that "Jesus did not trust himself to them" (John 2:24), because "he knew what was in a man" (John 2:25). Immediately John goes on to describe one of these same men, whose basic incapacity to belong to the kingdom is enunciated by Jesus himself (John 3:1–15, especially vv. 3 and 5).

Clearly John 3 follows John 2—particularly the verses

we have just considered, John 2:23–25—with most deliberate intent. Brown notes that John 3:1 begins with "And there was a man" and suggests: "Perhaps this use of 'man' is designed to recall the end of the last verse (2:25).[13] There is no "perhaps" about it; there is nothing random about this narrative order. John 3:1 does not even mention the name of the one Nicodemus visited at night. It only says, "He came to him at night and he said to him," obviously intending us to recall John 2:23–25.

Jesus' response to Nicodemus—a short-circuit response, as van den Bussche correctly perceives[14]—was a total rejection of Nicodemus's attitude. But this man was one of the "many" who "believed in the name of Jesus," as we have just been informed. To believe in the name of Jesus is a formula that characterizes the highest level of confession of Christian faith (see John 1:12; 3:18; 20:31; 1 John 3:23; 5:13; cf. John 14:13, 14; 15:16, 21; 16:24, 26). A simple reading shows that the significance of the transition from John 2 to John 3 goes beyond the anecdotal to the universal:

He needed no evidence from others about what there was *in man*, for he knew what was *in man*. And there was *a man* among the Pharisees, called Nicodemus, . . .

Moreover, the order of John 2:23–24 demonstrates its intraecclesial purposes: "Many believed in his name when they saw the signs that he did. But he did not trust himself to them."

In John 15 the intraecclesial intention is even more explicit. Commenting on the parable of John 15, Barrett accurately observes: "His major interest is in the life of the Church, in the question who are and who are not true disciples of Jesus."[15] The wording at the beginning of the parable has been very carefully studied, and it is unambiguous: " . . . Every branch that does not bear fruit *in me*, [the gardener] cuts away" (John 15:2). Jesus Christ is the vine; the Christians are the branches. The parable presupposes that the persons spoken of as branches are members of Christianity; they are *in Jesus*.

Barrett comments that this verse "shows that his primary thought was of apostate Christians."[16] But by comparing this comment to the main intention of the First Epistle we see that Barrett's statement is inaccurate, for these are not apostates or ex-Christians. They are people who are *in Jesus*. They are Christians who, while remaining Christians, do not produce the fruit described in John 15:16–17. This message has always been de-emphasized; therefore we define it exactly. It is not enough to explain, as Brown does, that the parable "emphasizes strongly love for others."[17] Lagrange had already said of verse 16: "We have, then, in this passage the key to the entire discourse."[18] The message of verse 16 continues in verse 17: "These things I command you: that you love one another."

Exegesis that disregards the direct connection—the unity—between the first use of "fruit" in John 15:2 and the "fruit" described in John 15:16-17 disjoints the pericope John 15:1–27; it treats verse 12 ("This is my commandment: that you love one another as I have loved you") as an erratic segment, connected with neither the preceding nor the following verses. But to do that is absurd. Ascertaining the preredactional history of the elements combined in John 15 should not prevent us from understanding the exact Johannine sense of the parable, which John explains immediately following the parable itself. Verses 9–13 describe what it means to bear "much fruit" (v. 8) and develop this typically Johannine thesis: I established the reality called "my love"; abide in it. To abide in my love is to keep my commandments, and my commandments can be reduced to this: Love one another.

Two other elements in the same verse confirm that this is the sense of "bear much fruit" in verse 8. First there is the explicative and synonymic "and" in the phrase "that you bear much fruit *and* that you be my disciples." In John 13:35 we have already been told explicitly, "By this all will know that you are my disciples: that you love one another." Thus to bear much fruit is to love one's neighbor. The other corroborating element in John 15:8 has been pointed out by Lagrange and Brown: "In this is my Father glorified: in that you bear much fruit." Nestle notes the parallel with Matt. 5:16: "That men see your good works and glorify your heavenly Father." As we demonstrated in our chapter 5 "good works" are specifically works of love of neighbor.

John is addressing not apostates but Christians. Having admitted that, the great temptation is to interpret his reproof evasively as Schnackenburg does the First Epistle: "The object of his attack is over and again simply the lack of fraternal love."[19] But it is impossible to reduce John's fierce censure to a routine accusation of lack of charity. In chapter 8, John is speaking to Christians, even when he affirms that the persons in question do not know the true God. It is clear that both Gospel and Epistle are directed against the Christians themselves and not against any heresy or erroneous doctrine.

1 John 2:19 says of heretics that they left our company "so that it might be clear that not all *are* of us." Grammatically we would have expected it to say: "so that it might be clear that not all *were* of us." Bultmann comments: " 'That all are not of us' does not mean: 'they all, the false teachers, do not belong to us,' but rather: 'not all (who so claim) belong to us.' The statement permits recognition of the distinction between the empirical and the true congregation: false members are therefore to be found in the empirical congregation. The sentence is thus also an admonition to critical examination and certainly to self-examination as well."[20] Since in this same verse (1 John 2:19) the verb "to be" was just used twice in the imperfect plural, the change to the present tense seems completely intentional: "so that it might be clear that not all *are* of us." John alludes to the Christians of that time, to the Christians themselves, not only to

those who had already separated themselves from Christianity. Schnackenburg minimizes this:

> The experience, painful in itself, of the Christian church toward the end of the first century—that its own front ranks were going astray—was mitigated by the knowledge that all those who did not belong to the church in the long run could not remain within it.[21]

This commentary might be appropriate to or supported by John 15:2 ("the gardener will cut it away") as referring to Christians who do not bear the fruit of love of neighbor. When 1 John 2:18–19, however, speaks of the Antichrists it in no way mitigates the calamity to the church. On the contrary, it says that Antichrists exist within the church. The Protestant distinction between empirical church and authentic church may be valid, but John goes beyond it: He affirms that there are Christians in the community who do not believe that Jesus is the Messiah. John says that some Christians who are authentic members of the community are Antichrists. Thus the question of whether or not the Epistle refers to heretics and apostates becomes irrelevant.

THE MESSIAH AND THE END OF HISTORY

The coincidence of the questions raised by the Epistle and the Gospel is noteworthy. The Epistle's accusations of failure to know God (for example, 1 John 2:4; 3:1; 3:6) and of failure to "believe that Jesus is the Messiah" need not be understood as accusations of formal heresies. Moreover, even if the Epistle does allude to formal heresies, we miss its message if we concentrate exclusively on them. The sense of the Johannine challenge is that both accusations can in equal degree be applied to Christians.

The reason is that one can ascribe to Jesus all the predicates, all the attributes, even divine ones, including the title of "Messiah," and nevertheless deny that with Jesus the end of history has arrived. Indeed Christians do so today. But if the end of history has not arrived, then the epithet "Messiah" is eviscerated. It becomes a nontemporal predicate *emptied of all meaningful content.* The end of history is what differentiates "Messiah" from all other attributes. It is clear that the Christians condemned by John did not question the epithet as a mere attribute, nor did the heretics either, in all likelihood. What they denied was the historical meaning of the content. What they denied—although they preserved a hollow notion of the linguistic meaning of the attribute in verbal form—was a historic fact that concerns all of history. But this is to deny the attribute all its content, for Jesus can *really* be the Messiah only to the degree that "the true light already shines," to the degree that the messianic kingdom that is the end of history has arrived in history.

The Christians condemned by John maintained the idea of Messiah as a mere idea, although they might swear that they professed it as a reality. The fact that they were not dedicated to accomplishing the worldwide kingdom of love and justice shows that "Messiah" for them was a nontemporal predicate. To keep the Messiah nontemporal means that they themselves have undertaken to prevent him from becoming reality. To keep him nontemporal is the same as to keep him eternally pre-existent or eternally future. What they refused to admit is that the Messiah can be *now*, and in this they exactly resembled the Nazarenes of Luke 4:16–30, who found Jesus quite acceptable (Luke 4:17–20) until he told them: *"Today* this Scripture has been fulfilled in your presence" (Luke 4:21). Then the persecution unto annihilation was unleashed (Luke 4:22–29). Attributes are all meaningless because they are ineffectual; in the last analysis they change nothing. The past and the future are likewise of no great moment, for they do not affect *us.* Likewise truth: We can profess anything as "true," and it will make no difference and there will be no real difference between those who profess it and those who do not. The irony of exegesis lies in its failure to understand that *logos* means "word." And the irony of being Christian is that twenty centuries of Christians have not understood that *Christos* means "Messiah." The Christians condemned by John were Antichrists because they did not act as if Jesus was the Messiah. Twenty centuries have passed, and the Antichrist has not changed.

"To deny the Son" (1 John 2:23) is to deny that Jesus is the Messiah.

Who is the liar? Who but he that denies that Jesus is the Messiah? He is the Antichrist, he who denies the Father and the Son, (for) anyone who denies the Son does not have the Father either (and) anyone who confesses the Son also has the Father (1 John 2:22–23).

To heighten and intensify his denunciation of the Antichrists, John adds—in the same breath—that those Christians who deny that Jesus is the Messiah are thereby also denying the Father. They only deceive themselves by believing, like the Jews, that they can deny that Jesus is the Messiah and yet know the true God.

We must now examine why those who reject the *eschaton* do not know the true God. The connection cannot be explained extrinsically nor as divine punishment for disobedience.

NOTES

1. Henri van den Bussche, *Jean* (Paris: Desclée, 1967), p. 98.

2. Ibid., p. 97.

3. A.E. Brooke, *The Johannine Epistles*, International Critical Commentary 38 (Edinburgh: Clark, 1912), p. 108.

4. Ibid., p. 109.

5. Van den Bussche, *Jean*, p. 98.

6. Ibid., p. 97.

7. Rudolf Bultmann, *Die drei Johannesbriefe* (Göttingen: Vandenhoeck, 1967), p. 73 n. 3 [Eng. trans.: *The Johannine Epistles*, trans. R. Philip O'Hara et al. (Philadelphia: Fortress Press, 1973), p. 68 n. 17].

8. C.H. Dodd, "Behind a Johannine Dialogue," *More New Testament Studies* (Grand Rapids: Eerdmans, 1968), p. 52.

9. C.K. Barrett, *The Gospel according to St. John* (London: SPCK, 1955), p. 287.

10. Ibid.

11. Rudolf Bultmann, *Das Evangelium des Johannes* (Göttingen: Vandenhoeck, 1964), pp. 237–38 [Eng. trans.: *The Gospel of John*, trans. A.R. Beasley-Murray et al. (Philadelphia: Westminster, 1971), pp. 433ff].

12. Barrett, *Gospel according to St. John*, p. 284.

13. Raymond E. Brown, *The Gospel according to John (i–xii)*, Anchor Bible 29 (Garden City, New York: Doubleday, 1966), p. 129.

14. Van den Bussche, *Jean*, p. 162.

15. Barrett, *Gospel according to St. John*, p. 393.

16. Ibid., p. 395.

17. Raymond E. Brown, *The Gospel according to John (xiii–xxi)*, Anchor Bible 29A (Garden City, New York: Doubleday, 1970), p. 676.

18. M.J. Lagrange, *Evangile selon Saint Jean*, 3rd ed. (Paris: Gabalda, 1927), p. 408.

19. Rudolf Schnackenburg, *Die Johannesbriefe*, 3rd ed. (Freiburg: Herder, 1965), p.110 n. 1.

20. Bultmann, *Johannesbriefe*, p. 42 [Eng. trans: *Johannine Epistles*, p. 37].

21. Schnackenburg, *Johannesbriefe*, p. 151.

Chapter 9

Demythologizing the Gospel

Bultmann, commenting on Schnackenburg's attempt to interpret 1 John 2:8—an attempt made by all the socially accepted, established churches of history—says: "Schnackenburg wishes to understand 'is already shining' not with reference to the eschatological event, but rather with reference to the historical process which takes place in the 'extension of the divine realm of light' in the 'victorious advancement of the power of Good.' He has thereby very likely misunderstood the paradox that consists of the historicizing of the eschatological event."[1] This criticism is valid—except for the word "paradox." In the Old Testament, in the Qumran scrolls, and in Jewish literature—in fact, since the idea of the *eschaton* was first conceived—the *eschaton* always means the last moment of *history*; it is not beyond history in some imagined atemporal and ahistorical world. John's thesis, which is also Jesus Christ's, and the entire New Testament's—that the *eschaton* has now begun to be realized—may be unacceptable to us, but it is not paradoxical, for the *eschaton* was never supposed to occur outside history.

Nevertheless Bultmann's criticism mainly hits its mark. The *eschaton* is not a progressive phenomenon. Nor is it a result of the "maturation" of humankind, from age to age after the fashion of the historical periods into which textbooks divide human events or the "history of the spirit."

As Günther Klein observes, the arrival of the Antichrists is referred to in 1 John 2:18–19 as an empirical fact, regardless of what Bultmann says.[2] From this fact, understood as historical, John deduces that we have already reached the last hour: "by which we know that this is the last hour." Therefore this cannot mean that the last hour is "a period of critical change, 'a last hour,' but not definitely 'the last hour,' "[3]—as the established churches would have it. The "last hour" refers precisely to the end, not to any extent of time prior to the end. Klein says that the First Epistle not only historicizes eschatology (as Bultmann admits), but it also eschatologizes history. The socially accepted churches do not want the end to come, but they want the period in which they exist and with which they are identified to be "eschatologically relevant." But unless a period is the end of history, it is no more eschatologically relevant than any other.

THE PRESENT ESCHATON

Klein bases his exegesis on Bultmannian premises and relegates the First Epistle to the group of decadent New Testament writings that had begun to deal with the "history of salvation." However, Klein and Bultmann notwithstanding, the eschatology of the Epistle is equally affirmed in the Gospel:

Jesus said to her: "Your brother will rise again."
Martha said to him: "I know that he will rise again, at the resurrection on that last day."
Jesus said to her, "I am the resurrection and the life" (John 11:23–26).

Martha professes the traditional eschatology of the Old Testament, of Judaism, and of Christianity: "I know that he will rise again, at the resurrection on the last day." But Jesus *corrects her:* The resurrection is already here; there is no need to wait for an ever postponable *eschaton.*

This is the difference between the Old Testament and the New: What the prophecies and promises of the Old Testament regarded as future, and rightly so, has become present. That is what established theology has never accepted. For many centuries—long before Bultmann—established theology has been waging an undeclared campaign of so-called demythologizing. But John did not write a history of salvation, neither in his Epistle nor in his Gospel; he affirms that history has arrived at its end and the end is already here.

In John 11:23–26 Jesus radically altered traditional eschatology with regard to the resurrection of the dead. In John 4:25–26 he stated the same correction with regard to the coming of the Messiah, which is another integral element of the *eschaton:*

> The woman said to him, "I know that the Messiah, the one called Christ, is coming; when he comes, he will tell us everything."
> Jesus said to her, "I am he, I who am speaking to you now."

It is impossible not to recognize the parallel between Jesus' correction of this woman's chronology and of Martha's eschatology; even the wording is similar. Schnackenburg has perceived the progressive deepening of the Samaritan woman's insight. In John 4:9 Jesus is a "Jew" to her; in verse 11 he is "sir"; in verse 12 she asks if he is "greater than our father Jacob"; in verse 19 she says, "I see you are a prophet"; and finally she approaches the truth in verses 20–26, 29: Could Jesus be "the Messiah"?

John 4:27–38 refers to nothing other than the true scope of the messianic event: "Raise your eyes and look at the fields, which are already white for harvest" (v. 35). "Harvest" or "reaping" or "crop" is a specialized term used to designate the eschatological event by Isa. 27:12; Joel 4:13; Mark 4:29; 13:28–29; Matt. 3:12; 13:30, 37ff.; Rev. 14:15–16. John dwells self-indulgently upon his subject in John 4:39–41 ("many," v. 39; "many more," v. 41), indicating that the Messiah is the salvation of the whole world: "We know that this is truly the savior of the world" (v. 42). Van den Bussche observes: "In fact the accent should fall more on the word 'world' than on the word 'savior.' "[4] Schnackenburg specifies quite exactly: "The question of Messiahship is already involved in the process."[5] The compositional center of this passage is John 4:25–26, which we have transcribed.

The chronological approach is here the key: He who "is to come" is already here. In verse 21 Jesus said: "Believe me, woman, the time is coming when you will worship the Father neither on this mountain nor in Jerusalem." In verse 23 he became more explicit: "The time is coming *and it is now* when the true worshippers will worship the Father in spirit and in truth." Even confronted with this direct and unequivocal eschatological statement, the woman again managed to postpone the *eschaton*, using the traditional tranquillizing affirmation: "I know that the Messiah is to come; when he comes, he will tell us everything" (v. 25). This is traditional eschatology. With it we can postpone the *eschaton* indefinitely, keeping it a pure and permanently unreal truth. We are prepared to admit and "believe" whatever we are told—about some future time. In the future nothing is truly real, not even the Messiah, because if the Messiah is always future, the epithet is emptied of all content. Jesus blocked the escape: This Messiah who you say is to come is already here; I am he, I who am speaking to you. He said exactly the same thing to Martha: This resurrection and this last day of which you speak, it is already here.

In John 9:35–37 we again find Jesus proclaiming the inescapable "presentness" of the *eschaton*, although the blind man, unlike Martha and the Samaritan woman, has not explicitly formulated the contrasting traditional escapist eschatology:

> Finding him Jesus said, "Do you believe in the Son of man?"
> He answered and said, "And who is he, sir, that I might believe in him?"
> Jesus said to him, "You have seen him; the one who is speaking to you, it is he."

The debate over the term "the Son of man" is currently in its apogee, but in this passage the expression unquestionably designates the bearer of eschatological salvation. Perhaps the question of the one who was blind was intended to elicit some "pure," nontemporal truth as answer. (We have customarily been taught to believe in such truths, regardless of their content.) But Jesus replied, "the one who is speaking with you," asserting the chronological "presentness" of the Son of man as forcefully and unequivocally as he did to the Samaritan woman in John 4:26: He was not referring to another world nor to an awaited future, however imminent; he was speaking of his historical time, which had arrived.

The thesis of 1 John 2:18—"we know that this is the last hour"—was formulated as early as John 1:41 in Andrew's words to Simon: "We have found the Messiah." For the affirmation that a historical man is the promised Messiah makes sense only insofar as that man brings into the world all the conditions of the messianic kingdom described in the Old Testament: complete justice, knowledge of the true God, life, the resurrection of the dead, the cure of physical ills, love of neighbor. Jesus was not simply the protagonist of John's narrative who passed through the Fourth Gospel amassing an anthology of attributes, "titles," and "names of Christ." Had he been only that, he could not also have made present the Last Judgment, the Parousia, the kingdom, knowledge of God, and the time of the true worshippers. John's message throughout the Gospel and the First Epistle is that *Messiah* is a great *now*.

"THE TIME IS NOW"

This brings us to the hermeneutical problem par excellence. The New Testament thesis of John 11:23–26; 5:24; 12:31; 16:11; and 1 John 2:18–19 has only one possible meaning: The Messiah is now. But how are we to reconcile this meaning with the indisputable fact that in the nineteen centuries of human history since the Messiah entered the world there has been no perceptible realization of the resurrection and of justice? The tension induced by this apparent contradiction has led us customarily to look for some other interpretation of John, because it does not seem possible that the Bible would affirm what history shows to be obviously false. In this well-meant assault on John's true meaning, the most disparate theological factions join forces: traditional apologetics on the one hand and the modern demythologizing school on the other. The former attempts to keep the dogma of biblical inerrancy safe from Schweitzer and rationalism; the latter attempts to adapt the gospel message to modern times, whose self-understanding—according to this school—imposes conditions of possibility on every message. The conservatives do not admit to violating the obvious meanings of the texts. The demythologizers perhaps do, but as extenuation they plead their demythologizing intention, which the biblical authors, especially John, can be shown to have shared.

To distort the meaning of the Bible on pretext of "correcting" it, making it conform to extrabiblical criteria, is not sound exegesis. Scientifically speaking, the history of the last nineteen centuries, along with the other extrabiblical data, would perhaps cause us to deduce that the Bible is mistaken and must be consigned to oblivion; but denying that 1 John 2:18–19 and John 11:23–26 affirm the end of history in the time of Christ is to make the Bible assert what it does not assert, and such a method is called falsification, not exegesis.

The pericope John 5:21–30 is the occasion of a crisis of

modern biblical science, because in it the Johannine Jesus affirms that the *eschaton*, with the Last Judgment and the resurrection of the dead, is chronologically present:

(21) As the Father raises the dead and gives them life, so too the Son gives life to those he loves,

(22) for the Father does not judge anyone, but has given the whole judgment to the Son,

(23) so that all might honor the Son as they honor the Father. Anyone who does not honor the Son does not honor the Father who sent him.

(24) In truth, in truth, I say to you: Anyone who listens to my word and believes in the one who sent me has eternal life and does not come to judgment but rather has crossed over from death to life.

(25) In truth, in truth, I say to you that the time is coming, and it is now, when the dead shall hear the voice of the Son of God, and hearing it they will live.

(26) For as the Father has life in himself, so too has the Son, by the Father's gift,

(27) and he has given him power to judge, because he is the Son of man.

(28) Do not wonder at this, because the time is coming when all those in the grave shall hear his voice,

(29) and those who have done right will rise to life, and those who have done wrong will rise to judgment.

(30) I can do nothing on my own account; I judge as I am bidden. And my judgment is just because I do not seek my own will but the will of the one who sent me.

In the first place, note that verses 22–23 sustain the same thesis as 1 John 2:23: "Anyone who denies the Son does not have the Father either." In 1 John 2:23, as we pointed out, denying the Son means denying that Jesus is the Messiah. But in John 5 that denial is related to the Last Judgment: The only Last Judgment is that which occurs in the time of Jesus, in relation to that concrete bit of human history called Jesus of Nazareth.

Exegetes traditionally handled this passage in one of two ways. Some of them implicitly decided that when

John says "and it is now" (v. 25) he does not mean "now," but rather "in some undetermined future." This —whatever name they call it—is demythologizing pure and simple. Other exegetes explicitly interpreted "and it is now" as meaning an inchoative present; thus neither John nor Jesus Christ were saying anything new, for the *eschaton* was inchoate from the time of Adam. Both of these traditional interpretations are tantamount to postponing the *eschaton* indefinitely. Each in different words repeats Martha's eschatology, which Jesus rejected: "I know that he will rise in the resurrection of the last day."

Modern exegetes have seen that such tergiversations of John 5:25 are untenable. So, in a continuing effort to postpone the *eschaton*, they resorted to dismembering the pericope, making John 5:21–25 and John 5:26–29 into separate discourses mistakenly combined by a later compiler or redactor. This is the solution offered, with variations, by the Catholic scholars Boismard, Gächter, Brown, and others, and by Protestants of the Bultmannian school. (Bultmann himself prefers to extirpate verses 28–29 as interpolations of a later redactor who attempted to reduce John's work to ecclesiastical orthodoxy.) Both Bultmann and Boismard believe that John 5:21–25 teaches an interior eschatology of mental experiences—the "spiritual life," which indeed can be present. Once John is "demythologized," the exegetes have no difficulty accepting what he says.

Boismard, unlike Bultmann, gives priority to John 5:26–30, believing it alone to be authentic. Boismard believes that the interior eschatology of John 5:21–25 was conceived by later generations of Christians when they saw that the Parousia, or second coming of Christ, had not arrived, and that John 5:26–30 expresses the view of the early Christian who, he says, originally thought of the eschaton as future.

But such an interpretation does not fit the available

evidence, which demonstrates that the historical process was, in fact, the other way around: The eschatology of the future is the latest of all eschatologies. Matt. 11:2–6 and Luke 7:18–23 (in the responses to John the Baptist's emissaries) make clear that Jesus himself, as well as Matthew, Luke, and Q, considers the resurrection *of the dead* as present. Jesus responds to the question whether they should continue to wait or not by adducing present facts. Moreover and most convincingly, Matthew's account of the moment of Jesus' death includes the resurrections of many dead (Matt. 27:51–53).

The expression "resurrection of the dead" (not "from among the dead"; the case is genitive) can be found in Paul (1 Cor. 15:12, 13, 21, 42 and Rom. 1:4). *Anastasis nekron* designates an entire epoch, an entire definitive eon of human history. Therefore Paul argues: "If there is no resurrection of the dead, then neither has Christ been raised" (1 Cor. 15:13). If the *eschaton* has not arrived, then Jesus could not have risen.

In Rom. 1:4, where "Son of God" is a messianic title,[6] a document that predated Paul himself[7] maintains that Jesus was constituted Messiah "in virtue of the resurrection of the dead." In fact, the messianic appellative would be completely lacking in real content if Jesus did not bring to history the messianic kingdom, in which the resurrection of the dead (in the plural) is prominently included. Jesus is constituted Messiah by this collective dimension that embraces all humankind; it is the end of all human history, the definitive age, the *eschaton*, the *ultimum*. One might hypothesize (although it would be absurd, according to Paul) that Jesus' individual resurrection could occur without forming part of the collective era of the resurrection; but Jesus' own resurrection would not be sufficient to make him Messiah. He is constituted Messiah by the arrival of the *eschaton* to human history. Without this the word "Messiah" makes no sense. According to Paul and to the pre-Pauline hymn utilized in Rom. 1:3–4, the age of the resurrection of the dead is present. Therefore they affirm in the aorist tense that Jesus "has been constituted Messiah."

Thus the most ancient Christian eschatology known conceives the *eschaton* as present, not future. Our analysis of John confirms Käsemann's statement: "John has not yet learned to understand Jesus' resurrection as an individual event limited to Jesus only."[8] Documentary evidence indicates that this interpretation of resurrection was developed later. Boismard's contention that in Christianity the eschatology of the future antedates the eschatology of the present is historically inaccurate.

The principal argument of Bultmann and Boismard for reading an eschatology of the future into John 5:26–30 is that verse 28 says only "the time is coming," while John 5:25 says "the time is coming and it is now." But such an argument ignores the fact that Jesus' conversation with the Samaritan woman also contains both formulations (John 4:21 and 4:23), and in this conversation both expressions obviously mean the same thing. No one could postulate—and in fact no one does—that John 4:21 and John 4:23 indicate two different dates on which worship in spirit and truth rather than in the temples will begin. The formula "the time is coming and it is now" is simply a further specification of the meaning already expressed by the formula "the time is coming."

In the same fashion Bultmann and Boismard interpret "life" and "they will live" in John 5:24, 25 as referring to interior experiences and the spiritual life—alienation from God as the death of the soul. This they contrast to "life" and "resurrection" in John 5:28, 29, where the terms unequivocally refer to real, physical life. But to do this Bultmann and Boismard have to ignore John 11:24–26, where "he will rise" and "resurrection" (v. 24) are perfectly interchangeable with "life" and "he will live" (vv. 25–26). And this passage refers, not to the spiritually "dead," but to physically dead people whose bodies stink of decomposition.

Likewise, any difference between "when the dead shall hear the voice of the Son of God" (John 5:25) and "when all those in the grave shall hear his voice" (John 5:28) escapes me completely. There is absolutely no literary basis for holding that the content of John 5:21–25 differs from that of John 5:26–30. To give life to the dead, which is recognized as the theme of John 5:28–29, is treated thematically from John 5:21 on: "He raises the dead and gives them life." Thus the pericope John 5:21–30 is a unified whole.

TOTAL TRANSFORMATION

Only extrabiblical motives could induce careful exegetes to interpret John's use of the same expressions sometimes metaphorically and sometimes literally. For conservatives like Boismard the extrabiblical motive is to supply some explanation for the evils of the past nineteen centuries. For liberals the motive is to supply currently acceptable, "rational" interpretations of the "miracles" that strain modern credulity. But let me repeat: Extrabiblical data allow us—at the very most—to conclude that the Bible is mistaken. Period. In no way do these data allow us to distort what the Bible says so that we may comfortably profess our "belief" in it while denying its real meaning.

Käsemann puts his finger on the problem with a question about Gaugler's commentary on John 5:21–30: "E. Gaugler . . . interprets in the liberal fashion . . . : 'For the loving community the idea of judgment is bankrupt.' But then what happens to the resurrection of the dead?" This gets to the heart of the matter: A Last Judgment that occurs during the lifetime of Jesus can—with sufficient rationalistic ingenuity—be denatured into an event of "spiritual life" or invisible "justification," whether Lutheran or Tridentine; this kind of event changes nothing. But John 5:21–30, in accordance with Old Testament tradition, has the Last Judgment and the resurrection of the dead occurring together in a single stroke. This cannot be understood as an interior or experiential change. The rationalist fashion in exegesis has been proved useless.

Barrett points out that *ou me apolontai eis ton aiona* ("they will never die," John 10:28) does not mean "they shall not perish eternally" but rather "they shall never perish,"[9] and he makes the same point regarding John 11:26.[10] In fact, this Greek phrasing, meaning "will never," occurs frequently in the New Testament, especially in John. For example, *ou me nipses mou tous podas eis ton aiona* (John 13:8) cannot possibly be translated as "you will not wash my feet eternally"; it can only mean "you will never wash my feet." The same translation is inescapable in John 4:14; 8:51–52; Luke 2:26; and Psalm 89:48.

Nevertheless certain spiritual writers distort "whoever believes in Jesus Christ will never die" to mean the negation either of eternal death or of spiritual death. But such an interpretation renders the contrast in John 6:48–49 completely meaningless: "I am the bread of life; your fathers in the desert ate the manna and died." As van den Bussche says: "Eternal life is not life after death, but rather life that knows no death."[11]

Bultmann (more consistent than his Catholic predecessors and those spiritual directors whose present-day heirs abominate him) finds it necessary to eliminate John 18:9 as a later interpolation, although there is no textual basis whatever for this opinion. After Jesus had identified himself to his captors and said, "If I am the man you want, let these others go" (John 18:8), the evangelist adds: "This was to fulfill the word he had said: 'I did not lose one of those you gave me.' " The verb *apollymi* ("to lose," and in the passive, "to be lost") as used here unequivocally means physical death. John has already used this verb five times to express the idea that anyone who believes will never die, will not be lost, nor will ever perish (John 3:16; 6:39; 10:28; 12:25; 17:12). Although John 18:9 quotes only the words of 17:12, John interprets himself as having spoken of the suppression of physical death every time the issue was touched upon. Bultmann would strike out John 18:9 because it conflicts with traditional idealistic exegesis: He cannot accept that the realization of faith and justice in this world is capable of modifying the physical conditions of humankind. Such exegetes forget that according to the Bible human beings are the instruments of God in the task of transforming this world. Ancient and modern demythologizing reduces the biblical message to interior experiences or to ever postponable futures; the demythologizers do not realize that these indeed are myths, not the realistic struggle to transform life.

In contrast, the French Dominican Braun comments on John 5:24:

It would be incorrect to interpret the crossing over from death to life as if John had only the soul in mind. For him, the judgment effected by the Word has to do with the entire person, whether the unbeliever or the believer. By embracing it, the believer becomes a new being, a being in God, over whom natural death has no power. Bearing in mind the divine activity, indispensable for coming to Christ (John 6:44–45), one would be tempted to say that, in virtue of his self-determining decision, the believer makes for himself a nature that engages him to the core. And since this is permanent, the *eschaton* for him has been achieved.[12]

Our only objection to this interpretation of Johannine thought is its individualistic concept of the *eschaton*. For John, as for all biblical authors, the kingdom is a collective, supra-individual reality; it is a definitive age for all of humankind. The justice that will be capable of transforming even the physical order is a mutual justice among all people (once the unjust are eliminated). Freud's profound observation that human beings die because of their own conflicts demonstrates how greatly reason assists biblical hope in the struggle against

Platonic idealism, which separates the material and spiritual orders.

John's ideas are clear. But spiritualism cannot accept that faith and justice determine our very being as well as our relationships with others and with the material order (as if we were not part of the material order). The demythologizers cannot accept the miracle. Instead they prefer to adopt idealistic philosophy and anthropology as the supreme exponent of what humanity is. The anachronism of this belief is made obvious by their claim that idealistic philosophy constitutes the implicit philosophy of the modern era. Few assertions have been so far out of touch with their times as this anthropological dogma.

It is understandable that idealism and spiritualism are unable to link moral transformation with the material transformation of humankind: Capacity to make such a connection would necessitate a change of genus, *metabasis eis allo genos*. From their perspective the material order is completely heterogenous to the moral order. I believe that modern times, however, are characterized by the quest that Sartre sees in Marxism: "What constitutes the strength and richness of Marxism is that it has been the most radical attempt to clarify the historical process in its totality."[13] To be certain of the worldwide achievement of justice is of course to believe in miracles much greater than the future defeat of death. For the Bible the two go together, and this is indeed to confront history in its totality. We have already seen that existentialism is concerned only with the field of being that, in order to be, demands our decision. The reason why only that "part" of being is of any concern is precisely because that part can change by our decision. But if other fields of being are of no concern to us, it is not because they cannot be changed, but rather because their change depends on the new field of being that, in order to be, demands a decision of us.

The truly modern person cannot accept the dichotomy

of the human being into two disconnected genera. If the achievement of justice and love in the world is possible, the transformation of the material order is not heterogenous to it. There are not two unrelated orders. If we believe in the possibility that the moral order can be transformed, we have to accept the possibility that the material order can be as well, for they are one and the same in a much more realistic and profound sense than we had thought. We can no longer dissever the moral from the physical order.

Let us not forget, however, the profound reason for modern demythologizing. Stuhlmacher summarizes it thus:

> Invoking Luther and using as a criterion the thesis that the foundation of faith should coincide with the content of faith, Bultmann has challenged the New Testament proclamation (broadly based on the tradition of the Old Testament and Judaism) of the kingdom of God and of Christ, of the Last Judgment and the new world of God. For he asks if the pure relationship of faith with the God who by grace alone makes us just might not be hindered and even annulled by fantasies that try to link God's future action to human yearnings and desires. As Bultmann answers this question affirmatively, he has demythologized to the extreme the eschatology of the New Testament.[14]

A more recent origin of Bultmannian thought is Kant. But it is not enough to say simply that Kant's motive is justified, for the Kantian imperative is the very essence of the God of the Bible (although Kant does not explicitly state the biblical origin of his moral imperative). Notwithstanding the concealed eudemonism and hedonism of "Christian" theology, the authority of the God of the Bible is unquestionably not grounded on reward and punishment nor on the well-being or happiness produced by the achievement of justice. Those who do not perceive this confuse the moral imperative with utilitarianism or simply do not know what the moral imperative is. The moral imperative *stat in indivisibili*.

The true God is grounded in himself, not in an apologetics of miracles or in the satisfaction of human desires.

But it is precisely this implacable imperative that demands the transformation even of the physical order, the elimination of injustice and death. And it demands it now, unpostponably. "The hour is coming and it is now."

A god who intervenes in history to elicit religious adoration of himself and not to undo the hell of cruelty and death that human history has become is an immoral god in the deepest sense of the word. A god who is reconciled or merely indifferent to the pain of human beings is a merciless god, a monster, not the ethical God whom the Bible knows. We would be morally obliged to rebel against such a god, even if our defeat were inevitable. Equally immoral is the god for whom the end of injustice and innocent suffering is a secondary or subordinate imperative. Hence the New Testament intransigence with regard to the *eschaton*. It is not for apologetical reasons nor to gratify less-than-divine yearnings and desires that the God of Jesus Christ comes to establish justice and life now; it is because that is God's unmistakable essence.

Though idealistic anthropology denies it, the most outstanding characteristic of our time is the demand for total justice. This does indeed impose conditions of possibility: For a message, any message, to deserve attention, the kingdom of justice must be achieved. But it has not been made sufficiently explicit that this justice includes the transformation of nature and the defeat of death. For sentimental recollection does not do justice to the worker-martyrs who were gunned down in Haymarket Square. Nor is it justice that people should be born crippled. The tortures we voluntarily or involuntarily inflict on one another, the sufferings we mutually cause, will cease only when humanity's age-old egoistic instinct and mistrust are eliminated. A materialist should be the last to deny the possibility of a miracle: If justice is attainable, surely the defeat of death is not in a compartment distinct from that realization. Human beings could not carry out reforms and revolutions if material being itself were not compelling them. Their basis for action, their impulse toward revolution, is the very being which of itself tends toward an *eschaton* and of which people form the medium.

In the same vein, Sartre says, "As an internal negation, man must by means of matter make known to himself what he is not and consequently what he has to be."[15] One could not suffer—even die of a heart attack due to interpersonal conflict—unless one's very materiality were conditioned by one's relationship with other people. If the body itself were not molded and modeled in its being and in its being-such by interpersonal relationships, suffering or any bodily disease resulting from disillusion or frustration would be impossible.

PROCLAIMING THE GOOD NEWS

Bultmann has failed to understand true demythologizing. To demythologize is to make realizable, and this the New Testament authors explicitly and thematically do, as Braun notes (in the paragraph quoted above).

The western mind defines biblical "news" like Greco-Roman news: It is "information" about events whose occurrence is independent of human action or intervention. For the Greeks this autonomy is the "objective" element of an affirmation. The western mind cannot admit what the gospel says—that the time is coming and it is now when injustice and death will be defeated —for by the Greco-Roman definition of "news," this affirmation means that justice and life will triumph even if we do not "believe" it, even if human "subjectivity" refuses to participate in their triumph. But the New Testament expressly and repeatedly teaches that it is our faith (that "subjectivity") that will cause the announced events to be accomplished! A myth is an event that occurs independently of human will and action, regardless of what we do, but the news *that the kingdom arrives* means that we must *make it arrive*.

Of what value, then, are Jesus' indisputably authentic affirmations: "It is your faith that has saved you" (Mark 5:34; Matt. 9:22; Luke 8:48; Mark 10:52; Luke 18:42) —each uttered after a cure, which is a modification of physical nature? Of what value is the statement that "everything is possible for the one who believes" (Mark 9:23)? If we bear in mind the deliberateness and the emphasis with which John recounts Jesus' resuscitation of Lazarus (chap. 11), then the following assertion leaves no room for doubt about the nature of faith: "In truth, in truth I say to you: Anyone who believes in me will do the works that I am doing, and will do still greater works than these (John 14:12). The term "greater works than these" (*erga meizona touton*) had previously occurred only in John 5:20 and was exemplified in 5:21 by the resurrection of the dead. When Jesus performed the miracle of resurrecting Lazarus, he said to Martha, "Did I not tell you that if you believed you would see the glory of God?" (John 11:40).[16] The condition is always belief: "if you believe," "anyone who believes." John's strongest affirmation of the causal efficacy of faith is John 14:12; only Mark 9:23 expresses it more fervently.

In the Synoptic passages cited above "salvation" has a material, this-wordly sense (see also Matt. 8:25; 9:21; 14:30; 27:40, 42, 49; Mark 3:4; 5:23, 28; and John 11:12; 12:27). If we keep in mind that for John "to live" and "life" can also be expressed as "to be saved" (see John 3:16–17; 11:12, 23, 25),[17] then the thesis that life and resurrection will be caused in this world by faith becomes apparent throughout the Fourth Gospel (John 3:15, 16, 36; 4:50–51 [cf. Mark 9:23; 2:5]; 5:24; 6:35, 39, 40, 47; 11:25, 26, 40; 20:31). Brown is justified in claiming a relationship between John 14:1 and Jesus' words in Mark 5:35–36 and Matt. 8:25–26 ("Do not fear, only have faith") and likewise between John 14:12 and the words of the historical Jesus about the faith that moves mountains (Matt. 21:21).[18]

The good news called gospel is not Greek news. It is the most purely biblical news that can be imagined. It is a word signifying action, not information; it seeks to *achieve what it says*, not simply to notify. The announcement itself enjoins: "Be converted and believe in the news" (Mark 1:15); "Be converted because the kingdom has arrived" (Matt. 4:17). Only this conversion and this faith will cause the kingdom to come.

Among New Testament authors there exist minor differences, but they express clearly and unanimously the idea that "first the good news must be proclaimed to all peoples" (Mark 13:10). Given that the good news constitutes the sole object and content of faith, and given the real efficaciousness of this faith, Mark 13:10 means that predicting the Parousia bears no resemblance to Greek-style teaching about events that would occur independently of human action. Such preaching is not auto-suggestion or subjectiveness, but the bringing about of real universal interpersonal justice.

This conviction of the causal efficacy of faith, enunciated by Jesus, can be documented as persisting until the middle of the second century: "In your holy conduct and piety, should you not be waiting and hastening the coming of the day of God?" (*speudontas ten parousian tes tou Theou hemeras* [2 Pet. 3:11–12]).

In this passage it is expressly stated that human beings make the Parousia take place. We find substantially the same idea in Luke, who according to Conzelmann was well rooted in history:

> Repent, then, and be converted, so that your sins may be wiped out, so that the time of consolation might come from the Lord and he might send Jesus Christ who was announced to you (Acts 3:19–20).

John is much more incisive than Luke as we shall see. But it is of utmost importance that authors as disparate as Mark, Luke, and the author of 2 Peter say that the Parousia, the total realization of the *eschaton*, is brought about by the evangelization and conversion of human beings. Jesus Christ expressed the same conviction when he proclaimed the "good news" (Mark 1:14–15). This causative relationship pertains to the very essence of "gospel." If we understand the indicative in the Greek fashion, that it simply "informs," then the "gospel" is more imperative than indicative. No, the achievement of justice and life is not the myth; the myth is rather to imagine (as disillusioned Christians have imagined for the last nineteen centuries) that justice and life could be achieved without faith and without human participation.

True being, the demythologized field of being, is that which demands decision, that which requires our decision in order to be. Heidegger says it well: Only that which presents itself as possibility-for-me, as something that I can decide, has meaning.[19] Kierkegaard learned this by reading the New Testament, which was written with this precise intention: to make us decide for the "possibility" that John affirmed as necessary for humankind. The New Testament cannot be separated from this intention. Its purpose is to make Jesus the Messiah. Antichrists are those who oppose an *eschaton* of justice and life for all. If a genuine "possibility" does not arise when we are faced by Christ, then it does not arise at all, for only Christ demands that we bring about the *eschaton*. Any other "possibilities" are individualistic trivialities that really do not summon.

Thus we can understand the Johannine intransigence with regard to the *eschaton*. God is revealed only in the implacable "now" of the moral imperative of justice and love for all. To postpone the kingdom, to postpone the Messiah, is to prevent them from ever being real. This is the eternal stratagem employed to separate us from the only real otherness that summons us. It is to fall back again into the eternal return, into the self's grand deception that enables us to continue enclosed in our own immanence, whispering to ourselves assurances that there is nothing new, that everything that happens we already knew and have summarized in the concepts that equip our self-absorbed self-sufficiency.

We have already seen that in 1 John 2:8 the presence of the *eschaton* is the reason for the commandment of love of neighbor. If there is no *eschaton*, the word ceases to be transcendent; its summons is neutralized and ceases. If I can postpone the realization of the commandment, I reassimilate it into the archive of the self and I continue in my solitude and immanence. Therefore 1 John 2:22–23 tells us that anyone who denies the Messiah does not have God either. If I do not believe that Jesus is the Messiah, if I do not believe that the *eschaton* has come, then the imperative of love of neighbor becomes an intra-self concept. It does not speak as a real otherness, because anodyne time, even if it is present, truly has no reason to command me any more than any other time. I can postpone the realization of the commandment to any other time, so that reality will continue being the same as now. It is always "the same"; there is no "other," and God is not revealed. I will continue to speak "of him who I say is my God, and I do not know him." I have again converted God into an idol always available at my pleasure for my purposes. God is no longer nonassimilable otherness who commands. Anyone who denies the Messiah does not have God either.

THE ONE TRUE GOD

John 17:3 reads, "And this is eternal life: that they know you, the only true God, and the one whom you sent, Jesus Christ." Brown comments on this verse: "Elsewhere in the Bible the adjectives 'one' and 'true' may be applied to God to distinguish Him from the pagan gods."[20] Then he adds simply that in John this is not the case, but he does not support this assertion. Elsewhere in the Bible the expression "the one true God" is used to distinguish God from false gods. Without evidence it cannot be maintained that John 17:3 constitutes an exception. Acknowledging Jesus Christ is related to knowing the one true God in contradistinction to the false gods. We have already seen that according to 1 John 2:22–23 anyone who denies that Jesus is the Messiah does not have God either.

1 John 5:20–21 is even more perplexing, but it is precisely this passage that demonstrates that John is arguing against the neutralization and idolization of a God who thereby ceases to be God:

We know that the Son of God has come to give us understanding so that we might know the true one. And we are in the true one, in his son Jesus Christ. This is the true God and eternal life. Little children, be careful of idols (1 John 5:20–21).

Note that knowing the true God depends on the historical, contingent appearance of Jesus Christ. The word was so utterly made flesh that without this bit of human history there is no longer any God. Without the *eschaton* there is no God; there is no transcendence. John is not unaware that the true God was already known before Jesus' historical birth. If he asserts that anyone who denies the Messiah does not "have" God either (1 John 2:22–23), his extraordinary purpose must be to tell us what God really is.

1 John 5:20–21 refers to the true God in polemical contradistinction to false gods. This could be denied only by holding that the last phrase ("be careful of idols") is a fragment unrelated to the preceding passage, and there is no evidence whatsoever for this opinion.

Eidola can mean either images of false gods or the false gods themselves.[21] But, as Bultmann notes, in this context it cannot mean "images," for if it did "the sense of the admonition would have to be not to participate in pagan cults,"[22] and pagan cults are nowhere remotely alluded to in the Epistle. The redaction clearly indicates that "the admonition of v. 21 is a suitable conclusion for the whole writing." In this passage *eidola* can only mean "false gods." Moreover, this translation is strongly suggested by the contrapuntal phrases "the true one," "the true God," in this same climactic passage of the Epistle.

Even so, the very exegetes who recognize that *eidola* refers to false gods find this conclusion unexpected and astonishing. Bultmann says, "Most striking, however, is the phrase *apo ton eidolon.*" Schnackenburg writes, "The concluding warning against idolatry quite frankly sounds strange." Their astonishment is most revealing. Let us credit John with meaning what he says: If the Johannine Jesus says to the Jews, "he who you say is your God, and you do not know him" (John 8:54–55), he obviously supposes that they have a conception of a false god. Otherwise what god are they speaking of, given that they do not know the true one? By the same token, let us look again at John 16:2–3: "Indeed the time is coming when anyone who kills you will suppose that he is worshipping God. And they will do this because they do not know either the Father or me." If they do not know the true God, then obviously the god they think they are pleasing by killing Christians is a false god.

Brooke is on the right track in his comment on *apo ton eidolon:* "The expression embraces all false conceptions of God. . . . If any limited reference is necessary, it must be found in the untrue mental images fashioned by the false teachers."[23] With regard to the passage "anyone who denies the Son does not have the Father either," Bultmann likewise comments: "Whoever, then, has a perverted view of Jesus, by that very fact also thinks wrongly of God."[24] But neither Brooke nor Bultmann gets to the root of the question; John is not talking about erroneous or defective doctrinal conceptions of God that permit people to worship the true God albeit with an imperfect conceptual instrument. John says, "Be careful of idols," and, "He does not have God either." He is not talking about imperfect awareness of God, but about the *denial* of God, even by persons who sincerely believe that they are worshipping the true God. The dilemma is this: God or idolatry.

Thus John 17:3, with its genuinely biblical expression "the one true God," in no way is an exception among the biblical passages in which this expression appears. Eternal life consists in knowing the true God—as distinguished from the false gods and mental constructs we invent to elude God—and in knowing Jesus as Christ, that is, as Messiah. John 17:3 is really the summary of the entire message of John and of the New Testament. Eternal life depends on this knowledge and will come to be throughout the world by this knowledge. This teaching cannot be vitiated so that it becomes rationalistically acceptable. On the contrary, as van den Bussche says: "Eternal life is not life after death, but rather life that does not know death."

The true God is accessible only in the historical fact called Jesus of Nazareth. This thesis of John and of the whole New Testament (beginning with Jesus Christ himself) cannot be understood in an extrinsicist way, as if God punitively withdrew knowledge of himself from those who rejected Jesus Christ. The true God reveals himself and consists solely in the imperative of love of neighbor. And love of neighbor is no romantic, individualistic sentiment: It means definitive justice for humankind; it means justice and life and heeding every cry of suffering. All other "possibilities-for-me" are trifles. They are prizes the soul awards itself for playing the love-your-neighbor game. They do not transcend.

At this point the "totality" combatted by Levinas regains all its rights. Levinas is correct when he says, "It is not I who resist the system; . . . it is the Other."[25] Existentialism that does not acknowledge this is incapable of discovering the new field of being that in order to be demands decision. But the "Other" that constitutes the summons of the infinite is all others, all those who were and are broken by history. And these others demand the totality called the messianic *eschaton.*

John 17:3 telescopes knowledge of the one God into the knowledge of Jesus Christ; it combines them. One thereby becomes impossible without the other. We find the same telescopic approach in 1 John 3:23:

And this is his commandment: that we believe in the name of his son Jesus Christ and that we love one another as he commanded us.

Exegetes have found this passage strange for including faith within the content of the commandment.[26] As we have seen, John considers love of neighbor to be the only content of the commandment, and he is saying nothing different here. Indeed, the phrase "as he commanded us" alludes to John 13:34. To believe in Jesus Christ, to believe that Jesus is the Messiah, is an *essential* component of love of neighbor. The sole object of faith is the "fact" or truth that Jesus is Messiah (see our chapter 4), and this truth is essential to the imperative of love of neighbor in which the God of the Bible consists.

The First Epistle has a single purpose: to confute the Antichrists. Or, as the Gospel puts it: "So that you might believe that Jesus is the Messiah" (John 20:31). The fact that Christians have not set out to conquer the world for love of neighbor shows that they do not believe that the messianic *eschaton* has arrived. They have adapted to the "world" and to history. Civilization has ensnared them so that they have made Christianity into a conventional religion, and by this very fact they deny that Jesus is the Messiah. They have withdrawn from the otherness of millions of hungry, tormented human beings, and they worship a mental idol invented by civilization itself.

THE "NOW" OF JESUS

In John 7:33 Jesus says, "For a little longer I shall be with you." Bultmann observes that this refers to the "contingency of revelation," for revelation "does not consist in universal truths, which can be grasped at all times and for all times, nor in dogma which one could invoke at any time."[27] The true God is knowable only in the segment of history constituted by the life of Jesus of Nazareth. But Bultmann not only fails to see that this contingency specifically and solely means that God is God only in the imperative of love of neighbor; his very interpretation of contingency in effect eliminates contingency. This brings us once again to the problem of Kierkegaardian contemporaneity.

Bultmann continues: "Of course in this symbolic scene John does not consider the fact that the word of Jesus is taken up again by the community, and that the revelation is again and again made present in time." But we cannot interpret John by saying that he is mistaken when a statement of his displeases or baffles us.

Bultmann holds, "In the word of proclamation [Jesus] is himself made present to the world (as in this Gospel), in the 'Now,' in the present moment in time. And the threat is always present, 'too late!' "[28]

By this statement Bultmann reveals that he does not have in mind the "now" of the historical Jesus, but rather an existential now ("existentive," as José Gaos would say) that is at all times available and that we can latch onto at any moment. True, he is not speaking of universal truths or dogmas, but he is referring to existential experiences that do not constitute an other different from the self. Rather, as objects that are conceived or "lived," they form part of the experiential, existential apparatus of the self, and the self uses them as it uses its own faculties and concepts. The "now" of which Bultmann speaks has been reassimilated by the subject. It is no longer the reality of the historical now of Christ that presents me with an irreducible otherness.

But when the Johannine Jesus says "now," John means the historical moment in which Jesus speaks. This alone demonstrates that Bultmann is not a faithful interpreter of John. For example, Jesus says to Peter, "You cannot follow me now; you will follow me later"

(John 13:36), and when John wrote his Gospel, Peter had already "followed" Christ. We find this same chronological "now" in 4:23; 5:25; 12:27; 12:31a, 31b; 13:31, 36; 14:29; 15:22, 24; 16:5, 22; 17:5, 7, 13. John's implacable insistence on the "hour" and *kairos* of Jesus (John 2:4; 4:21, 23; 5:25, 28; 7:6, 30; 8:20; 12:23, 27; 13:1; 16:4, 21, 25) is meaningless if we can separate this "hour" from the chronological, dateable time of the historical Jesus.

Anyone who determines that this historical moment can be repeated automatically lifts it out of time, detemporalizes it, makes it nontemporal and eternal, sets it in the Platonic world—a different and, moreover, nonexistent world. Time is the touchstone of any philosophy, and nonrepeatability is the touchstone of real time. Bultmann's distinction between the historical Jesus and the Christ-of-faith or the celestial, eternal Christ has always been an essential part of any theology that does not accept the *eschaton*. These theologies can be contemporaneous only with a nontemporal (and nonexistent) Christ. True demythologization includes denouncing this myth, which contradicts itself (someone *nontemporal* cannot be *contemporaneous* to anyone) and which is a tool deliberately used to prevent the realization of the messianic kingdom on earth. Bultmann, echoing his bitterest conservative opponents, explicitly detemporalizes Christ. John wants to tell us that the hour of justice and life for all humankind has already arrived. But the vested interests of the masters of this world have been passed off as Christian theology to drown out his message, silence it, and so prevent it from revolutionizing the world.

To rebut these theologies that treat Jesus' historical moment as repeatable or as continually available, we can say, like Jesus to his relatives: "Your moment [*kairos*] is always at hand" (John 7:6). And the very argument that Bultmann uses against "the world" in his commentary on this passage can also be used against him: "If their *kairos* is always there, then in reality it is never there, and their actions never decide anything, because everything is decided in advance."29

John's contemporaneity with Christ is not achieved by intellectual or psychic juggling. John did not use techniques of asceticism to "feel" or "imagine" himself in the "now" of Jesus of Nazareth, who died fifty or sixty years before John wrote. John's contemporaneity with Christ is not imaginary but real. Jesus is the definitive "now" of history, in which justice and life are to be achieved. But this achievement depends on our decision. John's commitment is to the historical Jesus, not to a celestial, eternal Christ.

Western civilization's overwhelming rejection of the historical Jesus might persuade us that the West lacks a historical sense. But the West is not *unable* to understand that the hour of the kingdom has already arrived; it is *unwilling* to understand it, because to understand it would oblige us to change. To circumvent this obligation we have invented and for centuries believed in a celestial Christ and an "eternal life." And this total distortion of the gospel has been accomplished with the tacit consent—indeed, the connivance and cooperation—of ecclesiastical authorities. The fate of our world depends on our believing Jesus Christ when he says that the hour of the kingdom has come (Mark 1:14–15), but the masters of our world lose their power if we believe it. Conservative theology counters Bultmann by affirming that its celestial Christ is identical to the historical Jesus, but clearly the only Christ that matters to conservative theology is the nontemporal, celestial one, for such theology does not take the "now" of Jesus seriously. This "now" is the historical Jesus. Conservative theology professes concern with time; but time is the unrepeatable "now" or it is not time.

To demythologize is to make realizable. This consists in proving that the good news is not Greek news but rather a reality that depends on our decision in order to be. Demythologizing also includes reintegrating into our historical world everything that has been projected into a so-called eternal "other world." To do this we must understand that the hour of justice and life has come to history. Such is the proclamation made by Jesus Christ, and it has not been abrogated. It is not repeatable. The hour of Jesus does not return. It is really present.

If existentialism rejects this indicative that is imperative, then being becomes unchangeable and "objective," as in the old ontology. In order to make the *eschaton* arrive, "first the good news must be proclaimed to all peoples." Existentialism can discover and make the new being, or it can become the ideological defense par excellence of the status quo. But if existentialism is to remain faithful to itself, it cannot reject the only summons that attempts to modify the entire being of history.

NOTES

1. Rudolf Bultmann, *Die drei Johannesbriefe*, 2nd ed. (Göttingen: Vandenhoeck, 1967), p. 33 [Eng. trans.: *The Johannine Epistles*, trans. R. Philip O'Hara et al. (Philadelphia: Fortress, 1973), p. 28].

2. Günther Klein, "Das wahre Liecht scheint schon," *Zeitschrift für Theologie und Kirche* 68 (1971), p. 302.

3. Brooke Foss Westcott, *The Epistles of St. John* (Cambridge: Macmillan, 1892), p. 69, as cited by Rudolf Schnackenburg, *Die Johannesbriefe* (Freiburg: Herder, 1963), p. 142. The German exegete rejects this interpretation, but neither does he accept the fact that it refers to the end. He says that John "wants only to characterize his own time as eschatologically relevant." However, if the end has not come, all times are eschatologically of the same relevance—or irrelevance.

4. Henri van den Bussche, *Jean* (Paris: Desclée, 1967), p. 197.

5. Rudolf Schnackenburg, *Das Johannesevangelium* (Freiburg: Herder, 1965), 1:489 [Eng. trans.: *The Gospel according to St. John*, trans. Kevin Smyth (New York: Herder and Herder, 1968), 1:455].

6. Cf. Stanislas Lyonnet, *Exegesis epistulae ad romanos, Cap. I–IV*, 3rd ed. (Rome: Pontificio Istituto Biblico, 1963), pp. 37–40; Eduard Schweizer, "hyios," *TWNT*, 8:368 [Eng. trans.: *TDNT*, 8:367].

7. H. Zimmermann, *Neutestamentliche Methodenlehre* (Stuttgart: Katholisches Bibelwerk, 1967), pp. 192–213.

8. Ernst Käsemann, *Jesu letzter Wille nach Johannes 17*, 2nd ed. (Tübingen: Mohr, 1967), p. 34 [Eng. trans.: *The Testament of Jesus*, trans. Gerhard Krodel (Philadelphia: Fortress Press, 1968), p. 16].

9. C.K. Barrett, *The Gospel according to St. John* (London: SPCK, 1955), p. 317.

10. Ibid. p. 330.

11. Van den Bussche, *Jean*, p. 253.

12. F.M. Braun, *Jean le théologien* (Paris: Gabalda, 1959–66), 3:124.

13. Jean-Paul Sartre, *Critique de la raison dialectique* (Paris: Gallimard, 1960), 1:29.

14. Peter Stuhlmacher, "Neues Testament und Hermeneutik," *Zeitschrift für Theologie und Kirche* 68 (1971), p. 157.

15. J.-P. Sartre, *L'être et le néant* (Paris: Gallimard, 1943), p. 712 [cf. Eng. trans.: *Being and Nothingness*, trans. Hazel E. Barnes (New York: Citadel, 1968), p. 536].

16. Brown: "Didn't I assure you that if you believed, you would see the glory of God?" Westcott: "Said I not unto thee, that, if thou wouldest believe, thou shouldest see the glory of God?" This refers to the Old Testament concept of the glory of God ("that glory might dwell on our earth"), as I have shown in *Marx y la biblia* (Salamanca: Sígueme, 1972), p. 259–82 [Eng. trans.: *Marx and the Bible*, trans. John Eagleson (Maryknoll, New York: Orbis Books, 1974), pp. 229–50].

17. See this synonymy in Mark 5:23; Josh. 6:17; Lev. 18:5; Hab. 2:4; Rom. 1:16–17; 5:10; 8:13; 10:5; 10:9–10; Gal. 3:12; Ezek. 18:13, 21, 22; etc.

18. Raymond E. Brown, *The Gospel according to John (xiii–xxi)*, Anchor Bible 29A (Garden City, New York: Doubleday, 1970), pp. 624, 633.

19. Martin Heidegger, *Sein und Zeit* (Tübingen: Niemeyer, 1960), p. 395 [Eng. trans.: *Being and Time*, trans. John Macquarrie and Edward Robinson (New York: Harper & Row, 1962), p. 447].

20. Brown, *Gospel according to John (xiii–xxi)*, p. 752.

21. Cf. Walter Bauer, *Wörterbuch zu den Schriften des Neuen Testaments*, 5th ed. (Berlin: Töpelmann, 1963), cols. 438–39 [cf. William F. Arndt and F. Wilbur Gingrich, *A Greek-English Lexicon of the New Testament and Other Early Christian Literature* (Chicago: University of Chicago Press, 1957), p. 220]; and Schnackenburg, *Johannesbriefe*, p. 292.

22. Bultmann, *Johannesbriefe*, p. 93 [Eng. trans.: *Johannine Epistles*, p. 90].

23. A.E. Brooke, *The Johannine Epistles*, International Critical Commentary 38 (Edinburgh, T. & T. Clark, 1912), p. 154.

24. Bultmann, *Johannesbriefe*, p. 43 [Eng. trans.: *Johannine Epistles*, p. 38].

25. Emmanuel Levinas, *Totalité et Infini* (The Hague: Martinus Nijhoff, 1971), p. 10 [cf. Eng. trans.: *Totality and Infinity*, trans. Alphonso Lingis (Pittsburgh: Duquesne University Press, 1969), p. 40].

26. Cf. Schnackenburg, *Johannesbriefe*, p. 207.

27. Rudolf Bultmann, *Das Evangelium des Johannes* (Göttingen: Vandenhoeck, 1964), p. 232 [Eng. trans.: *The Gospel of John*, trans. G.R. Beasley-Murray et al. (Philadelphia: Westminster, 1971), pp. 307–08].

28. Bultmann, *Evangelium des Johannes*, p. 233 [cf. Eng. trans.: *Gospel of John*, p. 308].

29. Bultmann, *Evangelium des Johannes*, p. 220 [Eng. trans.: *Gospel of John*, pp. 292–93].

Chapter 10

Parousia or Presence?

This chapter is virtually an appendix for exegetes, though nonspecialists may find it an aid to understanding what has gone before. My purpose in writing it is twofold: First, to expose the conservatives' claim that John must be interpreted in relation to the Synoptics as a euphemism for suppressing John's message; second, to seek the corroboration of ecclesiastically sanctioned studies for the astonishing and revolutionary Christianity that has emerged from our objective analysis of Johannine writings.

Here, briefly, we shall attempt to accomplish both ends: to establish that the Synoptics support our interpretation of John and to cite recognized Catholic exegetes to corroborate the soundness of our interpretation. And we shall attempt to identify and summarize the problems posed directly or indirectly by our exegesis without making this chapter into a mere catalogue.

THE PARACLETE

Once we have understood that faith is *really* supposed to transform humankind and the world, then the delay of the Parousia—which has presented such a problem to twentieth-century exegesis—is not a problem of biblical error but of our infidelity to Jesus Christ. This we have already established. But a mistaken demythologizing maintains that John corrects the errors of Synoptic eschatology. Let us see.

Each sacred writer should be interpreted individually, as Käsemann has emphasized in his magnificent study of the canon.[1] There is no basis for the dogmatic presupposition that they must all be saying the same thing. Nonetheless, in a series of articles on Synoptic eschatology (Mark 13; Luke 21:5–36; Matt. 24–25) published between 1948 and 1950, the Catholic Feuillet definitively showed that according to the Synoptic Gospels the Parousia and the complete establishment of the kingdom take place during "this generation"; that is explicitly stated in Mark 13:30; Luke 21:32; and Matthew 24:34. That being the case, we must conclude that although John rectifies traditional eschatology, that is, the eschatology of Judaism, as when Jesus corrects Martha (John 11:24–26), he does not change that of Jesus Christ or the Synoptics. Both the Synoptics and John speak of "this generation," but for John its arrival is signalled by the death and resurrection of Christ, while for Jesus and the Synoptics it is signalled by the destruction of Jerusalem.

Regarding the "we will come" of John 14:23, Barrett says, "To the man who becomes a Christian . . . both the Father and the Son . . . will come. This is the *parousia* upon which John's interest is concentrated."[2]

The Johannine Jesus insists on this teaching, which theology has yet to take seriously:

Because you have seen me you have believed. Happy are those who believed without seeing (John 20:29).

As the Catholic van den Bussche says, "the Spirit is not a substitute for the Christ who has gone away. It puts them [the disciples] in contact with the Master much more radically than when they were at his side

every day during his public life. The later Christian
generations will not have less good fortune than the
eyewitnesses."[3] We should add: Not only is their good
fortune no less; rather the intentionally emphatic contrast in John 20:29 indicates that the later Christian
generation, who did not see Christ, enjoyed greater fortune. John 16:7 reinforces this message:

> But I tell you the truth: It is better for you that I go away,
> because if I do not go away the Paraclete will not come to you,
> but if I go away I will send him to you.

Brown has perceived the key idea in this passage:
"The Paraclete is the Spirit understood as the presence
of the absent Jesus. . . . It is our contention that John
presents the Paraclete as the Holy Spirit in a special
role, namely, as the personal presence of Jesus in the
Christian while Jesus is with the Father."[4] Granting
that, however, we still must explain why Jesus' presence
as Holy Spirit is better for us than his actual bodily
presence, as John 20:29 and John 16:7 clearly stress.

The continuation of the latter passage gives us the
answer: "And when he comes, he will reproach [or
denounce] the world about sin and about justice and
about judgment" (John 16:8). But this denunciation of
the world the disciples themselves are to carry out, as is
shown by the explicative "and" in John 15:26–27: "He
will bear witness to me *and* you will bear witness because you have been with me from the beginning." The
Catholic exegete Mussner recognizes the role of the disciples: "In *their* testimony the testimony to Christ of the
Spirit goes forth in the world."[5] So does Lagrange,
another well-respected Catholic: "And since this Spirit
was to remain in them (John 14:16), should they not
understand that the Paraclete would use them to convince the world?"[6]

To believe that Jesus' presence as Paraclete will be
made real by specific works of his followers does not

diminish in the least the reality of the Holy Spirit. The striking thesis of John 16:7 and 20:29 is consistent with that of John 14:12:

In truth, in truth, I say to you: Anyone who believes in me will also do the works that I do, and even greater ones, because I am going to the Father.

If, as we have seen, the Father is revealed only in a certain type of works, then it is not strange that Christ should say that it is better for us if he goes away: Obviously his followers could do more God-revealing works than he alone, and his sole intent was to reveal the true God to the world. John's basis for this assertion we have elucidated in the preceding chapters: The God who is "the word" not only does not need to be perceptible to the senses; he needs the distance of otherness to reveal himself and to be truly God. Only across this distance is God "the word" that summons. Without this distance I can encompass God within my worldview and my system, and I convert him into an idol; he ceases to be God. The Parousia, or true presence, is the full realization of this status of "the word."

Regarding the parallel in series between John 14:15–17 (presence, in the disciples, of the Spirit that the world cannot see) and John 14:18–21 (presence, in the disciples, of Christ whom the world cannot see), Brown notes: "Such parallelism is John's way of telling the reader that the presence of Jesus after his return to the Father is accomplished in and through the Paraclete. Not two presences but the same presence is involved."[7]

That is really the least that can be deduced from this strange parallel that has caught the attention of all exegetes. In John 14:18 Jesus assured the disciples of his presence (he will not leave them as orphans, etc.), speaking as someone who has *already explained what he means* by not abandoning them but returning to them: His presence, of which he assures them, *consists* in the presence of the Paraclete, whom—like the historical Jesus—the world cannot know but the disciples can. That is the nature of Christ's return.

We find the same parallel between John 16:12–15 (the coming of the Paraclete) and John 16:16–21 (the return of Christ). John 14:21–24 and John 14:25–26 present the same parallel but in reverse order. The only possible interpretation is that the Parousia coincides with Pentecost.

John does not use the Synoptic expression "this generation." He seems, in fact, not to know the word "generation." But in other, more incisive ways he affirms that the Parousia and the Last Judgment will occur during the same generation as Jesus Christ. For example, he shows us that the second coming of Christ is Pentecost.

This is the meaning of the scene in John 20:19–23. It is the first appearance of the risen one to the assembled disciples, and its climax and significance is this: "Having said this he breathed upon them and said, 'Receive the Holy Spirit'" (John 20:22). John uses this symbolic scene to tell us that the Pentecost coincides with the Resurrection of Jesus Christ, having previously told us that while Jesus was alive on earth "there was not yet any Spirit because Jesus had not yet been glorified" (John 7:39).

Note the seven facts or events involved here: Crucifixion, Resurrection, Ascension, Pentecost, Parousia, Last Judgment, and eternal life. We customarily represent them as occurring in that order one after the other. But John's sole concern is that they all occur "in this generation," as the Synoptics say, or "in the hour of Jesus," as John says, that is, during the generation of Jesus of Nazareth.

To state the historical simultaneity between Pentecost and the Resurrection, John invented the scene 20:19–23 mentioned above. To express the simultaneity, within one period or generation, between the Crucifixion, the Resurrection, and the Ascension, he assigned double meanings to the verbs *hypsoo* ("to lift up") and *doxasthenai* ("to be glorified") (see John 8:28, 12:32, and 7:39, as well as many other passages in which the verb "to glorify" occurs).

The best known usage of *hypsoo* is this:

When I am lifted up from the earth,
I will attract all toward me.
He said this to signify the death he would die (John 12:32–33).

These two verses are the continuation of 12:31, which says, "*Now* is the judgment of this world; *now* the prince of this world will be cast out," indicating John's intention to show both the chronological and simultaneous nature of these events. But this passage also shows that the Last Judgment coincides historically with the Crucifixion, Resurrection, and Ascension of Jesus Christ. In light of this verse we can see in John 16:8–11 the simultaneity of Pentecost and the Last Judgment. The Last Judgment and eternal life are simultaneous, as John 5:20–22 says (see our chapter 9). Moreover, the presence of eternal life in the hour of Jesus is the theme of John 5:24 and 1 John 3:14.

Given that the Parousia is indisputably simultaneous with the Last Judgment and with eternal life, the cited passages are sufficient to document the presence of the Parousia. By putting these three events in the present, John contradicts the eschatology of Judaism, which sees them as future. But Judaic eschatology was soon reestablished within Christian theology, where it became accepted and orthodox as if the New Testament had never existed.

The occurrence of the Parousia during the generation of Jesus Christ is especially relevant to the relationship between John and the Synoptics. By identifying the Parousia with Pentecost, John affirms that the Parousia is present. John also affirms and demonstrates the presentness of the Parousia in other ways.

DWELLING-PLACES

The initial verses of John 14 have been much misinterpreted: "I am going to prepare a place for you"; "in my Father's house there are many dwelling-places"; "I will return and I will take you with me." Over half a century ago the Catholic Lagrange observed: "We have tended to explain the confidence as due to what Jesus will do first: He goes to prepare places. But this is no more than an initial idea that prepares for a more complete understanding."[8] In verse 2 the term "dwelling-places" "does not refer in any way to levels of heavenly happiness. There are many places; this is all that matters."[9]

I think, however, that the redactional form of John 14 suggests an additional meaning. The opening verses allow of our customary and comfortable otherwordly interpretation, but subsequent verses compel us to understand the true meaning of these initial phrases. The form of Jesus' conversation with his disciples here is similar although not identical to that of his conversation with Martha. The term "dwelling-place" reappears in verse 23, and there its meaning is explained: It is located in the believers themselves who live in this world; the Father and Jesus will come to the believer and "they will make a dwelling-place in him." Their dwelling-place is here, not in heaven or another world.

Traditional theology's error has been to divide John 14, as if its opening verses were not part of a compositional whole. But the dwelling-places referred to in these verses cannot be in another world, for verse 16 promises that Jesus will *send* to believers the Spirit to remain with them "forever" *(eis ton aiona)*.

In verse 12 Jesus assures them that the believers will do "greater works" than his, which would be meaningless in another world. The presence of the Paraclete, which synthesizes the presence of the Father and the return of Jesus, will consist precisely in these works that challenge the world. The goal is to change the world; for this "greater works" are needed. But the world to be changed is this world, not another. Lagrange demonstrates that "chapter 14 is perfectly delimited."[10] It is an indestructible redactional unit. Brown has seen that verses 1–3 and verses 27–28 form an intentional "bracketing," or inclusion "marking the beginning and end of a section."[11] In fact, John uses triple brackets: "I am going away and I come to you" (v. 3 and v. 28, quoting v. 3); "believe" (v. 1 and v. 29); and "set your troubled hearts at rest" (v. 1 and v. 27).

The formulation of the first of these three bracketings demonstrates John's genius. Feuillet has seen "le paradoxe de 14:28: 'Je m'en vais et je viens vers vous.'"[12] This is the paradox of "the word," which we have already described: Only across an impassable distance can absolute otherness be made present. I return to you by going away. The "and" is consequential: "I am going away and I am coming to you." The first "and" of the key verse of the chapter is likewise consequential:

If anyone loves me, he will keep my word,
and my Father will love him,
and we will come to him
and make a dwelling-place in him (John 14:23)

The first "and" functions as "therefore" and controls the rest of the verse. Note that "the word" is mentioned in this verse, which is the linchpin of the whole chapter. The "word" in this verse is to love one another, as we already have seen in our chapter 7, for this verse refers to the phrase "keep the commandments" in verses 15 and 21 and also to the "greater works" in verse 12.

Moreover, John is referring to a change in this world, as we see in verses 13–14:

And whatever you ask for in my name I will do so that the Father is glorified in the son. If you ask me for something in my name, I will do it.

It does not make any sense to say, "When you are in heaven your prayer will be efficacious." Thus the "dwelling-place" of verse 3 cannot refer to another world. The exegete who refuses to relinquish an otherwordly bias has to say, with Brown, "Verses 13–14 are a problem," and to confess, with Lagrange, "I am unable to determine the context."[13] But if one accepts that verses 13–14 refer to changing this world by "the word" and "good works," then the "ask-and-you-will-receive" theme fits perfectly. Indeed, it is a necessary attribute of the true "dwelling-place" and the true Parousia.

The "peace" of John 14:27 is the worldwide eschatological peace of Isa. 54:13; 57:19; Ezek. 37:26; and Rom. 2:10; 8:6; 14:17. Its eschatological character is manifested in the words "not like that of this world" (John 14:27).

That John is referring to the Parousia is demonstrated by his deliberate use of the expression "on that day," which throughout the Bible indicates the day of the final intervention of Yahweh. John says:

On that day you will know that I am in my Father and you are in me and I am in you (John 14:20).

Brown has noted: "In 20 Jesus used the OT phrase 'on that day,' implying that his indwelling with his disciples after the resurrection would fulfill the eschatological dreams of the prophets."[14] This gets to the heart of chapters 13–17, the Johannine Last Supper. "Probably," Brown says, "in the final stage of Johannine theology, all these indwellings were thought to be accomplished through and in the Paraclete"[15]—an accurate statement without the initial "probably." Even more precise is his commentary on John 17:23: "Apparently in Johannine thought the believers are to be brought to completion as one *in this life*, for this completion is to have an effect on the world."[16]

Lagrange comments on John 14:18 ("I will not leave

you orphans; I come to you"): "Even after the [Easter] appearances, the disciples felt like orphans, as if Christ had again completely abandoned them. Therefore this passage refers to a coming that would not end during their lifetimes."[17] Let us repeat Barrett's words in his commentary on the "we will come" of John 14:23: "To the man who becomes a Christian . . . both the Father and the Son . . . will come. This is the *parousia* upon which John's interest is concentrated."[18]

THE DISCIPLES' ROLE

The etymological sense of the word "parousia" is presence. The parousian, definitive presence of Christ consists in the Paraclete, which in turn consists in the "greater works" that the believers will do and that will eventually suffuse the world and give it life. If we keep in mind that John writes after the resurrection of Christ, then we can understand why in 14:19 he has Christ say "because I live" and not "because I will live":

(18) I will not leave you orphans; I come to you.
(19) In a little while the world will not longer see me,
but you see me
because I live and you will live.

Primordial Christianity's Paschal message is that Christ lives. John (like Rom. 5:10 and Acts 3:15) asserts that Christians live from the life of the risen Jesus. But he adds that Jesus' return, his Parousia, consists in the believers' lives of good works. What John states in verse 18, he explains in verse 19.

Judas (not Judas Iscariot) understood that Jesus was speaking of the Parousia. Surprised, he asked, "Lord, how is it that you will show yourself to us and not to the world?" (John 14:22), for he knew that the Parousia had to affect the whole world; it is not an inner state of a privileged group. It is commonly assumed that Jesus' answer does not respond to the question:

If anyone loves me, he will keep my word,
and my Father will love him,
and we will come to him
and make our dwelling-place with him (John 14:23).

But Jesus does indeed respond to the question. If the disciples "keep my word" (which includes the "even greater works" of verse 12), then Christ will in fact also be made manifest to the world, for keeping "the word" constitutes an unconcealable reality, as we saw in our chapter 7.

When Jesus asked his Father that the disciples become as one, he specified: "as you, Father, in me and I in you" (John 17:21). He used this superb formula once before, echoing Psalm 82, in John 10:38: "Believe the works, so that you might recognize and know that the Father is in me and I am in the Father." As we saw, the works mentioned are the "good works" that make the true God unmistakable. Thus John 17:21 ends by saying: "so that the world might believe that you sent me" (and the formula is repeated almost exactly in John 17:23). The central theme is that the disciples will relieve Jesus of his function as "the word." Therefore John has Jesus add: "so that the world might know that . . . you loved them as you loved me" (John 17:23). The profound meaning that John attaches to "the word" is stunningly suggested when he has Jesus add: "because you loved me before the constitution of the world" (John 17:24). Before the world existed, according to John, there was nothing but "the word" (John 1:1–3). John spells out the disciples' function when he says: "so that the world might recognize that you sent me and you loved them as you loved me" (John 17:23). He had just said: "I gave them your word" (John 17:14), and then, in a most significant parataxis:

Your word is truth. As you sent me to the world, I also have sent them to the world (John 17:17–18).

That is why in John 17:24 Jesus did not say, "I want them to be wherever I might be" or "to go wherever I might go" or "to be wherever I will be." Rather he said, "I want them to be where I *am*." The disciples are to take Jesus' place. Saint Augustine recognized his meaning: "Nec dixit, ubi ero; sed ubi *sum*."[19] At that moment Christ functioned as the transcendent "word" in the world and addressed to the world. The world is where his disciples must be.

Because of the disciples' good works—along with "the word" that is addressed to the whole world and is not heterogenous to these good works—not only Jesus but also the Father is in them, and more than before. Therefore, referring to God, John says: "From now on you know him and you have seen him" (John 14:7). Both the Parousia and eternal life are already a present fact in our history. The qualitative identity of the works and the nonresorbable summons of "the word" are able authentically to reveal God and to transcend insofar as they are *eschaton*, insofar as we can no longer postpone the realization of justice and unending life, insofar as we need wait for nothing else. All theological efforts to postpone the *eschaton* and confine God to "heaven" founder upon this absolute proclamation: "From now on you know him and you have seen him."

PAROUSIA IN THE SYNOPTICS

According to John, the Parousia takes place during the generation of Jesus Christ. Let us turn now to the Synoptics.

The time of the Parousia is made explicit in all three of the Synoptics. After describing the ruin of Jerusalem and the following Parousia, the Marcan Jesus solemnly affirmed:

In truth I tell you that this generation will not pass away until all these things happen (Mark 13:30; cf. Matt. 24:34 and Luke 21:32).

This was said in a discourse expressly dedicated to the question: "Tell us *when* this will happen and what the sign will be that all these things are to be fulfilled" (Mark 13:4; cf. Matt. 24:3 and Luke 21:7). Matthew reformulates the question more explicitly: "Tell us *when* this will happen and what the sign will be of your Parousia and the end of the age." Today it has been established that "this generation" does not refer to the Jews, as conservative exegesis has held for centuries, but means what we commonly understand by the term. This can be shown by Mark 8:12, 38; 9:19; Luke 7:31; 11:29, 32, 50; 17:25; Matt. 11:16; 12:39; 17:17; 23:36. The only instance where the term "generation" could have another meaning is Luke 16:8. But in the first place this is not truly an exception ("astute in dealing with their contemporaries"),[20] and in the second place the context demands that "generation" here indicate a specific time, excluding any other meaning. Mark 13:30, moreover, does not simply say "generation," but rather "this generation," whose meaning is clear.

For centuries an incorrect and unwarranted interpretation of Mark 13 has assigned to certain verses the prediction of the Parousia (vv. 24–27 or vv. 20–27 or vv. 21–27 or vv. 19–27), while to other immediately preceding and following verses has been assigned the prediction of the destruction of Jerusalem. Proponents of this interpretation adduced a prophetic enthusiasm which, they held, telescoped events actually occurring over a very long time. But such a literary genre does not exist, and as early as 1933 the respected Jesuit Ferdinand Prat called this "the most arbitrary of interpretations."[21] The Dominican Lagrange recognized that the eschatological discourses of Mark and Luke "do not seem to have in mind more than one event; it asks [in Mark 13:4] when it will take place and what the sign will be."[22] With regard to Mark 13:30 ("this generation") Lagrange says this: "It is useless to take *genea* in some sense other than the normal one, the generation that was alive at the moment when Jesus uttered this discourse."[23]

In Mark 13:4, 7, 8, 10, 14, 24, 26, 27 we find locutions that are used expressly to determine time: "then," "in those days," "when," "and then." The intention to indicate chronological sequence is clear throughout the chapter. The same intention can be detected in Matthew and Luke. Grundmann says, "The composition demonstrates an unequivocal temporal concatenation in vv. 4, 7, 8, 10, 14, 24, 26, 27. The content is the sequence of events in a chronological period."[24] Feuillet concludes from his own analysis: "Thus, to the eyes of Christ, the judgment of condemnation against the chosen people appears as the great sign of the establishment of the messianic kingdom and its extension to the whole world (cf. the conclusion of the parable of the murderous winegrowers, as well as Luke 13:22–30 and Matt. 8:11–12)."[25] The expression "after that tribulation" (Mark 13:24) and the Matthean equivalent "*immediately after* the tribulation of those days" (Matt. 24:29) compel us to consider the Parousia and the establishment of the kingdom (Mark 13:24–27 and parallels) as events immediately subsequent to the destruction of the temple of Jerusalem.

The thesis that "nobody knows the day or the hour" (Mark 13:32) heartens those who would postpone the *eschaton,* as if Mark himself had not just told us (13:30) that it will all happen during "this generation." In this regard we need only note with Feuillet that the Greek wording *Peri de tes hemeras ekeines e tes horas* ("However, about the day and the hour") clearly "shows that the accent falls on the exact character of the chronological indications."[26] The adversative particle *de* ("however") is very important: Verse 30 tells us that everything will happen during this generation; verse 31 simply emphasizes what is being affirmed and the indefectibility of its fulfillment; verse 32 adds adversatively that only the exact day and hour are still unknown. In sum, the Parousia will occur during the present generation, but it is impossible to specify on what day or hour. As Feuillet observes, "There is no contradiction between Mark 13:30 and Mark 13:32, which can both perfectly well refer to the same historical event: Of this event Jesus says that it will take place during the lifetime of the present generation, but he refuses to specify further."[27]

Regarding the cosmic scenic effects omitted by John but preserved by the Synoptics, the Catholic Bonsirven notes that Peter applies the prediction of Joel 3:1–5 —that the sun will be changed to darkness and the moon to blood—to the Pentecost event (Acts 2:16–21): "None of that occurred on that clear morning of early summer; but this did not stop the Apostle from declaring that they were present at the fulfillment of the prophecy of Joel."[28] With similar grandiloquence the Mexican national anthem says, "and the earth trembles at its core." Such an expression may seem shabby and excessive to us, but it is simply a literary device. We find a similar example in Isa. 13–14: The reality is the destruction of Babylon, undoubtedly an event with enormous historical consequences, but the author says that the tumult of it affected the entire universe, including the stars and their constellations. Mic. 1:2–7 ascribes the same cosmic concomitants to the devastating punishment of Samaria and Judea; according to the author the whole world trembled (see also Jer. 4:23–26; Wisd. 18:14–19; Ezek. 32:7–8; Amos 8:9; Isa. 34:4). As Lagrange notes, such expressions "had long been simply metaphors, for Isaiah uses them with regard to the ruin of Babylon and Edom, and Ezekiel does so in speaking of Egypt."[29] We find expressions like those in Luke 21:11 and Mark 13:19 and in Flavius Josephus's coolly historical account of the fall of Jerusalem—the critical event for the Synoptics.[30]

We cannot here analyze Mark 13, Luke 21 and Matt. 24–25. Such a project would require a study of each of them as intensive and extensive as our study of John. We will simply mention two small points and one major issue.

The Lucan modifications of Mark's text—which some exegetes find tantamount to a postponement of the *eschaton*—are in fact intended to prohibit Luke's readers from postponing it. For example, Luke omits "these things will be the beginning of the birth pangs" (Mark 13:8, Matt. 24:8), because when Luke was writing "these things" had already occurred. Therefore he warns, "They must happen first, but the end will not come immediately" (Luke 21:9). He speaks of wars and rebellions (21:9) and persecutions (21:12–19). We must not forget that Luke puts these words into the mouth of Jesus Christ, and if his readers understood these events to signal the immediate irruption of the Parousia their expectations would be frustrated. Therefore he warns that this is not the meaning of Christ's words. Similarly the long siege of Jerusalem means for Luke only that the destruction of Jerusalem is occurring (21:20–24). Luke distinguishes all these catastrophes from the *eschaton*, because when he wrote they had already occurred, that is, because he did not want his readers to become discouraged about the imminence of the Parousia.

Luke's verbs in the future tense do not signify an indefinite time nor even a long time. After describing the Parousia (21:25–28) and the definitive coming of the kingdom (21:29–31), Luke expressly states, "The present generation will not pass away until all this happens" (21:32). This he would not have said if his modifications were an attempt to postpone the *eschaton*. Note that Luke, unlike Matthew, omits the parenthetical Mark 13:32, which says that the exact time of the *eschaton* has been set by God but is as yet unknown to anyone else. Luke leaves his readers with the positive affirmation that the *eschaton* will occur during the present generation.

In Matthew all of chapter 25 deals with the definitive establishment of the kingdom (cf. vv. 1, 34,40). It is clear that Matthew elaborates on Marcan eschatology and gives greater emphasis to the fact that the destruction of the temple leads into the coming of the kingdom. From the initial question of the disciples the entire discourse explicitly refers to Christ's "Parousia and the consummation of the age" (24:3), and the word "parousia" appears four times in all (24:3, 27, 37, 39). "The consummation of the age," as Feuillet notes, refers in the prophets to "the establishment of the kingdom of God, the definitive economy."[31]

THE TEMPLE

The major point—and here we return to John—is that the Synoptics did not invent the notion that when the temple of stone was destroyed it would be replaced forthwith in the world by the messianic kingdom. The Samaritan woman asked Jesus where to worship, on Gerizim or in Jerusalem (John 4:20). Jesus responded: Neither here nor in Jerusalem but in spirit and in truth (John 4:21-24: "the hour is coming and it is now"). By his response, Jesus clearly indicated that when the messianic hour arrived the stone temple would be replaced by the people of the kingdom, who would worship God in spirit and in truth. The point of the anecdote is the contrast between the temple "made with hands" and the temple "not made with hands," which Mark 14:58 has Jesus express. As we read in the book of Revelation, in the new Jerusalem "there will be no temple" (21:22), but the columns and stones of the true temple will be human beings themselves (3:12).

It is essential to recall that these anticultic tendencies did not originate with Jesus of Nazareth in the first century, nor with the prophets of Israel in the eighth century B.C. They derive from the very essence of Yahweh as distinguished from other gods. When David first thought to build a temple or house of God, Yahweh said to him through Nathan: It is not you who will build a house for me; rather I will build a house for you and give you a posterity that will dwell there forever (2 Sam. 7:5–16). The people gathered together by the Messiah will be the true temple. This conviction was always present in Israelite tradition. When Jesus was accused before the Sanhedrin of wanting to destroy the temple (Mark 14:58; Matt. 26:61), the high priest understood perfectly that the temple's destruction was equivalent to the Messiah's arrival (Mark 14:61; Matt. 26:63). The accusers had not mentioned the Messiah, yet apparently everyone took the high priest's interpretation for granted, including Christ and the evangelists.

In Mark 13:2, Jesus says, "You see these great buildings? Well, not one stone will be left upon another; all will be thrown down." Lagrange comments: "The critics, even the most radical, agree in recognizing the authenticity of this prophecy. Jesus predicted the ruin of the temple; it was even one of the accusations they used against him (Mark 14:58; Matt. 26:61)."[32] But if the historical Jesus truly predicted the ruin of the temple, it would be natural, according to Israelite tradition, for him to announce that the definitive establishment of the messianic kingdom would follow immediately upon the ruin of the temple.

This is not exactly equivalent to the Johannine eschatology that identifies the Parousia with "the hour" of the death and resurrection of Christ. But the difference is insignificant, because both John and the Synoptics, along with the historical Jesus, assert that the Parousia occurs during the "present generation," and this assertion, however stated, prevents postponement of the *eschaton*.

THE SIGN OF JONAH

John and the Synoptics may concur even in details, according to Feuillet. In Luke 11:29–30 the sign of

Jonah—the only sign to be given to "this generation" —is the risen Jesus Christ:

> With the crowds swarming around him he went on to say: "This is a wicked generation; it demands a sign, and the only sign that will be given it is the sign of Jonah. For just as Jonah was a sign to the Ninevites, so will the Son of man be for this generation (Luke 11:29–30).

According to the parallel passage Matt. 12:39–40 the sign of Jonah is the resurrection of Jesus:

> But he answered, "It is a wicked, adulterous generation that asks for a sign, and the only sign that will be given it is the sign of the prophet Jonah. For just as Jonah was in the whale's belly for three days and three nights, so too the Son of man will be in the bowels of the earth for three days and three nights (Matt. 12:39–40).

Outside chapter 24, Matthew utilizes the term "sign" *(semeion)* only in 12:38–42 and 16:1–4, both passages that speak of the sign of Jonah. Therefore when he speaks of "the sign of the Son of man" in 24:30, it is not merely probable that he is referring to the resurrection of Jesus Christ; he cannot be referring to anything else, because in 12:39 he had expressly stated that no other sign but this would be given to the present generation. But in 24:30 "the sign of the Son of man" is the sign of the presence of the Parousia. Therefore Matthew identifies the resurrection of Jesus with the presence of the Parousia.

Comparing Matt. 24:30 with Matt. 26:64, Feuillet says: "Obviously in these two texts 'to see' and 'to appear' should be understood in the metaphorical sense of experiencing the incomparable dignity of Jesus—which will be manifest in all its splendor from today onward by the course of events: The sign of the Son of man in heaven will not be seen with bodily eyes, nor will Jesus be seen seated at the right hand of the Father."[33] It is significant that at this moment Matthew employs the demythologizing temporal particle *ap'arti* ("from now on"), which John uses in the expression "from now on you know him and you have seen him" (John 14:7). The Parousia cannot be postponed, for Matthew maintains, "*From now on* you will see the Son of man seated at the right hand of power and coming on the clouds of heaven" (Matt. 26:64). Matthew adds explicit chronological precision to Mark's rendering of Jesus' words at the climactic moment of his trial (Mark 14:62). The eschatology of Matthew and Mark is the same as that expressed in John's use of the verb *hypsoo* ("to lift up") and the verb *doxasthenai* ("to be glorified").

As Feuillet says, in the book of Daniel "the Messiah, the 'Son of man,' is presented as an incarnation of that form of supernatural appearance known as 'divine glory,'" and glory "will be shown in the Messiah himself, who will be like the spiritual temple of the long awaited age."[34] If this is true, then the response of the Synoptic Jesus to the high priest (Matt. 26:64) seems to identify, substantially and chronologically, the death and resurrection of Jesus Christ with the Parousia of the Messiah and the definitive establishment of the kingdom of God on earth.

NOTES

1. Ernst Käsemann, "Begründet der neutestamentliche Kanon die Einheit der Kirche?" *Evangelische Theologie* 11 (1951/52), pp. 13–21.

2. C.K. Barrett, *The Gospel according to St. John* (London: SPCK, 1955), p. 389.

3. Henri van den Bussche, *Jean* (Paris: Desclée, 1967), pp. 410–11.

4. Raymond E. Brown, *The Gospel according to John (xiii–xxi)*, Anchor Bible 29A (Garden City, New York: Doubleday, 1970), pp. 710, 1139.

5. Franz Mussner, *Die Johanneische Seheweise*, Quaestiones Disputatae 28 (Freiburg im Breisgau: Herder, 1965), p. 58; Mussner's emphasis [cf. Eng. trans.: *The Historical Jesus in the Gospel of St. John*, trans. W.J. O'Hara, Quaestiones Disputatae 19 (New York: Herder and Herder, 1967), p. 62].

6. M.-J. Lagrange, *Evangile selon Saint Jean*, 8th ed. (Paris: Gabalda, 1948), p. 420.

7. Brown, *Gospel according to John (xiii–xxi)*, p. 645.

8. Lagrange, *Evangile selon Saint Jean*, p. 372.

9. Ibid., pp. 372–73.

10. Ibid., p. 370.

11. Brown, *Gospel according to John (xiii–xxi)*, p. 608.

12. André Feuillet, "L'heure de Jésus et le signe de Cana," *Ephemerides Theologicae Lovanienses* 36 (1960), p. 11 [Eng. trans.: *Johannine Studies* (Staten Island, New York: Alba House, 1965), p. 24].

13. Brown, *Gospel according to John (xiii–xxi)*, p. 623; Lagrange, *Evangile selon Saint Jean*, p. 404. Lagrange refers to John 15:7, but his admission is equally applicable to all the supplicatory passages of the Last Supper (John 14:13, 14 [26]; 15:7, 16; 16:23, 24, 26).

14. Brown, *Gospel according to John (xiii–xxi)*, p. 653. Regarding "that day" as a designation of the Last Judgment, see José Porfirio Miranda, *Marx y la Biblia* (Salamanca: Sígueme, 1972), pp. 137–66 [Eng. trans.: *Marx and the Bible*, trans. John Eagleson (Maryknoll, New York: Orbis Books, 1974), pp. 111–37].

15. Brown, *Gospel according to John (xiii–xxi)*, p. 643.

16. Ibid., p. 771; Brown's emphasis.

17. Lagrange, *Evangile selon Saint Jean*, p. 385.

18. Barrett, *Gospel according to St. John*, p. 389.

19. Augustine, *Patrologia Latina* 35, 1640 ad John 7:34. Brown comments on 7:34: "One would expect 'where I *go*' " (*The Gospel according to John (i–xii)*, Anchor Bible 29 [Garden City, New York: Doubleday, 1966], p. 314). And Lagrange: "*Eimi* au présent . . . suggère aussi . . . que déjà Jésus est dans cette sphère inaccessible" (*Evangile selon Saint Jean*, p. 212).

20. "Gegenüber ihrem eigenen Geschlecht d.h. gegenüber ihren Zeitgenossen" (Walter Grundmann, *Das Evangelium nach Lukas*, 4th ed., THKNT 3 [Berlin: Evangelische Verlagsanstalt, 1966], p. 321).

21. Ferdinand Prat, *Jésus–Christ* (Paris, 1933), 2:252 [Eng. trans.: *Jesus Christ*, trans. John J. Heenan (Milwaukee: Bruce, 1950), 2:242].

22. M.-J. Lagrange, *Evangile selon Saint Marc*, 4th ed. (Paris: Gabalda, 1929), p. 458.

23. Ibid., p. 348.

24. Walter Grundmann, *Das Evangelium nach Markus*, 4th ed. THKNT 2 (Berlin: Evangelische Verlagsanstalt, 1968), p. 260.

25. André Feuillet, "Le discours de Jésus sur la ruine du temple," *Revue Biblique* 56 (1949), p. 70.

26. Ibid., p. 87.

27. Ibid.

28. Joseph Bonsirven, *Les enseignements de Jésus-Christ*, 8th ed. (Paris: Beauchesne, 1950), p. 338.

29. Lagrange, *Evangile selon Saint Marc*, p. 345.

30. Flavius Josephus, *Bell. Jud.*, preface and 5,10,5; 6,5,3; see also Tacitus, *Histories*, 5, 13.

31. André Feuillet, "La synthèse eschatologique de Saint Matthieu (xxiv–xxv)," *Revue Biblique* 56 (1949), p. 344; and he cites Gen. 49:1; Num. 24:14; Deut. 4:30; Hos. 3:5; Isa. 2:2; 8:23; 46:10; Mic. 4:1; Jer. 23:20; Ezek. 38:18; Dan. 2:28; 10:14. Feuillet's testimony is of particular value, because—since he is still writing along apologetical lines—he denies that the Parousia is the Last Judgment. Matt. 25, which is part of the same discourse as Matt. 24, makes such a denial insupportable.

32. Lagrange, *Evangile selon Saint Marc*, p. 332. Bultmann's unwillingness to accept the authenticity of this logion of Jesus completely overlooks the fact that Jer. 26:6, 18 and Mic. 3:12 had already predicted the destruction of the temple (see Bultmann's *Geschichte der synoptischen Tradition* (Göttingen: Vandenhoeck, 1957), pp. 126–27 [Eng. trans.: *The History of the Synoptic Tradition*, trans. John Marsh (Oxford: Blackwell, 1963), pp. 120–21].

33. Feuillet, "Synthèse eschatologique," p. 354.

34. Feuillet, "Discours de Jésus," pp. 70–71.

Abbreviations

ATD   Das Alte Testament Deutsch
NTD   Das Neue Testament Deutsch
RNT   Regensburger Neues Testament
THKNT   Theologischer Handkommentar zum Neuen Testament
TDNT   *Theological Dictionary of the New Testament* (translation of *TWNT*)
TWNT   *Theologisches Wörterbuch zum Neuen Testament*

Bibliography

Allard, Michel. "Note sur la formule "ehyeh aser 'ehyeh.' " *Recherches de Science Religieuse* 45 (1957): 79–86.

Asensio, Felix. *Misericordia et veritas*. Rome: Gregoriana, 1949.

Assmann, Hugo. "Teología de la liberación." In *Teología desde la praxis de la liberación*, pp. 27–102. Salamanca: Sígueme, 1973 [Eng. trans.: "Theology of Liberation." In *Theology for a Nomad Church*, pp. 43–108. Trans. Paul Burns. Maryknoll, New York: Orbis Books, 1976].

Barrett, C.K. *The Gospel according to St. John*. London: SPCK, 1965.

Bauer, Walter. *Wörterbuch zu den Schriften des Neuen Testaments*. 5th ed. Berlin: Töpelmann, 1963 [In Eng. see William F. Arndt and F. Wilbur Gingrich. *A Greek-English Lexicon of the New Testament and Other Early Christian Literature*. Chicago: University of Chicago Press, 1957].

Black, Matthew. *An Aramaic Approach to the Gospels and Acts*. 3rd ed. Oxford: Clarendon, 1967.

Blank, Josef. *Krisis*. Freiburg: Lambertus, 1964.

Blass, F., and A. Debrunner. *A Greek Grammar of the New Testament*. 3rd ed. Trans. Robert W. Funk. Chicago: University of Chicago Press, 1967.

Böcher, Otto. *Der johanneische Dualismus im Zusammenhang des nachibiblischen Judentums*. Gütersloh: Mohn, 1965.

Boismard, M.-E. "La connaissance de Dieu dans l'alliance nouvelle d'après la première lettre de Saint Jean." *Revue Biblique* 56 (1949):365–91.

———. "L'évolution du thème eschatologique dans les traditions johanniques." *Revue Biblique* 68 (1961):507–24.

Bonsirven, Joseph. *Les enseignements de Jésus-Christ*. 8th ed. Paris: Beauchesne, 1950.

Botterweck, G. Johannes. *"Gott Erkennen" im Sprachgebrauch des Alten Testaments*. Bonn: Peter Hanstein, 1951.

Braun, F.-M. *Jean le théologien*. 3 vols. Paris: Gabalda, 1959, 1964, 1966.

Braun, Herbert. *Gesammelte Studien zum Neuen Testament und seiner Umwelt*. Tübingen: Mohr-Siebeck, 1962.

———. *Qumran und das Neue Testament*. 2 vols. Tübingen: Mohr, 1966.

Brooke, A.E. *The Johannine Epistles*, International Critical Commentary 38. Edinburgh: T. & T. Clark, 1912.

Brown, Raymond E. *The Gospel according to John.* Anchor Bible 29 and 29A. New York: Doubleday, 1966, 1970.

———. "The Qumran Scrolls and the Johannine Gospel and Epistles." *Catholic Biblical Quarterly* 17 (1955):403–19 and 559–74.

Bultmann, Rudolf. "aletheia." *TWNT*, 1:239–51 [Eng. trans.: *TDNT*, 1:238–51].

———. *Die drei Johannesbriefe.* Göttingen: Vandenhoeck, 1967 [Eng. trans.: *The Johannine Epistles.* Trans. R. Philip O'Hara et al. Philadelphia: Fortress, 1973].

———. *Das Evangelium des Johannes.* Göttingen: Vandenhoeck, 1941 [Eng. trans.: *The Gospel of John: A Commentary.* Trans. G.R. Beasley-Murray et al. Philadelphia: Westminster, 1971].

———. *Die Geschichte der synoptischen Tradition.* Göttingen: Vandenhoeck, 1957 [Eng. trans.: *The History of the Synoptic Tradition.* Trans. John Marsh. Oxford: Blackwell, 1963].

———. *Glauben und Verstehen.* Tübingen: Mohr, 1933 [Eng. trans.: (vol. 1) *Faith and Understanding.* Trans. Louise Pettibone-Smith. New York: Harper & Row, 1969].

———. "Neues Testament und Mythologie." In H.W. Bartsch, ed. *Kerygma und Mythos I.* Hamburg: Reich, 1960 [Eng. trans.: *Kerygma and Myth.* New York: Harper, 1961].

———. "pistis." *TWNT*, 6:175–82, 197–230 [Eng. trans.: *TDNT*, 6:174–82, 197–228].

———. *Theologie des Neuen Testaments.* 2nd ed. Tübingen: Mohr, 1954 [Eng. Trans.: *Theology of the New Testament.* Trans. Kendrick Grobel. New York: Scribner's, 1970].

Burkitt, Francis Crawford. *Church and Gnosis.* Cambridge: University Press, 1932.

van den Bussche, H. *Jean.* Paris: Desclée, 1967.

Conzelmann, H. *Grundriss der Theologie des Neuen Testaments.* Munich: Kaiser, 1968 [Eng. trans.: *An Outline of the Theology of the New Testament.* Trans. John Bowden. New York: Harper & Row, 1969].

———. "Was von Anfang war." In *Neutestamentliche Studien für R. Bultmann,* Beiheft zur Zeitschrift für die neutestamentliche Wissenschaft 21. Berlin: Töpelmann, 1954.

Cranfield, C.E.B. *The Gospel according to Saint Mark.* Cambridge: University Press, 1959.

Delling, G. "archo." *TWNT*, 1: 476–88 [Eng. trans.: *TDNT*, 1: 478–89].

Dewailly, L.M. *Jésus-Christ, parole de Dieu.* Paris: Cerf, 1945.

Dodd, C.H. *Historical Tradition in the Fourth Gospel.* Cambridge: University Press, 1963.

———. *The Interpretation of the Fourth Gospel.* Cambridge: University Press, 1953.

———. *More New Testament Studies*. Grand Rapids: Eerdmans, 1968.

Dupont, Jacques. "L'ambassade de Jean-Baptiste." *Nouvelle Revue Théologique* 83 (1961):805–21 and 943–59.

———. *Les béatitudes*. Paris: Gabalda, 1969.

Fensham, F. Charles. "Widow, Orphan and the Poor in Ancient Near Eastern Legal and Wisdom Literature." *Journal of Near Eastern Studies* 21, no. 2 (April 1962):129–39.

Feuillet, André. "Le discours de Jésus sur la ruine du temple (Mc 13 et Lc 21, 5–36)." *Revue Biblique* 55 (1948):481–502; 56 (1949): 61–92.

———. "Les *ego eimi* christologiques du quatrième évangile." *Recherches de Science Religieuse* 54, no. 2 (April–June 1966):5–22 and 213–40.

———. "L'heure de Jésus et le signe de Cana." *Ephemerides Theologicae Lovanienses* 36 (1960):5–22 [Eng. trans.: "The Hour of Jesus and the Sign of Cana," in *Johannine Studies*. Staten Island, New York: Alba House, 1965].

———. *Le prologue du quatrième évangile*. Paris: Desclée, 1968.

———. "La synthèse eschatologique de Saint Matthieu (xxiv–xxv)." *Revue Biblique* 56 (1949):340–64.

Friedrich, Gerhard. "euangelizomai." *TWNT*, 2:705–35 [Eng. trans.: *TDNT*, 2:707–37].

———. "keryx." *TWNT*, 3:682–717 [Eng. trans.: *TDNT*, 3:683–718].

Fuentes, Carlos. *Tiempo mexicano*. Mexico City: Mortiz, 1971.

González, A. "Le Psaume LXXXII." *Vetus Testamentum* 13, no. 3 (July 1963):293–309.

Grundmann, Walter. *Das Evangelium nach Lukas*. 3rd ed. THKNT 3. Berlin: Evangelische Verlagsanstalt, 1966.

———. *Das Evangelium nach Markus*. 3rd ed. THKNT 2. Berlin: Evangelische Verlagsanstalt, 1968.

———. *Das Evangelium nach Matthäus*. 3rd ed. THKNT 1. Berlin: Evangelische Verlagsanstalt, 1968.

———. "kalos." *TWNT*, 3:539–53 [Eng. trans.: *TDNT*, 3:536–50].

Heidegger, Martin. *Nietzsche*. 2 vols. Pfüllingen: Neske, 1961.

———. *Sein und Zeit*. 9th ed. Tübingen: Niemeyer, 1960 [Eng. trans.: *Being and Time*. Trans. John Macquarrie and Edward Robinson. New York: Harper & Row, 1962].

Hoffmann, Paul. *Die Toten in Christus*. Münster, Aschendorff, 1966.

Ibargüengoitia, Jorge. "Con el Laberinto en la mano." *Excelsior* (Mexico City), February 7, 1972.

Jeremias, Joachim. "geenna." *TWNT*, 1:655–56 [Eng. trans.: *TDNT*, 1:657–58].

———. "hades." *TWNT*, 1:148–49 [Eng. trans.: *TDNT*, 1:148–49].

———. *The Parables of Jesus*. New York: Scribner's, 1963.

———. "Die Salbungsgeschichte Mk. 14:3–9." *Zeitschrift für die neutestamentliche Wissenschaft* 35 (1936):77ff.

Joüon, Paul. *Grammaire de l'hébreu biblique.* 2nd ed. Rome: Pontificio Istituto Biblico, 1947.

———. "Notes de lexicographie hébraïque." *Mélanges de la Faculté Orientale* 5 (1911–12): 405–15.

———. "Notes philologiques sur les Evangiles." *Recherches de Science Religieuse* 17 (1927):537–40.

Käsemann, Ernst. *Exegetische Versuche und Besinnungen.* 2 vols. 5th ed. Göttingen: Vandenhoeck, 1967.

———. *Jesu letzter Wille nach Johannes 17.* 2nd ed. Tübingen: Mohr, 1967 [Eng. trans.: *The Testament of Jesus: A Study of the Gospel of John in the Light of Chapter 17.* Philadelphia: Fortress, 1968].

———. *Der Ruf der Freiheit.* 4th ed. Tübingen: Mohr, 1968 [Eng. trans.: *Jesus Means Freedom.* Philadelphia: Fortress Press, 1970].

Klein, Günther. "Das wahre Licht scheint schon." *Zeitschrift für Theologie und Kirche* 68 (1971):261–326.

Lagrange, M.-J. *Évangile selon Saint Jean.* 8th ed. Paris: Gabalda, 1927.

———. *Évangile selon Saint Marc.* 4th ed. Paris: Gabalda, 1929.

Lenin, V.I. *Obras escogidas.* Progreso: Moscow: 1969 [In Eng. see *Selected Works.* New York: International Publishers, 1967].

Levinas, Emmanuel. *Totalité et infini. Essai sur l'extériorité.* 2nd ed. The Hague: Nijhoff, 1965 [Eng. trans.: *Totality and Infinity: An Essay on Exteriority.* Trans. Alphonso Lingis. Pittsburgh: Duquesne University Press, 1969].

Liddell, Henry George, and Robert Scott. *A Greek-English Lexicon.* 9th ed. Oxford: Clarendon, 1940.

Lyonnet, Stanislas. *Exegesis epistulae ad romanos, Cap. I–IV.* Rome: Pontificio Istituto Biblico, 1963.

Marx, Karl. *Ausgewählte Schriften.* Munich: Kindler, 1962.

Michl, Johann. *Die Katholischen Briefe.* RNT 8/2. 2nd ed. Regensburg: Pustet, 1968.

Minette de Tillesse, G. *Le secret messianique dans l'évangile de Marc.* Paris: Cerf, 1968.

Miranda, José Porfirio. *Marx en México.* Mexico City: Siglo XXI, 1972.

———. *Marx y la Biblia.* Salamanca: Sígueme, 1972 [Eng. trans.: *Marx and the Bible.* Trans. John Eagleson. Maryknoll, New York: Orbis Books, 1974].

———. *Strukturveränderung. Die Unmoral der abendländischen Moral.* Wuppertal: Jugenddienst Verlag, 1973.

Moran, William L. "The Ancient Near Eastern Background of the Love of God in Deuteronomy." *Catholic Biblical Quarterly* 25, no. 1 (January 1963):77–87.

Mowinckel, Sigmund. *Die Erkenntnis Gottes bei den alttestament-lichen Propheten.* Oslo: Universistets-Forlaget, 1941.

Mussner, Franz. *Die Johanneische Seheweise.* Questiones Disputatae 28. Freiburg im Breisgau, 1965 [Eng. trans.: *The Historical Jesus in the Gospel of St. John.* Trans. W.J. O'Hara. Questiones Disputatae 19. New York: Herder and Herder, 1967].

Noth, Martin. *Das zweite Buch Mose.* 3rd ed. ATD 5. Göttingen: Vandenhoeck, 1965 [Eng. trans.: *Exodus: A Commentary.* Trans. J.S. Bowden. Philadelphia: Westminster, 1969].

O'Connell, Matthew J. "The Concept of Commandment in the Old Testament." *Theological Studies* 21, no. 3 (September 1960): 351–403.

Paz, Octavio. *El laberinto de la soledad.* 7th ed. Mexico City: Fondo de Cultura Económica, 1969 [Eng. trans.: *The Labyrinth of Solitude.* Trans. Lysander Kemp. New York: Grove Press, 1961].

Potterie, Ignace de la. *Adnotationes in exegesim Primae Epistulae S. Ioannis.* 2nd ed. Rome: Pontificio Istituto Biblico, 1966–67, mimeographed.

———. "De sensu vocis 'emet' in vetere testamento." *Verbum Domini* 27 (1949):336–54; 28 (1950):29–42.

———. "L'emploi dynamique de *eis* dans Saint Jean et ses incidences théologiques." *Biblica* 43 (1962):366–87.

Prat, Ferdinand. *Jésus-Christ.* 2 vols. Paris, 1933 [Eng. trans.: *Jesus Christ.* Trans. John J. Heenan. Milwaukee: Bruce, 1950].

Quell, Gottfried. "aletheia." *TWNT* 1, 233–37 [Eng. trans.: *TDNT*, 1: 232–37].

von Rad, Gerhard. *Das erste Buch Mose.* 7th ed. ATD 2–4. Göttingen: Vandenhoeck, 1964 [Eng. trans.: *Genesis: A Commentary.* Trans. John H. Marks. London: SCM, 1961].

———. "Das theologische Problem des alttestamentlichen Schöpfungsglaubens." In *Gesammelte Studien zum Alten Testament,* pp. 136–47. Munich: Kaiser, 1965 [Eng. trans.: "The Theological Problem of the Old Testament Doctrine of Creation." In *The Problem of the Hexateuch and Other Essays.* Trans. Rev. E.W. Trueman Dicken. New York: McGraw-Hill, 1966].

Sartre, Jean-Paul. *Critique de la raison dialectique.* Paris: Gallimard, 1960.

———. *L'être et le néant.* Paris: Gallimard, 1943 [Eng. trans.: *Being and Nothingness.* Trans. Hazel E. Barnes. New York: Citadel, 1968].

———. *Les mains sales.* Paris: Gallimard, 1948 [Eng. trans.: "Dirty Hands." In *No Exit, and Three Other Plays.* New York: Vintage, 1956].

Sasse, Hermann. "aion." *TWNT*, 1:197–209 [Eng. trans. *TDNT*, 1:197–209].

232   BIBLIOGRAPHY

——. "kosmeo." *TWNT*, 3:867–98. [Eng. trans.: *TDNT*, 3:867–98].

Schmid, Josef. *Das Evangelium nach Lukas*. 3rd ed. RNT 3. Regensburg: Pustet, 1955.

——. *Das Evangelium nach Markus*. 3rd ed. RNT 2. Regensburg: Pustet, 1954 [Eng. trans.: *The Gospel according to Mark*. New York: Alba, 1968].

——. *Das Evangelium nach Matthäus*. 3rd ed. RNT 1. Regensburg: Pustet, 1956.

——. "Joh. 1, 13." *Biblische Zeitschrift* 1 (1957):118–25.

Schmithals, W. "Empirische Theologie?" *Evangelische Kommentare* 8 (1969):447–52.

Schnackenburg, Rudolf. *Die Johannesbriefe*. 3rd ed. Freiburg: Herder, 1965.

——. *Das Johannesevangelium*. 2 vols. Freiburg: Herder, 1965 [Eng. trans.: *The Gospel according to St. John*. 2 vols. Trans. Kevin Smyth. New York: Herder, 1968].

——. *The Moral Teaching of the New Testament*. London: Burns and Oates, 1964.

Schneider, Johannes. *Die Kirchenbriefe*. NTD 10. Göttingen: Vandenhoeck, 1967.

Schweizer, Eduard. "*Ego eimi*." Forschungen zur Religion und Literatur des Alten und Neuen Testaments 56. Göttingen: Vandenhoeck, 1939.

——. "hyios." *TWNT*, 8:355–57 and 364–95 [Eng. trans.: *TDNT*, 8: 354–57].

Spicq, Ceslaus. *Théologie morale du nouveau testament*. 2 vols. Paris: Gabalda, 1965.

Stoebe, H.J. "Die Bedeutung des Wortes Hasad." *Vetus Testamentum* 2 (1962):244–54.

Strack, Hermann L. and Paul Billerbeck. *Kommentar zum Neuen Testament aus Talmud und Midrasch*. 6 vols. Munich: C.H. Beck, 1922–63.

Stuhlmacher, Peter. "Neues Testament und Hermeneutik." *Zeitschrift für Theologie und Kirche* 68 (1971):121–61.

Taylor, Vincent. *The Gospel according to St. Mark*. 2nd ed. London: Macmillan, 1957.

de Waelhens, Alphonse. *La philosophie de Martin Heidegger*. 7th ed. Louvain: Nauwelaerts, 1971.

Wahl, Jean. *Études kierkegaardiennes*. Paris: Vrin, 1949.

Westcott, Brooke Foss. *The Gospel according to St. John*. London: Clarke, 1958; first published in 1881.

Wolff, Hans Walter. " 'Wissen um Gott' bei Hosea als Urform von Theologie." *Evangelische Theologie* 12 (1952–53):533–54.

Wrede, William. *Das Messiasgeheimnis in den Evangelien, zugleich ein Beitrag zum Verständnis des Markusevangeliums.* Göttingen: Vandenhoeck, 1901 [Eng. trans.: *The Messianic Secret.* Trans. J.C.G. Greig. Cambridge: Clark, 1971].

Zahn, Theodor. *Das Evangelium des Matthäus.* 3rd ed. Leipzig: A. Deichert, 1910.

Zerwick, Max. *Analysis philologica novi testamenti graeci.* 2nd ed. Rome: Pontificio Istituto Biblico, 1960.

Zimmermann, H. *Neutestamentliche Methodenlehre.* Stuttgart: Katholisches Bibelwerk, 1967.

Index of Scriptural References

New Testament

234

New Testament

Apocrypha

Index of Authors